ORGANIZATIONAL MISBEHAVIOR

The Case for Personal Integrity

J. RONNIE DAVIS, PH.D.

NA

NorthAmerican
Business Press
Atlanta – Seattle – South Florida – Toronto

In Memoriam

Marion Fuller Davis
Daddy

Ida Belle Butler Davis
Mother

Dedicated To

Arthurine Payton
Wifey

Dorothy Payton
Mom

North American Business Press, Inc
Atlanta, Georgia
Seattle, Washington
South Florida
Toronto, Canada

Organizational Misbehavior: The Case for Personal Integrity
ISBN: 9780988919327
© 2013 All Rights Reserved.

Along with trade books for various business disciplines, the North American Business Press also publishes a variety of academic-peer reviewed journals.

Library of Congress Control Number: 2013932948
Library of Congress
Cataloging in Publication Division
101 Independence Ave., SE
Washington, DC 20540-4320
Printed in theUnited States of America
First Edition

Contents

Chapter One
PROPER UNDERSTANDING OF PERSONAL INTEGRITY

Chapter Two
THE PHYSICAL JOURNEY

Chapter Three

THE INTELLECTUAL JOURNEY

Chapter Four
THE EMOTIONAL JOURNEY

Chapter Five

THE SPIRITUAL JOURNEY

Chapter Six
TEN RULES FOR PERSONAL INTEGRITY

FOREWORD

Integrity is important to me, so essential to my life that I decided to write my own prefatory comments rather than ask someone else. I was blessed with a mother and father of integrity in the sense of honesty and trustworthiness. Throughout childhood, adolescence, and early adulthood, my understanding of integrity was limited to this selfsame sense of fair dealing with people. After taking my doctorate in economics at the University of Virginia, I began a career in academics, eventually a fifteen-year stint as a business school dean at three different universities. In 1971, I began a robust management consulting practice alongside my academic career. Consulting reshaped my understanding and sense of integrity.

Working with companies to improve productivity, cost, and profit as well as to facilitate strategic planning, I became concerned about organizational integrity, actually appalled at lapses in organizational integrity that I observed. This concern led to more thinking about integrity itself. First, I realized that integrity comes from the same Latin root as "integer," meaning a whole number. I then realized that integrity implies parts that must join, combine, and unite to make the whole. Next, I realized that organizational integrity joins, combines, and unites persons of integrity. In other words, organizational integrity is based on personal integrity. Finally, I realized that my understanding of integrity was too narrow, too limited. Honesty and trustworthiness are not integrity. The characteristics of honesty and trustworthiness are outward signs of integrity. When a person has integrity, he or she is honest and trustworthy.

Business consulting continued. I also began public speaking on the integrity topic and started training managers to pursue their own personal integrity and to understand that organizational integrity flows from personal integrity. I was asked repeatedly to write it down. After the catharsis of Hurricane Katrina, I formed a concept for manuscript development, starting with an explication of the proper understanding of integrity followed by a narrative of personal integrity as a journey and an articulation of ten rules for personal integrity. Afterwards, I began to write it down. The final work product is this treatise on personal and organizational integrity.

Organizational Misbehavior is wordplay. A required course in the business curriculum is Organizational Behavior. Particularly after the Enron scandal, I was shocked by the personal lapses in integrity evidenced in fabulously wealthy men such as Kenneth Lay. Failures in personal integrity led to organizational misbehavior that eventually brought the company down. Organizational misbehavior follows personal misbehavior. To put the same point in a positive sense, organizational integrity follows personal integrity.

I want to depart from the usual acknowledgments of people who read the manuscript and helped in its development. Instead, I want to acknowledge people who have greatly impacted my life, showed me personal integrity by example, and contributed to my life with their own life of personal integrity.

Let me begin with family. Dad was a humanist who valued all people. He taught me to treat all people with courtesy, respect, and dignity, regardless of their circumstances, their accidents of birth or their choices. He taught me how to be a real man with true masculinity, not the testosterone-driven, ostentatious manliness of machismo. My daughter, Amanda Davis Hughes, is the most spiritual person I know, although not religious. Her strong sense of right, wrong, and duty is inspirational if not sacred. Knowing her, she probably attributes this sense to me, but I believe her sense of right and wrong rises above and transcends her upbringing. I have the wonderment of marriage to a wife of integrity, Arthurine Payton. She holds the parts together to make us whole, complete, sound, and thus untouched by compromises with integrity. The encouragement and support of her husband are the stuff of which marriage dreams are made. Her mother, Dorothy Payton, is Mom to me, too. She raised four daughters on her own after her husband died before Arthurine was born. The upbringing she gave her daughters is a case study in integrity.

Outside my family, three men contributed immeasurably to my understanding of integrity, my sense of integrity, and my life of integrity. First, Dr. W. Edwards Deming enkindled a deep inner commitment to be the man I could be, the man I ought to be, and the man I was meant to be. Reverend O. Dean Martin, the late pastor of Trinity United Methodist Church, Gainesville, Florida, fueled my spiritual growth with his positive ministry at a time when I had left spiritual growth lagging behind physical, intellectual, and emotional development. Finally, Father Roy Pollina, priest of St. Michael's Episcopal Church, Mandeville, Louisiana, lifted my integrity as a platform for further growth, development, and maturity. He manifested propriety, seemliness, and grace while confronting the ugly face of perfidy, betrayal, and rejection directed at him by people who lost their integrity if they ever had any. His unfailing character elevated the animating integrity of those who were true to him and to his calling.

J. Ronnie Davis

Chapter One
PROPER UNDERSTANDING OF PERSONAL INTEGRITY

THE HAWTHORNE EXPERIMENTS

Academicians and Western Electric managers made the Hawthorne Works complex in Cicero, Illinois, the location of one of the most famous industrial studies of the twentieth century. The studies began in 1924. The National Research Council of the National Academy of Sciences conducted illumination tests to determine if lighting was a significant factor in worker productivity. No consistent correlation was found between lighting level and product output. This surprising outcome suggested that other factors must be involved.

In 1927, a team of academics from the Harvard Business School was invited to continue the studies. Leading the team was Elton Mayo, a professor of industrial research. Mayo stressed noneconomic factors involved in worker productivity and criticized business methods that took no account of human nature and human relations. From 1927 to 1932, Mayo and Fritz Roethlisberger, Mayo's research assistant, undertook controversial studies centered on the effects of working conditions on worker morale and productivity. Results of these studies indicated that output jumped significantly when resources provided workers were improved, when trust and cooperation between workers and supervisors were fostered, when fear in the workplace was eliminated, and when monotony was reduced.

The findings of the Hawthorne studies ran counter to "scientific industrial management" developed by, *inter alia*, Frederick Winslow Taylor. The experiments also challenged widely held assumptions about worker behavior. In particular, findings of the Hawthorne experiments indicated that workers were not motivated solely by narrow self-interest, *e.g.*, pay and benefits. The importance of worker behavior had to be understood.

Organizations and individuals who were threatened by findings of the

Hawthorne experiments sought ways to discredit the evidence that workers were motivated by factors other than pay and benefits. Eventually, the intent to discredit findings led to attacks on the methodology and conclusions of the Hawthorne experiments. After years of brushing aside findings of the Hawthorne experiments, a new term entered the English language. In 1950, Henry Landsberger originated the term "Hawthorne effect." By the 1960s and beyond, Hawthorne effect was a term meaning stimulation of output or accomplishment of any kind that ensues from the mere fact of being under observation. In other words, upholders of the Hawthorne effect insisted that when people know they are part of an experiment and thus are being observed, their behavior is different. These detractors claimed that results or findings of the Hawthorne experiments cannot be trusted because people will give their best efforts to accomplish whatever the experiment expects of them.

Despite decades of heated criticism, detraction, and other attempts to discredit results of the experiments, the Hawthorne findings survived in the quality movement, lately Six Sigma. Indeed, the Hawthorne findings not only survived, they became the heartbeat of management and leadership in the quality movement. From the beginning of the quality movement, the focus has centered on providing workers with materials, tools, equipment, machinery, and training suitable for the job, thus facilitating their pride of workmanship; building trust and cooperation throughout an organization; eliminating fear in the workplace; and more that was motivated by the Hawthorne experiments and findings. Moreover, the Hawthorne experiments led to disciplines such as industrial sociology, industrial psychology, and to academic courses and programs in organizational behavior commonly offered in business schools. Indeed, organizational behavior is one of the curriculum standards for business school accreditation by AACSB (Association to Advance Collegiate Schools of Business).

Organizational Behavior

An organization is an assemblage of interrelated and interacting human and nonhuman resources striving to advance common interests within a framework of structured relationships. Organizational behavior deals with aspects of how an organization influences and affects the behavior of people in the organization and how people in turn influence and affect the organization. As Mayo emphasized, people are social animals. Thus, organizational behavior is interdisciplinary, drawing liberally from social sciences such as anthropology, psychology, and sociology. The preoccupation of organizational behavior has been to improve if not maximize the effectiveness and efficiency of organizational operations, particularly functions and processes.

From Organizational Behavior to Organizational Misbehavior

The *idée fixe* of organizational behavior is centered on improving if not maximizing effectiveness and efficiency of people in an organization. Little if any focus is on organizational misbehavior, improper behavior that transgresses moral or civil law. Yet, recent history has shown that organizational misbehavior has led to corporate scandals, including misconduct that led to the ruin and demise of whole companies and imprisonment of their founders. The misdeeds are well known. Universities and business schools are organizations, and reports of misconduct such as cheating are growing. In some ways, organizational misbehavior should be the focus of concern and study more than organizational behavior.

Organizational misbehavior does not imply or in any way suggest that organizations misbehave. People embedded in the organization misbehave. The misbehavior is personal. Organizational misdeeds are transgressions of people, originated and carried out by people within structured relationships of an organization. Organizational misbehavior is originated and carried out by people in an organization who have personal lapses of integrity. The cure for the disease of organizational misbehavior is the medicine of personal integrity. Indeed, organizational integrity is built on the shoulders of personal integrity. Organizational integrity prevents and forestalls organizational misbehavior, but the nutrient medium of the culture of organizational integrity is personal integrity.

PERSONAL INTEGRITY IS A JOURNEY

This treatise has purpose. The treatise is meant first to develop a proper understanding of integrity, which deals with the whole person. Someone once said, "A man should be greater than some of his parts." This humorous wordplay at least recognizes that people have parts, *viz.*, physical, intellectual, emotional, and spiritual parts. Wholeness, completeness, and thus personal integrity result from growth, development, and maintenance of these parts. Growth, development, and maintenance imply that the pursuit of personal integrity is a journey, dynamic rather than static.

In this treatise, the physical, intellectual, emotional, and spiritual journeys to personal integrity are depicted through personal and business experiences. Afterwards, ten rules for personal integrity are articulated. In this way, the case for personal integrity is propounded and postulated. The case for personal integrity ultimately rests on a preventive for personal misdeeds that lead to organizational misbehavior.

Even the Longest Journey Begins From Where We Stand

Lau-tzu told us, "The journey of a thousand miles begins beneath one's feet." In America, we usually mistranslate the Chinese. We say, "The journey of a thousand miles begins with a single step." However, Lau-tzu had no knowledge of miles and did not emphasize the first step. He regarded action as a natural departure from stillness just as emotion is a departure from calm. So, we understand Lau-tzu better if we translate that even the longest journey begins from where a person stands. In this treatise, I begin from where we stood in the late 1880s with the rise of the modern enterprise, spurring the professionalization of management as well as business schools to meet the rising need for managers.

RISE OF THE MODERN ENTERPRISE

In the mid-nineteenth century, American business firms typically were enterprises owned by an individual or perhaps a family. Manufactured goods, for example, were produced by small, family-owned businesses that were personally managed. The same was true outside manufacturing, *e.g.*, shops, stores, mills, banks, and farms. Few salaried managers were employed in the mainstream of business. In manufacturing, an owner might hire salaried workers to oversee day-to-day operations. Essentially, these salaried workers had duties equivalent to modern first line supervisors. However, in the mid-1800s, there were no middle managers who supervised the work of other managers who in turn reported to top managers.

Continuous Process Machines

In the latter half of the nineteenth century, mass production was introduced in several industries. Large volume production was made possible by continuous process machinery. Output per worker increased greatly, and unit costs of production were reduced sharply. Enterprises that first adopted such machinery, so-called first movers, acquired vast and immediate market power difficult to overtake by later entrants.

An example of continuous process machinery is found in the tobacco products industry. In September 1880, one month shy of his twenty-first birthday, James Albert Bonsack, son of a Virginia tobacco plantation owner and third-generation machinist, applied for a patent on a cigarette-making machine capable of producing over 70,000 cigarettes in a 10-hour day. It was registered as the Bonsack Cigarette Machine. The patent for his rotary cutter and rolling machine was granted in 1881.

In 1883, twenty-seven year old James Buchanan "Buck" Duke leased two Bonsack machines. By 1887, Duke's engineers had improved the Bonsack machine to turn out 120,000 cigarettes in a ten-hour day. At that time, the most highly skilled hand workers, known as "cigarette girls," were capable of making 2,400 to 3,000 cigarettes a day. In this way, *one* Bonsack machine could do the work of *forty or fifty* of the most highly skilled hand workers! Duke himself invented a "crush-proof" package as well as machinery for packaging cigarettes. The Duke machine made packages for cigarettes and mechanically placed cigarettes in the package. His cardboard sliding tray package was intro-duced in 1886.

The first two firms to adopt the Bonsack machine were Duke's American Tobacco Company in the United States and the Imperial Tobacco Company in England. Cost reduction was spectacular. At the American Tobacco Company, cost per thousand cigarettes was quickly reduced from eighty cents to thirty cents and then to twenty-four cents, which was less than one-third of the cost of cigarettes made by hand workers. The price of a package of ten cigarettes, which was standard, was reduced from ten cents to five cents. At the Imperial Tobacco Company in England, Bonsack machines reduced cost per thousand cigarettes from sixty pence to ten pence, an astonishing cost reduction of more than *eighty* percent! Each of these firms, American Tobacco and Imperial To-bacco, consequently dominated the cigarette industry in its own country.

Continuous Process Factories

Creation of a continuous process factory was more complicated than a con-tinuous process machine since such factories involved a number of intricately arranged processes that had to be synchronized with exactness in operation. An important example was the gradual reduction mill used to process wheat into flour. Independently, Cadwallander Colden Washburn and Charles Alfred Pillsbury developed such mills. Before such mills, flour was milled from one grinding by stones set close together. The new gradual reduction mills utilized three to five grindings by stones progressively closer together, resulting in finer flour with fewer impurities. Moreover, these mills produced more flour per bushel of wheat.

Washburn built his first flourmill in 1866 and, with a partner named John Crosby, formed Washburn, Crosby & Company in 1877. By 1890, Washburn and Pillsbury had perfected these mills, which used steel rollers to replace grindstones. Both men first harnessed the churning falls at St. Anthony on the upper Mississippi River to thresh their wheat into flour. As Duke did in to-bacco, Pillsbury and Washburn began to package and brand their products as part of the production process. After Washburn won the gold medal for flour at the 1880 Millers International Exhibition in Cincinnati, he thereafter used Gold Medal as the brand for his flour, a brand that has endured.

The "new process" mills produced high quality wheat flour in large volume and at low unit cost. In 1928, after acquiring a number of other mills, General Mills was formed under Washburn, Crosby leadership. In 2001, General Mills acquired Pillsbury. A century earlier, the two companies had flourmills in Minneapolis on opposite banks of the Mississippi River. The "merger" of the two companies basically doubled the size of General Mills.

The Can Line

In 1883, a different kind of continuous process innovation was developed for processing agricultural crops. Edwin Norton built the first automatic-line canning factory. The "can line" consisted of special-purpose machines and a conveyor system. Norton's can line machines were capable of soldering cans at the rate of 3,000 per hour along with other machines that added tops and bottoms at the rate of 2,500 to 4,400 units per hour. The Norton automatic can line had spillover effects to other industries. Others noted that the can line brought work to the worker. For example, in 1913, Henry Ford's machine tool expert, Oscar C. Bornholdt, pointed out that the sequential arrangement of machine tools at the Ford factory was comparable to the layout of food canning machinery.

In 1901, Edwin Norton purchased sixty tin container companies and their 123 factories, and he founded the American Can Company. Afterwards, a number of these factory sites were shut down or sold. Nevertheless, American Can soon accounted for more than ninety percent of all cans produced in the United States. After retiring in 1902, he backed his son to form the Continental Can Company in November 1904.

Firms that first used the new canning system on a year-round basis were Borden, Campbell Soup, and Heinz. These "first movers" became some of the largest canners in the United States. Each is an example of first mover advantage, which is an insurmountable advantage gained by the first significant company to enter a market or first to adopt an innovative technology. In this case, first movers included Gail Borden, who enlarged facilities for canning milk and expanded the capacity for marketing milk. The Dorrance family of Philadelphia did the same for Campbell soup products. Henry John Heinz in Pittsburgh did likewise with his "57 varieties" of pickles, sauces, and other products.

Mass Production, Branding, and Multi-Market Distribution

Other companies also turned to mass production, branding, and multi-market distribution. Distributing and selling into several markets were necessary to sell large volumes. Procter & Gamble became a first mover in consumer chemicals. Sherwin-Williams in paints and Parke, Davis in pharmaceutical drugs also expanded their production facilities and built international marketing networks.

Producers of fresh meat and other perishable products took action to enlarge their distribution channels. Gustavus V. Swift, a Chicago meatpacker, financed the development of the refrigerator car and built a nationwide distribution organization. At the same time, Milwaukee and St. Louis beer brewers expanded by creating comparable networks. Their expansion was facilitated by development of specialized railroad cars for transporting beer. The Fleischmann Company developed a refrigerated network for the daily distribution of yeast to more than a thousand large bakeries. United Fruit Company began to build a network of refrigerated cars, ships, and depots comparable to the networks of meatpackers and brewers.

RISE OF MANAGERS

Increased volume of output and sales, branding of products, and establishment of far-reaching distribution networks became commonplace. Developments such as continuous process machinery and factories increased an owner-operator's responsibilities in functional areas of business such as purchasing, operations, sales, distribution, and finance. In turn, these developments led to establishment of a central office to ensure that everything from acquisition of raw materials to production runs and deliveries of finished products was accomplished smoothly and seamlessly. Manufacturing firms increasingly chose to acquire raw materials and distribute finished products themselves rather than rely on independent principals such as factors, agents, and brokers.

To administer their extensive, unprecedented investments in large-scale production and distribution facilities and networks, producers required lower-level managers to operate the several units of production as well as to take charge of marketing, purchasing, and so forth. Next, they needed middle and top managers to coordinate and monitor the activities of these operating units and to allocate financial wherewithal for growth of the enterprise.

RISE OF BUSINESS SCHOOLS

In the mid-nineteenth century, business schools in colleges had not been established to accommodate the rapidly rising need for managers. Furthermore, no programs for advanced study in business had been instituted. Medicine and law had been professionalized and medical schools and law schools provided the necessary curriculum and training for practice in these traditional professions. A need to professionalize management was growing, however, and a corresponding need to provide programs to prepare young people for practice in the profession of management was evident. In this way, young people, mostly young men at the time, would have an alternative to practice in the professions of medicine and law.

Responding to this emerging need, America's first business school, the Wharton School of Business of the University of Pennsylvania, was formed in 1881. In 1900, the Tuck School of Business of Dartmouth College offered the first postgraduate program in commercial sciences, *i.e.,* management, the forebear of the modern MBA. With the onset of such programs of study, fulfilling the rising need for managers had begun, and a new profession was birthed as the equal of medicine and law. To date, the MBA is regarded as a professional degree.

BUSINESS SCHOOL DEANS

Nowadays, business schools and MBA programs are standard fare for all colleges and universities except traditional liberal arts institutions. The chief academic officer of these schools and programs is the business school dean, whose job is to provide administrative control and professional leadership within the business school and to represent the business school and university within the business community. Mostly, these roles are fancy and fiction. Reality is the modern business dean exhausts most of his or her time raising money. Consequently, if the business school dean is in his or her campus office, the dean is not doing the expected job of raising money outside the office.

Most business school deans do not teach and do not write for publication. In this sense, they are hardly faculty members. Indeed, business school deans are set apart from their own faculty, although they occasionally preside over faculty meetings. Matters such as academic curriculum and academic requirements are discussed, debated, and decided by faculty members. On such occasions, the dean sees his or her role simply as maintaining order and assuring the agenda is completed without going over the allotted time.

A Personal Exception

In 1981, I began a stint spanning fifteen years as business school dean at three different universities, Western Washington University, University of South Alabama, and University of New Orleans. I was an exception to the archetypal business school dean. In the first place, I am highly academic. I took my doctorate in economics from the University of Virginia, and my academic experience there dealt with economics as a social science rather than a business discipline. My doctoral dissertation dealt with intellectual history. My first academic appointment at Iowa State University was in the College of Sciences and Humanities. At the time, Iowa State did not have a business school.

I never have believed in power "by virtue of the authority vested in me." When understood as power vested in someone who can demand obedience to orders and who can make judgments regarding those subjected to this power, authority is hardly a virtue. In business, of course, many managers direct people based on the authority of his or her position. Such managers see management as highly directive, and they rely on the authority of their position for their power to boss people around. These managers delight in managing people while seldom if ever considering that people generally hate the feeling of being managed or bossed around.

"Amazing" Grace Hopper, who made a career of the U.S. Navy, retired as a Rear Admiral after the nomenclature of her rank was changed from Commodore. She once said, "You manage things, and you lead people." In other words, her prescription was to manage work and to lead people. Managers who lead people rely on the virtue of their character. They have vision and a strong sense of mission, what is supposed to be accomplished. They articulate the vision and mission in concrete terms that people can understand. They inspire, motivate, and otherwise align people to achieve the vision and accomplish the mission. The same people who hate being managed do not mind being led. In fact, people who hate being managed and being bossed around generally like responding to leadership. In the case of leadership, power and respect do not ensue from the authority of a position. The power and respect due to a leader ensue from character. Character is a virtue.

As a business school dean, I always tried to lead by example. Even after becoming a business school dean, I always taught a course, almost always Managerial Economics in the MBA program. If I asked faculty members to do a good job of teaching, then I thought I also should teach and do a good job of teaching. After becoming a business school dean, I kept writing for publication, including textbooks, scholarly books, and scholarly articles for publication in refereed journals. Again, I thought I should be published if I expected faculty members to be published. Indeed, while a business school dean, I was the editor of a scholarly journal, *Public Finance Review*, on the list of Sage Publications in California.

In these and other ways, I was a typical business school faculty member even when I was a business school dean. In my role as business school dean, I raised a fair amount of money, lobbied successfully in 1990 for state legislative approval of a new business school building finally occupied in 2005 a week before Hurricane Katrina. I was nice to everybody, including a few to whom I did not feel like being nice. However, I did not give up being a faculty member to be a business school dean. After all, my reasons for going into academics were to teach and to write. I was not willing to forsake those seminal interests and commitments to take on an administrative role as one of the officers of a university.

WHAT BUSINESS STUDENTS REALLY NEED TO KNOW

After four years at Iowa State University, I joined the business school faculty at the University of Florida in 1971. In fall of that year, I was engaged as an expert witness for a case headed eventually to the U.S. Supreme Court. In the course of this engagement, I met other expert witnesses who were consultants with a national accounting firm. After our expert testimony in the case, they asked if I would be interested in doing some work with their consulting practice. Of course, I said I'd like to work with them again. I expected to hear nothing further from them.

Two weeks later, they were preparing a proposal to conduct a management audit of a large public school system. They simply wanted my credentials to improve on their chances of winning the engagement. We were engaged, and I tagged along with the team. I began to learn management consulting. For a while, I worked on a number of engagements with this firm and with another management consulting firm headquartered in New York City. Soon, I began working on my own. From the downright fluke beginning, the experiences blossomed into a robust management consulting practice, mainly cost and productivity improvement and strategic planning. Over the years, this consulting practice kept me engaged for fifty to a hundred hours monthly during the academic year and fulltime during summers.

Based on my consulting experience, I am committed to teaching MBA students what they really need to know and thus what they really will use in a business career. I stay away from textbook "mumbo jumbo," stuff they will never need to know and will never use. Instead of teaching Managerial Economics based on economic theory, I teach the course based on economics actually used in business practice.

In the 1980s while still a business school dean, I wrote a Managerial Economics textbook with Semoon Chang. Since I teach only Managerial Economics in the MBA program, adopting my own book would have been natural. However, I have never used the textbook that Semoon Chang and I wrote! *Principles of Managerial Economics* was written "for the market," *i.e.,* what professors teaching Managerial Economics typically wanted in a textbook. Most professors who teach Managerial Economics do not have any business experience whatsoever. They are academic economists. They teach what they know, academic economics. What they want in a textbook is a lot of elegant, esoteric theories that are irrelevant for making business decisions and crafting business strategies.

Instead of adopting my own textbook written for the market, I wrote a comprehensive "course packet" for my Managerial Economics students. The course packet, *Economics for Executives: Principles, Practices, and Strategies*, was the reading material for Managerial Economics. It contains what I found from consulting experience that students really need to know and really will use. I eschewed the beauty and elegance of those esoteric economic theories irrelevant to making business decisions and crafting business strategies. Instead, the course packet focused on the economics used in business practice by business practitioners. The course packet evolved into publication of *Economics for Executives: Principles, Practices, and Strategies.*

Beyond Business Topics and Business Language

As in an epiphany a few years ago, I suddenly had a flash realization that MBA students really need to know more than business language, business principles, business practices, and business strategies. Of course, MBA students needed to know about demand and supply; demand elasticity; diminishing returns; economies of scale, scope, and experience; learning curves and progress ratios; principles of profit maximization; economic value added; breakeven analysis; degree of operating leverage; Six Sigma; pricing strategies; competitive analysis;

competitive advantage; antitrust; and more. All of these business topics and associated business language are important to MBA students preparing for a business career. However, I experienced a sudden perception and comprehension that business students needed more than mastery of business topics and business language to succeed in business and in life. The epiphany was realization that to prepare for a business career, business students also really needed to know something about personal integrity.

THE DECLINE OF BUSINESS ETHICS
IN THE BUSINESS CURRICULUM

In the 1990s, I knew students preparing for careers in management really needed to know about integrity, particularly personal integrity. I began to integrate stories about life experiences into my class lectures and to devote as much as three hours of each semester to the topic of personal integrity. At the time, one of the curriculum requirements for AACSB accreditation was coverage of business ethics. Most schools at first complied with a course in business ethics. However, I knew that many schools were watering down their course offering drip by drip. Some schools reduced their business ethics course from three semester credits to two, perhaps to one, whereas other schools did away with the course altogether. With a wink and a nod, an abundance of smoke and mirrors, these schools claimed the topic of business ethics was covered "across the curriculum."

Even at those schools where business ethics was being taught in a course, topics often centered on standards governing the conduct of managers. More often than not, topics dealt largely with what managers must do to stay out of trouble. Indeed, the approach often became serial classes centered on "Let me tell you how to get around this or get away with that so you don't violate an organization's rules or laws of the land." The exceptions to this approach were truly exceptional, providing genuine education in the fundamental tenets of ethics applied to business practice.

The Incline of Need for Personal Integrity

Integrity, particularly personal integrity, was lost in this discussion of business ethics, a little like Hamlet without the Prince. Yet, students really need to know about personal integrity and really should use their knowledge of personal integrity as surely as they need to know about and should use their knowledge of business concepts and business language. Seeing the need, I used as much as three hours in my MBA course to tell students what personal integrity is, tell them a little about my own personal journey, and tell them what I regard as ten rules for personal integrity.

Students responded favorably. Almost every year, I am recognized as "Professor of the Year" or "Teacher of the Year" in the University of New Orleans Executive MBA program on campus in New Orleans as well as in Puerto Rico and Jamaica. Twice, I also was recognized as "Mentor of the Year," the only two years the nomenclature ever was designated. In 2007, the Executive MBA class honored me as Professor of the Year "in recognition of outstanding guidance in Managerial Economics *and Life's Lessons.*" Emphasis is mine. Every semester, students swarm to me afterwards, many of them imploring me to write "life's lessons" and include them with the course packet. Many of them have urged publication of life's lessons.

The Shocking Reports of Cheating

After teaching a little about personal integrity in my MBA course and in my Executive MBA course for more than ten years, I think the need for personal integrity is greater now than ever. The Academy of Management Learning and Education surveyed more than five thousand students in the United States and Canada. Results showed that graduate students in business are cheating more than graduate students in general, and graduate students in general are cheating at an alarming rate. Cheating was defined as plagiarizing, copying another student's work, or bringing prohibited material into an exam. According to the study, many students believe that cheating is an accepted practice in business. More than half of students surveyed admitted cheating in the past year.

Actually, the percentage is probably higher than the reported fifty-six percent. Some cheaters undoubtedly don't admit to cheating or if they do admit to cheating undoubtedly underreport their cheating. After all, if junk food addicts were asked how many Twinkies they ate in the past week, they undoubtedly would underreport their consumption just as alcoholics probably would underreport how many cans of beer they drank in the past week. Authors of the study were quoted as saying, "To us that means that business school faculty and administrators must do something, because doing nothing simply reinforces the belief that high levels of cheating are commonplace and acceptable."

However, even published reports of the study focused almost solely on punishment and other forms of discipline when students are caught cheating. These reports concentrated on fear of litigation that holds faculty and administrators back from taking action. To me, this focus is misplaced. It is like saying we need to find a way to scrape the burnt toast. This misplaced focus is on fixing instead of preventing. It is like turning the clock back by decades and returning to mass inspection as the sole means of quality assurance. Instead of scrapping defective product (expelling students caught cheating) or reworking defective product (requiring students caught cheating to repeat a course), what about a focus on prevention? Laying a foundation of personal integrity is preventive in nature.

Business students and business practitioners have a need to learn about and practice personal integrity. After all, cheating in an MBA program or cheating in business practice is one form of violating basic principles of honesty and trustworthiness. Dishonesty and untrustworthiness are outward evidence of an underlying lack of or failure of personal integrity. Certainly, the corporate scandals and accounting scandals of 2002 alone are a clarion call for attention to personal integrity.

CORPORATE SCANDALS

Enron, WorldCom, Adelphia. In a wave of corporate scandals centered on 2002, each of these corporate names became a household word for corruption, deceit, and fraud. These organizations systematically violated laws of the land, not to mention callously disregarded manifold principles of moral and ethical behavior, even standards of humanity. On a personal level, high-ranking members of top management were convicted of serious crimes, people such as Kenneth Lay, Jeffrey Skilling, and Andrew Fastow; Bernard Ebbers; as well as John and Timothy Rigas. At the behest of its founder and other top executives, Enron boosted reported profit and hid debt through improper and illicit off-the-books partnerships; WorldCom improperly and illicitly overstated its cash flow and granted its founder vast off-the-books loans; and Adelphia improperly and illicitly overstated earnings, hid debt, and made immense off-the-books loans to the founders backed by the company.

A question that comes to the mind of anyone who followed these corporate scandals is "Why?" Why would fabulously wealthy men violate the law and put themselves as well as their companies in legal jeopardy as means to accumulate still more wealth? Why would the founders of Enron, WorldCom, and Adelphia violate the law and thus act to bring down the companies they birthed? The superficial answer is greed. Excessive desire to acquire more material wealth than deserved is a symptom rather than the underlying disease. Unlawful actions taken to enlarge personal wealth were accommodated by convenient lapses of conscience, a willful urge to tolerate if not prefer wrong to right. Founders and others of these companies lost their way if they ever had a way. The lodestar they followed was clouded and darkened by lapses of integrity, particularly personal integrity.

The Foundation for Organizational Integrity

Honesty is not merely truthfulness. Honesty is also fairness in dealing with others as well as principled refusal to engage in fraud or deceit. Yet, integrity is not honesty. We are honest when we have integrity. Integrity is not trustworthiness. We are worthy of trust when we have integrity. Honesty and trustworthiness are outward indications of integrity. Core values of an organization are standards that the organization expects to be respected and practiced in all activities and at all times without compromise. In an incomplete way, these core values are meant to codify organizational integrity. Yet, accomplishment of organizational integrity cannot be based on mere articulation of core values. Organizational integrity must be built on the foundation of personal integrity.

Character

Character evidences moral and ethical qualities. Some companies look to character before any other attribute in their hiring, evaluating, and promoting decisions. These companies have a vision of organizational integrity that can be achieved only by investment in the personal integrity of its employees. Hiring people of character, evaluating people based on character, and promoting people based on character are the nutrients that feed organizational character. In this sense, character is in the first rank of considerations, placing personal integrity first and foremost even before university degrees and experience.

Personal integrity is more than moral uprightness, however. Personal integrity is moral uprightness *plus*. It is character *plus*. Personal integrity, the cornerstone on which the architecture of organizational integrity is built, deals with the inclusive configuration of the whole person, a gestalt of physical, intellectual, emotional, and spiritual parts.

PERSONAL INTEGRITY

"Know thyself" is an ancient Greek aphorism. Know thyself can be made so unnecessarily complex to be baffling and perplexing beyond ordinary human comprehension. On the other hand, water can be squeezed from know thyself to arrive at its existential elements. Once done, know thyself can be considered in the simplest terms possible, ultimately reduced to its intrinsic least common denominator.

Eventually, this reductionism unfolds the uncomplicated conclusion each of us is configured by distinct personal characteristics that constitute our unique individuality. These distinct personal characteristics have dimensions as surely as the spatial extents of height, width, and depth. Indeed, the totality of these distinct personal characteristics that constitute and define each of us can be disaggregated into four fundamental dimensions: physical, intellectual, emotional, and spiritual. In the same way that material objects can be seen in the spatial terms of height, width, and depth, each of these four dimensional aspects shows a different side of us. Each is a side of our respective individuality, and the sides taken together configure our individualities.

When seen in this light, the perspective is analogous to a box placed in a room with four windows. If someone perceives the box through one window, he or she sees only one side of the box but not all sides. With regard to ourselves, if someone looked through the physical window, for example, he or she sees only the physical side, and the other sides of our individuality would remain unseen and thus remain a mystery. Seeing our own integral individuality requires looking through all four windows at once, seeing at once the physical, intellectual, emotional, and spiritual sides that configure our total individuality. In this way, the manifold aspects of their relations can be discerned.

Striving for Wholeness

Each of us is the totality and integrality of distinct physical, intellectual, emotional, and spiritual characteristics. Each of these dimensional characteristics is subject to and is governed by maintenance, growth, development, and maturity over our lifetimes. As a simplification, consider growth. Growth of one characteristic is not necessarily at the same rate as growth of others. At one time in our lives, we may not grow or develop in the area of one characteristic as the others. At another time in our lives, growth may lead to development in the area of three characteristics, but the remaining characteristic may be left underdeveloped or undeveloped altogether. At such times in our lives, the unbalanced growth and development rob us of our sense of wholeness. We live a fractionalized life, the sum of our parts not completing the whole.

When we leave one characteristic or another behind the growth of others and thus experience lagging development in that one characteristic, we feel we do not have our act together or do not have our [expletive deleted] together, as young people say. We do not feel complete. We do not feel whole. We do not feel that the sum of our parts add up to complete the whole. For example, if we are well developed physically and intellectually and spiritually, but poorly developed emotionally, we will not feel whole and complete. If we are well developed physically and intellectually and emotionally, but poorly developed spiritually, we will not feel whole and complete. We feel that something is missing from our lives and, indeed, something is missing. What is missing is the realization of wholeness and fullness. Because of what is missing, we are fractions of ourselves, and we lead fractionalized lives. We do not have personal integrity that makes us whole.

INTEGRITY

The word "integrity" comes from the same Latin root, *integritas*, from which the word "integer" comes. An integer is a "whole number" such as 13, 52, 101, or 5,280. The Latin root *integritas* means whole. It also means untouched. When we have integrity, we have completeness, wholeness. When we have integrity, we are unbroken, we are entire, and we are sound. Integrity infers the existence of parts and indicates the interdependence of these parts and the completeness of the whole. The parts act on each other. The parts add up to complete the whole. Integrity means that we are so entire, whole, complete, and sound that we are incapable of being false to or of betraying a trust, a responsibility, or a pledge. Integrity means that we have such rectitude that we cannot be touched, that we are untouched by compromises with trust and responsibility.

None of us can leave one part of the whole person behind and still maintain our sense of personal integrity. When we grow and develop, we must grow and develop in balanced proportions if we grow in personal integrity and with personal integrity. As we move from physical characteristics to intellectual, emotional, and spiritual characteristics, we also move more and more away from genetics and towards choices we make, more and more towards characteristics under our control. "Under our control" means that the characteristic is less genetic and more behavioral. For example, the physical aspect of our individuality is far more genetic than the spiritual aspect. Moving from physical to intellectual to emotional to spiritual means more and more is up to us to decide. As Adam Trask said to Cal in the movie *East of Eden*, "A man has a choice. That's where he's different from an animal." Control begins with awareness. In turn, awareness begins with a look at and a consideration of each aspect of our respective individualities.

Physical

The word "physical" comes from a Greek root, *physikos*, translating as "pertaining to nature." In its usual usage, "physical" pertains to the body as opposed to the mind, although another usual usage also pertains to natural or material things. One characteristic of our individualities deals with our bodies. To a degree but not altogether, the physical characteristic of our individualities takes care of itself. Physically, we spring up and mature physically as surely as the lowliest morning glory from a seed planted in fertile soil and watered properly. For the most part, we are born to be tall or short, white or black or brown in skin color, and blond or brunette in hair color. We inherit a wide range of physical characteristics from our parents, grandparents, great grandparents, and so on. How we relate to nature is determined in part by nature itself. How we relate to nature also is determined in part by choices we make.

A realization of genuine integrity, which is to say wholeness and fullness, is based in part on physical maintenance. In other words, as we grow and develop physically according to our genetic makeup, our personal integrity increasingly depends on choices dealing with how well we maintain our bodies. We cannot leave the physical side of our individualities behind and still have the personal integrity we seek.

We do not need to run marathons to maintain our bodies or take care of ourselves. Indeed, we do not need to run at all, but we do need to follow some sort of sensible regimen of physical exercise of sufficient intensity and duration to have proper cardiovascular effect and to prevent muscle loss as we age. For most of us, walking will produce the cardiovascular effect, but choosing to jog, cycle, swim, or to undertake some other similar activity also produces this effect. Modest weightlifting at home or at an athletic club will keep the muscle mass we otherwise lose over the years.

We also must follow a regimen of good sense and judgment regarding our habits. Drinking alcoholic beverages only in true moderation. Eating whole grains, limiting fat intake, and following other practices that we now know contribute to good health. This regimen also includes no smoking. Period. In his poem, *The Hunting of the Snark*, Lewis Carroll (pen name of C. L. Dodgson) says, "What I tell you three times is true." Following this tradition, no smoking, no smoking, and no smoking. Therefore, it's true.

Intellectual

The word "intellect" comes from a Latin root, *intellectus*, which in verb form translates as "to understand." The word "intellect" thus deals with the power of understanding, knowing, reasoning, comprehending, and judging. Intellect deals with the ability to perceive relationships. The word "intelligent" implies success in solving problems through the power of understanding, knowing, reasoning, comprehending, and judging. The word "intellectual" refers to belonging to, relating to, or performed by the intellect. To a degree, our intellectual characteristic takes care of itself. In other words, our intellect is determined genetically to some extent but to another extent is determined by environment and experience. Some of us are more adroit, more alert, more quick-witted, and more knowing than others. As in the case of our physical side, however, our intellectual side and our respective intellectual growth and intellectual development also are dependent on choices that we make.

All of us have an intellectual side, an intellectual characteristic to our respective individualities. Intellectually, we cannot grow, develop, mature, or even maintain by standing still. In fact, we cannot stand still by standing still. The late Methodist minister O. Dean Martin once said, "We grow every day. We grow either forwards or backwards." If we are content to stand still intellectually, we grow backwards. To grow forwards intellectually requires intention, commitment, effort, and exercise.

So many people spend much of their lives watching vacuous entertainment programs on television, going to mindless movies, playing meaningless video games, or otherwise squandering time in a similar manner. Any of these activities is worthy of a mind, an intellect that is growing and developing. Some of life should be entertaining rather than informing. If these activities are undertaken at the exclusion of growing and developing intellectually, however, then these activities are destructive. Reading a book, listening to an opera, attending an art exhibit, visiting a museum, watching a dramatic stage play, learning a new skill, studying for a degree, qualifying for a certification are activities that contribute to a mind that is not standing still but rather is growing forwards. To grow forwards, we must find a means of evolving the possibilities of our minds more fully, making the resources of our minds more available and usable, making our latent thoughts more active. My father, Marion Fuller Davis, was the equivalent of the village wise man. He had his own take on the old saying, "You can't teach an old dog new tricks." He said, "As long as you are learning new tricks, you will never be an old dog."

Muriel Spark wrote a splendid novel, *The Prime of Miss Jean Brodie*, made into an equally splendid movie of the same title. Indeed, Maggie Smith was awarded the Best Actress Oscar in 1969 for her peerless portrayal of the eponymous Miss Jean Brodie. Miss Brodie was a schoolteacher who was totally devoted in her own way to her girls, the *crème de la crème*. She believed in true education, pointing out correctly that the word "educate" comes from the Latin "*e-*," meaning "out," and "*ducere*," meaning "to lead." Educate means to lead out something already within us. An educator is one who leads out something within another person. Miss Brodie objected to thrusting something in, which she said was not education but rather intrusion.

It is so with intellectual growth. When we grow forwards, we lead out the intellectual possibilities and resources of our minds more fully. We lead out our latent thoughts and make them active.

Emotional

The word "emotion" comes from a Latin root, emovere, which in turn comes from "*e-*," meaning "out," and "*-movere*," meaning "to move." Emotion deals with feelings such as fear, anger, disgust, grief, joy, surprise, and yearning. Emotion means to move out, which is to say to move out feelings. When we say that we are moved, we literally mean it. In general, feelings and emotions are responses that are partly physical and partly mental.

Emotion generally refers to a departure from calm, a departure that includes strong feeling and an impulse toward open action. This departure from calm involves certain internal physical reactions. All of us have an emotional side to our individualities. As children, this emotional characteristic is undeveloped and immature. As we grow toward adulthood, our emotional characteristic should grow, develop, and mature. Otherwise, we remain emotionally as children. As Paul of Tarsus wrote in a letter to his followers in Corinth, "When I was a child, I spake as a child, I understood as a child, I thought as a child: but when I became a man, I put away childish things."

Many men in particular remain emotionally undeveloped or underdeveloped. Men tend to be guarded about showing emotion, which is to say that men tend to be guarded about feelings. When we are boys, some of us learn that men are supposed to be strong, and strong men do not show their feelings. As a result, many men do not even know their feelings. Indeed, they cannot even make a short list of feelings. If they find themselves in counseling, they find themselves at a total loss to answer the usual question, "How do you feel about that?" They answer the only way they know, saying, "Okay." Or "Good." Or "Bad." Or "Terrible." The counselor asks, "Yes, but how do you feel about it?" The man says, "What do you mean?" The counselor then has to give multiple choices to move the session along. "Do you feel happy, sad, frustrated, angry? How do you feel?"

We are every person we ever have been. Each of us is still the little boy or little girl we once were. Each of us is still the adolescent that we once were. The magic key to a healthy and successful emotional life is to keep the little boy or little girl in us happy without letting the little boy or little girl run our lives. We must keep the adolescent in us happy without letting the adolescent run our lives. A major problem for adults is that, if we did not have a successful childhood, we tend to keep repeating and reliving childhood in an attempt to get it right. If we did not have a successful adolescence, an adolescence in which we accomplished all of the tasks we are supposed to accomplish in our adolescence, we tend to keep repeating and reliving our adolescence as adults in the attempt to get it right this time, until we accomplish these tasks of adolescence.

Usually, when we say someone needs to grow up, we are talking about the emotional side of a person. He or she is behaving childishly. When a behavior always worked with your mother, when a behavior always got you what you wanted as a child, the behavior might be repeated over and over until you finally learn it no longer works. Learning that it no longer works can be costly and painful. Tantrums that always worked with your mother may cost you your job or your marriage when you are an adult. Someone who did not have a successful adolescence may keep repeating adolescent behavior over and over in a pubescent attempt to get it right. The person may be caught in a kind of time warp, not able to grow up emotionally to adulthood because he or she is not able to advance successfully beyond adolescence. The problem is that these people keep repeating the failures of adolescence. Going from girlfriend to girlfriend as an adolescent becomes going from wife to wife as an adult. Shirking responsibility for the consequences of one's own choices and actions becomes blaming others, thinking in terms of bad luck, or things just happening to us.

How we behave emotionally is a matter of how we act or change in relation to an environment. How we respond in relation to an environment has its physical, intellectual, and emotional aspects. Behavior implies a standard of what is proper. In terms of emotional maturity, behavior implies that adults grow and mature emotionally to the extent that our actions and behavior show that we can direct or control ourselves. We grow and mature to the extent that, as adults, we direct and control our emotions rather than be directed and controlled by our emotions, as we were when we were juveniles and adolescents. This kind of emotional growth and maturity does not just happen. Directing and controlling our emotions rather than being directed and controlled by them must be made to happen.

When we grow and develop physically and intellectually but not emotionally, we do not have the sense of integrity, the sense that the parts add up to make and complete the whole. When we leave emotional growth behind, our actions and behavior are often childish responses in relation to situations. Often, these situations are parallax in our minds to those of childhood, and our actions and behavior are childhood responses repeated over and over again to these situations. Grow up usually means grow up emotionally.

Spiritual

The word "spirit" comes from a Latin root, *spiritus*, which is related to a Latin root, "*spirare*," meaning "to breathe." As a word, therefore, spirit suggests the breath of life. Spirit suggests a kind of vapor that breathes life into flesh and bone, a kind of vapor that animates the body or mediates between the body and soul. Spirit is viewed as breath, a gift of deity, and thus the agent of vital and conscious functions in us. The breath given to us as spirit is the respiratory agent of the soul. Irrespective of religion, soul refers to the essence or substance, the animating principle or actualizing cause of life manifested in thinking, willing, and knowing. Spiritual is simply an adjective that describes something relating to or consisting of the spirit. Spiritual is an adjective dealing with the higher endowments of the mind and with the moral feelings or states of the soul.

All of us have a spiritual side to our individualities. As children, this spiritual aspect is immature and undeveloped. Based on the kind of upbringing by our parents and on the kind of schooling by our teachers, we develop a sense of values, a sense of right and wrong, and a sense of connection and relation to others and for some people to God. This sense of values serves as a lodestar that leads us in the right direction in making choices and decisions. This sense of values gives purpose to our lives and is teleological, meaning that our lives are directed toward an end and shaped by a purpose.

As we grow to and arrive at adulthood, we must grow spiritually. Our spiritual characteristic should grow, develop, and mature. Otherwise, we remain spiritually as children, having no internal sense of direction but instead requiring direction from others in authority, having no internal values but instead depending on the values of others around us, having no internal sense of right and wrong but instead behaving morally only to please others when they are watching, and having no internal sense of connection and relation to our fellow man but instead having other people in our lives only when necessary from a practical viewpoint. Otherwise, we do not fully develop these senses. Otherwise, we do not have a principle of life that animates us with spirit and vigor or a cause of life that actualizes and realizes in action what we think, will, and know. We do not have a sense of purpose. When efforts and actions and lives are not purposeful, they are not motivated and animated. When lives are not purposeful, they are meaningless, and no sense of fulfillment is possible because no purpose has been established.

THE BREATH OF LIFE MAKES US HUMAN

If what the author (or if the documentary hypothesis is correct, the authors) of Genesis tells us is taken literally, the issue of time, *viz.*, day, must be resolved first. Einstein turned to an outrageous example to illustrate that time is relative to the observer. Remember Einstein's twin paradox. One twin leaves Earth on a rocket ship traveling near the speed of light, the other remaining on Earth for many years. When the twin brother returns to Earth, he is still a young man whereas his twin left on Earth is an old man. Before humankind, time was relative to the only observer, God. Thus, day was a case of *kairos*, God's time, not *chronos*, mankind's time. In other words, before mankind, day was universal or cosmic time, not day in the sense of Earth time because man was not yet an observer. Day could not have meant day relative to man before mankind was an observer.

The sequence of events recorded in Genesis is fairly descriptive of what scientists tell us happened in the early universe. The first universal or cosmic day in Genesis, light separates from dark, *i.e.,* photons finally escape the gravity of a very dense universe, and light is first seen; the second day, the heavenly firmament forms, *i.e.,* the Milky Way, Sun and Moon form; the third day, oceans and dry land appear and plant life springs forth, *i.e.,* Earth cools enough for liquid water followed by first forms of bacteria and algae; the fourth day, the Sun, Moon, and stars become visible from Earth, *i.e.,* Earth's atmosphere becomes transparent and an oxygen-rich atmosphere is produced; the fifth day, animal life is abundant in waters followed by reptiles and winged animals, *i.e.,* animal life appears in waters, each having the basic body plans of future animals, and winged insects appear; and the sixth day, land animals, mammals, and humans appear, *i.e.,* land is populated or perhaps repopulated after massive extinction, including hominoids followed by human beings. Basically, this sequence found in Genesis is the same as the sequence of events proposed in the Big Bang theory of the universe.

In this way, Genesis tells us that humankind was created on the sixth universal or cosmic day. We are told that God made humankind from dust. In fact, heavy elements including all elements other than hydrogen and helium have come to Earth from exploding stars. In other words, all heavy elements on Earth are literally stardust. The implication is that each of us is composed of dust, stardust that is a carrier of various atoms that have come to us from those exploding stars.

Atoms are mostly space. In various analogies, this aspect of atoms can be appreciated. Someone suggested that if a hydrogen atom were expanded to the size of the Louisiana Superdome, its nucleus would be the size of a marble, and its electron would be smaller than a grain of sand. Another suggested that, if a hydrogen atom were the size of a basketball, its electron would be fifteen miles away. Still another imagines complex atoms in which outermost electrons are slower than innermost electrons. The slowest outermost electrons would be eight thousand miles away. Any of these analogies illustrate that atoms are mostly space, equivalent to saying atoms are mostly nothing.

Since we are composed of atoms, we are mostly nothing. The breath of life makes something from nothing. Genesis tells us that humankind was made from dust and that God breathed the breath of life into man's nostrils. Only after the breath of life did man become a human being. Our humanity comes from this final act, the breath of life. Spirituality, the breath of life, makes us human.

TRANSFORMATION

In the early 1970s, I partnered with an industrial psychologist. As consultants, we were engaged to change organizational cultures that ruled so many manufacturing, assembly, and chemical plants. Plant managers inculcated an acculturation of passing orders down through the ranks. Essentially, plant managers taught hourly workers to shut up rather than to encourage them to speak up. My partner and I believed the old saying, "The best ideas come from those who are closest to the work." Our consulting and training were centered on this belief. Our intent was to unhinge the meme that silenced hourly workers and to instill trust among salaried managers as well as hourly workers. With trust, hourly workers were no longer muzzled and thus were free to come forward with their ideas for improvement in processes and systems. Hence, we called our program "Companywide Employee Involvement."

One day, we were in a final meeting with chemical plant managers in South Carolina capping our lengthy engagement. When the meeting wound down and we were walking out the room, an engineer said to me, "What you do reminds me of Deming." I had never heard of anyone named Deming, but being a typical man, I didn't want to admit I didn't know something. For weeks after returning to the University of Florida, I asked around the business school. Nobody had heard of anyone named Deming.

My best friend at the University of Florida was Nancy Horowitz, an economist and wife of the Management Department chairman, Ira Horowitz. Every year on my birthday, Nancy invited me for dinner, and she prepared nonpareil leg of lamb. At the dinner table, Ira asked if I had found out anything about Deming.

"Nobody I've asked knows anything about anybody named Deming," I said.

Nancy, who was fiddling around with a garden salad, looked up and said, "Maybe it's Ed Deming. He was one of America's first experts in what was called at the time 'scientific sampling technique.' What we now call statistics. If you want to know more about him, go over to Industrial and Systems Engineering (ISE). They teach Deming over there."

I was slack-jawed, my mouth agape in amazement. My best friend knew all the time. I visited an engineer in ISE and learned enough about Deming to decide I wanted to learn more.

Dr. W. Edwards Deming was the spokesman and leader of the quality movement that evolved into its current organism of interrelated elements called Six Sigma. Deming regarded himself as merely a disciple of "the Master," Dr. Walter Shewart. By the 1970s, Deming's teachings were more widespread in Japan than in the United States. Among country people, there is a saying about a man who would rather tell a lie when the truth would make a better story. In the same vein, some would rather pass on a myth than to bother with veracity, which takes a little effort. The myth is that Deming went to Japan because his ideas were not accepted in America. In fact, his ideas were so acceptable in the United States that the War Department tasked him to train more than thirty-five thousand engineers during World War II. Afterwards, his ideas were so acceptable that Deming went to Japan *because he was sent there by the War Department.* As a consultant, Deming was unlikely to have struck out for devastated, war-torn Japan. Indeed, Deming is unlikely to have thought of Japan. So, why did Deming go to Japan? His ideas were so acceptable in the United States that his expertise, experience, and reputation led the War Department to send him there in the aftermath of World War II.

Weeks passed after learning a little about Deming from ISE faculty. At the time, I was doing agency work in Washington, D.C., mostly Treasury and Education. One day, I picked up the *Washington Post* and saw a little ad announcing that Deming would be offering a workshop in the Hilton Hotel. I signed up. The following week, I attended along with seventeen others. Deming offered this workshop before his famous four-day seminars he conducted in the 1980s and 1990s with hundreds if not thousands in attendance.

At the time, I was somewhat cynical about conventions, conferences, and other tax-deductible vacations. I often said all I wanted from these organized confabs was a new idea, a new friend, and a new joke, but of course in reverse order. That was all I expected from Deming. Instead, Deming changed my life.

Midst his presentation on the last day, Deming drew a schema projected overhead. In the lower left corner, he drew a small box. Inside the box, he wrote the word "Is." He said it represented an organization the way it is. He continued to say that the organization could be described in physical terms, e.g., number of plants, number of employees, volume of output, and in behavioral terms, e.g., what it is like to work there, what workers must do to be promoted, what workers must do to stay out of trouble. Next, he drew a diagonal line to a large box in the upper right corner of his overhead. Inside the box, he wrote "Can Be" and "Ought To Be." He said it represented what the organization can be and ought to be. He went on to say what the organization can be and ought to be could be described in physical and behavioral terms. His focus was on the behavioral aspect, e.g., what working there ought to be like. Then, he wrote the word "Transformation" along the diagonal line. He said going from the organization as it is to the organization as it can be and ought to be requires a transformation. He emphasized that transformation is not managed. Deming was highly critical of the term "change management." First, he said, what is required is not change but transformation, passing from one state to an altogether different state that is markedly converted in appearance and character. Moreover, he said, transformation is not managed. Transformation requires leadership. He also emphasized fourteen principles for the transformation.

That night, sitting alone in my hotel room, I could not keep from thinking about what Deming had done in his presentation. I realized what he said about organizations could also be said about people. I realized that I could be described in physical terms and behavioral terms, what it was like to be me. I also realized I was not the person I could be and ought to be. I was nowhere close to the person I was meant to be. Sitting there in my room late at night, I began to develop a vision of the person I could be and ought to be, the man I was meant to be. I needed a personal transformation from "is" to "can be and ought to be."

A transformation leading to the person I was meant to be. Although unformed and rudimentary, my personal transformation began at that moment. Deming had rerouted the path I was traveling through life. Deming transformed my life.

A JOURNEY, NOT A DESTINATION

Personal integrity is a journey, not a destination. Since personal integrity is dynamic rather than static, work on each of its components is a continuous, never-ending, lifetime engagement. Once achieved, personal integrity can be fleeting if nothing further is done to maintain that realization of wholeness. When we leave behind one component in our growth and development, we struggle until we do the work necessary to catch up that component with the others.

On the ensuing pages, I relate some experiences along my own journey, including struggles from time to time in my life. The experiences of the journey are not a mere collection of stories, not an anthology of omnibus self-serving narratives. Instead, the stories are meant to provide association, illustration, and repetition of salient points on which learning depends as well as to tell a typical story of the pursuit of personal integrity and struggle to maintain personal integrity once achieved, however fleetingly. Afterwards, I present ten rules for personal integrity. These rules address the needs of the four components making up wholeness. They are not a recipe for personal integrity but rather principled responses centered on choices and consequences that lead us in the direction of personal integrity. After all, recipes are merely directions or procedures. In other words, recipes tell people what to do, not why. Principles provide the why. Why implicitly suggests purpose.

Chapter Two
THE PHYSICAL JOURNEY

The word "physical" comes from a Greek root, physikos, translating as *"pertaining to nature." In its usual usage, "physical" pertains to the body as op-* *posed to the mind, although another usual usage also pertains to natural or ma-* *terial things. One characteristic of our individualities deals with our bodies. To a* *degree, but not altogether, the physical characteristic of our individualities takes* *care of itself. Physically, we spring up and mature physically as surely as the lowli-* *est morning glory from a seed planted in fertile soil and watered properly. For the* *most part, we are born to be tall or short, white or black or brown in skin color,* *and blond or brunette in hair color. We inherit a wide range of physical charac-* *teristics from our parents, grandparents, great grandparents, and so on. How we* *relate to nature is determined in part by nature itself. How we relate to nature also* *is determined in part by choices we make.*

OPERATING AND PLANNING DECISIONS

In business practice and in the context of ordinary discourse, references often are made to the short run and the long run. In business, the terms have particular meaning. In the first place, "run" is a reference to production run, thus
meaning a short production run or a long production run. Furthermore, short
run and long run should not be confused with time as kept on, say, a watch or a
calendar. A short run of production means making a product with use of given
facilities, *i.e.*, given plant and equipment. A long run of production involves
planning to make a product with new or enlarged facilities, *i.e.*, new plant and
corresponding equipment or enlarged plant size and additional equipment.

In business, short-run decisions are operating decisions because such decisions generally deal with operating fixed and given facilities, *i.e.*, plant and

equipment. For example, decisions to utilize more or less plant capacity are operating decisions. Long-run decisions are planning decisions because they deal with increasing scale, *i.e.*, the size of operations. Operating decisions deal with utilization of existing plant and equipment, but planning decisions deal with increasing available plant and equipment.

In business practice, authority usually differs for operating and planning decisions. A plant manager usually has full authority to make operating decisions. However, the authority to make planning decisions is limited. Planning decisions usually invoke the capital budgeting process, which ordinarily involves financial people at the corporate level.

It is so with life, particularly with respect to the physical component of our individuality. In effect, we make operating decisions when we are content to maintain our bodies. Choices we make to maintain our body weight and to prevent muscle loss are the equivalent of utilizing more or less of a given physical condition. When we adopt a regimen of fitness meant to improve our body weight, add muscle mass, and improve cardiovascular performance, we make planning decisions. These choices deal with improving our bodies, which can be considered as physical facilities.

The distinction between operating and planning decisions is a good one when applied to our bodies. Physically, operating choices keep us where we are. At times, we utilize more of our physical facilities when we exert ourselves. More or less exertion makes use of our given bodies. Planning choices, on the other hand, are based on a vision of what we want our bodies to be and strategies to realize the vision. Achieving the vision thus entails plans such as losing weight, lifting weights, and running on neighborhood streets. The critical aspects of planning decisions are vision, perceiving the physical capacity we want for ourselves; mission, deciding what we want to accomplish; core values, what we are willing to do and what we are not willing to do; and strategies, what must be done to achieve the vision and accomplish the mission while respecting the core values.

GOOD GENES

My mother's father was a Butler. He claimed the Butler tribe was Scotch-Irish. I doubt it. My Butler grandfather had a sixth grade education and a life tenancy on a farm outside Wesson, Mississippi, hidden deep amidst piney woods. He and his wife raised eleven children in an unpainted, tin-roofed house with no electricity and no plumbing. He was a tough old coot, wiry and grizzled. If cussing could solve a problem, he was your man. He didn't care too much for people, including his own children. When family visited, he disappeared into the piney woods. When he was in his nineties, he suddenly had blood in his urine. He had never been to a doctor in his life. Someone had to take him to see a doctor. His children caucused and decided I was the only person in the family he liked. I was designated. I took him to the doctor. He was diagnosed with bladder cancer, perhaps from all the moonshine whiskey he made and drank over numberless years. He lived a long life, a life made hard by working every day from "can see" to "can't see."

My mother's mother was a Waldrop. My grandmother also had a sixth grade education. She was a saint if ever there was one. She was taller and bigger than my grandfather, who was rather gnomish without the pointy hat. She was soft-spoken, mild mannered, and patient. She was given the gift of endurance. She was not given to vulgarity or profanity, although I once heard her exclaim "thunderation," whatever that means. She was a hard worker. Cooking every day on a wood burning stove, raising chickens, milking cows, feeding hogs, growing vegetables, and otherwise caring for a large farm family. She lived into her nineties and "died of old age." Someone said in the characteristic Mississippi piney woods manner, "Her body jus' plain played out on 'er."

My father's father was a Texas cowboy, growing up in Calvert, Texas. My grandfather homesteaded in the Arizona Territory before statehood in February 1912. During the early 1930s, he relocated to Mississippi to "ride out the Depression." There, he lived with his sister and her husband, Marion Douglas Fuller. My grandfather respected his brother-in-law so much that he named his first son Marion Fuller Davis after him. His sister and her husband owned a very large estate with cattle. My grandfather ran the day-to-day operations of the cattle side of business. He, too, lived to an old age, but a life cut a little short by a stroke that left him bedridden. A working cowboy, he looked a little like Gary Cooper and talked a little like Richard Farnsworth.

My father's mother was a Warren. My grandmother was a cowboy's wife, which was hard enough. She also had to endure without complaint all of the dangers of a woman living alone in the middle of nowhere when her cowboy husband was riding the range. Sometimes, Apache plunderers, Mexican bandits, or American outlaws would appear as though from nowhere, usually wanting nothing more than something to eat. She also had a small café in Bowie, Arizona, serving Mexican food. When I was a youngster, she and my grandfather lived separately, an arrangement that had lasted a long time and lasted the rest of their lives. She also relocated to Mississippi, where she lived to an old age.

My parents thus inherited genes that enabled a long life. Years of my father's life were surrendered to Camel cigarettes, which caused lung cancer when he was in his late 60s. Dad died in my arms when he was a mere sixty-seven years old. My mother passed away in her late 80s due to an acute onset of sepsis, a poisoned condition of the blood. Until then, she was as healthy as the proverbial mule. She led a robust, active lifestyle till the end, including brisk daily walks of five miles or more that challenged me to keep up with her even when I was a marathoner. According to my Garmin watch, she walked at a pace of thirteen minutes per mile! When she was a young girl, her father said she was his best worker. I'm sure she was. All she ever wanted of life was to be a good wife to her husband and a good mother to her children. Nothing more, nothing less, she just wanted to be a good wife to her husband and a good mother to her children. She was both. When asked her name, she gave it as Mrs. Marion F. Davis, her wifely name.

Genetically, therefore, I was gifted and blessed with generations of good physical genes enabling a long, healthy life. My grandparents, great-grandparents, and beyond were given good bodies, the kind of bodies that can live to old age in good health if given a chance. Consequently, both of my parents were given good bodies. The only requirement for a long, healthy life was to take good care of their bodies. My mother took good care of herself. She realized the genetic promise, living to old age in good health. My father did not take good care of himself.

A Heritage of Physical Wellness

As a beneficiary of good genes, I was born with a healthy body, although I was a breech-birth baby. My mother often said I had showed my behind ever since birth. When I was a boy, I was rarely sick. Even a slight fever, however, induced hallucinations. The hallucinations were appearances of horrifying disembodied spirits such as seemingly palpable skeletons and formidable specters that grabbed for me. My mother would hold me in her arms to restrain me from attempted flight. For a long time, I thought the hallucinations were caused by the damnable Vicks salve she rubbed on my chest, a palliative I still cannot abide. Thank goodness, I have had few fevers in my lifetime. My normal body temperature is well below 98.6 degrees, certainly well below 97 degrees. If my temperature ever reaches the average of 98.6 degrees, I personally have a fever of at least a couple of degrees. I have never had a headache in my life.

Throughout my life, I have been remarkably healthy, at first because of a heritage of good genes and afterwards because I eventually began to take care of myself physically. Eventually, meaning in the fullness of time. When I was a youngster and an adolescent, I was physically active and physically fit. For many years after I left home for college life first as a student and then as a professor, I muddled through a pendency of physical activity and physical fitness. My physical journey had discontinuities of laxity and dereliction, strange for one accustomed to soundness as the result of exercise and nutrition. Like the Phoenix, I later arose renewed from my ashes.

PHYSICALLY ACTIVE

When I was a boy and an adolescent, I was physically active. I played unorganized baseball in sandlots and open fields overcome by weeds and wild flowers. Later, I played organized baseball on Little League teams and beyond.

I played organized football from the time I was in the fifth grade through high school. I followed sports with fanaticism, reading the sports pages every day, listening to baseball and football games and boxing matches on the radio, later watching such games and matches on television.

In those days, parents were not responsible for entertaining their children. We were responsible for entertaining ourselves. If we were bored, we were faulted, not our parents. On Saturday mornings or during summer days, boys did not sleep late. We arose early from bed for a big country breakfast of eggs, bacon, ham, or sausage, grits, and biscuits, and then bolted outside where we would choose sides for a game or otherwise collectivize some kind of activity. Baseball; football; biking to the "pits," quarries now filled with water for swimming; hiking through the woods to Two Mile Branch with hope to see an alligator. We did not sit around watching television, and we were a couple of generations before video games. As a result, we were reasonably fit without ever thinking about it. We were just taking responsibility for keeping ourselves entertained and without knowing it keeping ourselves physically fit.

1952: IT WAS A VERY GOOD YEAR

Some years are better than others. The year 1952, when I was eleven years old, was the best in my recollection as a youngster. Yes, 1952 was a good year, a very good year, the kind of year that transcends matter and motion, space and time. The kind of year that when recalled seems to exist beyond the material world. I was maturing physically, expressing myself in team sports and developing an interest in girls, normal progressions towards physical maturity.

Eastlawn

In the fall of 1952, I was a sixth grade student at Eastlawn School in Pascagoula, Mississippi. Actually, Eastlawn School was under construction and would not be opened for classes until the following year in the fall of 1953. The boys and girls who lived in the forthcoming Eastlawn school district attended classes in a dilapidated federal government building that had been vacant, abandoned, and downright derelict until it was conscripted as temporary classrooms while the new Eastlawn School was being built. Our faux school was called "Eastlawn," but it was not Eastlawn. It was transparently spurious, an inferior imitation, an ersatz knockoff Eastlawn, but all the kids who went to the ersatz knockoff Eastlawn lived in the district of the real yet still future Eastlawn School. As sixth graders, my fellow students and I would be going to Pascagoula Junior High School the following year, but the fifth graders and down would be going to the new, real, and genuine Eastlawn School.

Many of the boys and girls who attended this ersatz knockoff Eastlawn School lived in the Bayou (we pronounced it BUY-oh) Casotte area, a marshy area east of town where shrimp boats were harbored, where oyster boats were tied to rotting piers, and where crab buckets seemed to multiply according to their own kind. The people who owned and operated these shrimp boats and oyster boats worked hard and lived hard lives. The people who crabbed lived even harder lives. Bayou Casotte was the place where a lot of shrimpers and oystermen lived with their families in rundown houses, often little more than roughly built shacks that looked like fishing camps. You did not want even to think about messing with these Bayou Casotte folks or their kids. I went to school with their kids. I was big for my age and needed to be. There was a curious novelty about those Bayou Casotte boys. When they grew up, many of these tough guys became policemen and deputy sheriffs. They were good at it.

The Warehouse

The old dilapidated government building that had been converted to ersatz knockoff Eastlawn School was a hundred feet or so behind and somewhat west of a stately, achromatic ivory white government warehouse. The warehouse loomed high like a Moorish alcazar over innumerable, identical, selfsame residential houses that surrounded it for blocks and blocks, from Eighth Street to Fourteenth Street and Taylor Avenue to Lincoln Avenue, now renamed Ingalls Avenue.

World War II began on September 1, 1939, the day that Hitler's forces in-

vaded Poland. America joined the war more than two years later. During the
buildup to World War II and after the American entry to the war, the U.S. Navy
had a sudden and large presence in Pascagoula, which still is a major shipbuild-
ing town. Over the years, Ingalls Shipyard, now part of Northrop Grumman,
has built incalculable, inestimable Navy ships, including nuclear-powered submarines and aircraft carriers. At the outbreak of World War II, housing was
in short supply in the face of military and civilian demands driven by the war
itself, and a housing project was built by the federal government to house Navy
personnel. After the War when the houses were no longer needed for military
personnel, the "Navy Project" was maintained for a time as rental housing for
civilians and then eventually sold to private owners in the 1950s. The warehouse stored materials, tools, and equipment needed by the men who maintained the Navy Project houses.

My father worked at the government warehouse when the rental housing
units of the Navy Project were being maintained. We lived across the street
from the warehouse at 614 Twelfth Street, which was on the corner of Twelfth
Street and Wilson Avenue. My childhood and adolescence were lived in the
Navy Project, making me a product of the project, thus a project kid.

I loved living there in that house. It was a modest, humble, inelegant residence, but it housed an exceptional, especial, magnificent home where voices
were never, ever raised in anger or otherwise, where two sons had total unsur-
passable respect for their parents. Across the street from our house, the warehouse itself was constructed of white jumbo cement blocks, and it rose about
thirty feet or more from street level to the roofline. I marked off a baseball strike
zone on the concrete wall, and I threw thousands of pitches at that wall. More
than fifty years later, my recollection is that all of those pitches were in the strike
zone. Of course, I was my own umpire.

I learned to throw a curveball by chucking a tennis ball toward the strike
zone marked on the warehouse wall. I could put enough spin on a tennis ball to
make it break about three feet. A baseball was a little more difficult to curve, but
every baseball that I threw broke at least a little. More than fifty years later, my
right elbow hurts more days than not. The orthopedic specialist I first consulted

as an adult told me I have "pitcher's elbow." Throwing curves is hazardous to the health of elbows. The orthopedist also told me that more than half of his practice was men "my age" who have aches and pains from old sports injuries. Eventually, I "threw my arm away," a term used before medical science discovered the rotator cuff. Nowadays, I cannot throw a small rock across a narrow street.

I was able to walk to ersatz knockoff Eastlawn every day and also walk home for dinner. When I was growing up, lunch was not in our household lexicon. My mother prepared three full meals a day. The noon meal was dinner, the evening meal supper. Dinner was never a sandwich, never a salad. Dinner was a full meal. My father, who I called "Daddy" as a boy and "Dad" as an adult, also walked across the street for dinner every day. My mother, who I called "Mother" as a boy and "Mother" as an adult, was a terrific cook, and these dinners were absolutely splendid. Almost always, we had fresh vegetables and a modest cut of meat.

Inexplicably, everyone at the warehouse and all of his buddies at filling stations, barbershops, and other places where men gathered to celebrate their masculinity and according to the mothers of their children set bad examples, called Daddy "Hank," although his name was Marion Fuller Davis. I think Hank was a term of endearment. One erudite man offered the explanation that Hank was a nickname given to Daddy based on Quintus Horatius Flaccus, the Roman poet known to us as Horace. He actually had a straight face when he told this whopper.

Baseball

In 1952, I played on the first Little League team organized in Pascagoula. The Pascagoula-Moss Point (PMP) Bank sponsored a team in Pascagoula and another one in Moss Point. The entire schedule of games that year was Pascagoula and Moss Point playing against each other. We played the first game at Pascagoula on the baseball field in front of War Memorial Stadium, where Pascagoula High School played its football games, the second game in Moss Point, the third game back in Pascagoula, the fourth in Moss Point, and so forth. I played the infield until the coaches learned I couldn't field grounders or hit. Other than that, they thought I was a swell infielder.

The good news was the coaches discovered I could pitch. By rule at the time, I was not supposed to throw a curveball in Little League, but by then I had thrown so many tennis ball curves that every pitch curved. The bad news, however, was another kid named Robert Earl Siedell. "Robert Earl reminds me of Carl Hubbell," said one of our coaches, Sam Leslie. He should have known since Sam Leslie played with the Giants when Carl Hubbell won 253 games for the Giants during a fifteen-year career that spanned 1928 to 1943. At one time, Sam Leslie held the major league record for home runs hit by a pinch hitter. I had a baseball card that said so.

Later, following brilliant pitching in high school, Robert Earl turned down a contract offer from the Pittsburgh Pirates and instead went to the University of Mississippi (Ole Miss) on a baseball scholarship. He was an all-SEC (Southeastern Conference) pitcher. If the coaches of our Little League team ever had needed a second pitcher in 1952, I would have been ready. They didn't. I did pitch later in Babe Ruth League baseball.

Football

In 1952, I played every down of every game in peewee football. Each elementary school in Pascagoula had a peewee football team, and I suppose these schools comprised the Peewee Football League. We even had peewee cheerleaders, and I suppose they had peewee megaphones and peewee pompons. The word is in fact "pompon," not to be confused with the word "pompom," which is the military term for a certain type of cannon.

In those days, my nickname was "Skint," which was not a reference to broke or busted. I had a buzz cut, a really close buzz cut. One of the coaches said my hair was buzzed so tight that I looked like I had a skint head. From then on, it was, "Come here, Skint." And, "Get in there, Skint." Some people still know me as Skint. My brother once sent me a Christmas present addressed to "Dr. Skint Davis." The mail carrier personally knocked on my door and hand delivered the package so that he could see firsthand the man named Dr. Skint Davis. He could not contain his amusement.

We were undefeated in 1952, won the peewee championship, played a team from Escatawba in a bowl game and won that game, too. Nobody on our team knew where or what Escatawba was, but, hey, it was a bowl game. However, something was wrong about this picture of an utterly triumphal season. The purity of our triumphal spirit was adulterated by the frustrating, distressing, and otherwise unsettling fact that we did all of this for Beach School! Ersatz knockoff Eastlawn did not have a peewee team until the following year when the new, real, genuine Eastlawn School was completed and occupied.

The boys of ersatz knockoff Eastlawn were conscripted to play for Beach School because the only boys who went to Beach School were SOBs, "Sons of the Beach" as we called them. SOBs were boys in families financially blessed enough to live on or near the beach in Pascagoula. These boys were either skinny or fat, and they were mostly blond. They had the pallid, wan skin associated with invalids and inmates. SOBs preferred to stay indoors and read a book or play chess rather than go outdoors to play ball of any kind. They also talked funny, kind of like girls. As a rule, these boys were more suited for cheerleading than playing football. I don't think Beach School had ever won a peewee football game before 1952. Once the boys from Bayou Casotte and the boys from the Navy Project suited up for dear old Beach School, however, Beach School was the scourge of peewee football in 1952. We savaged every opponent, every peewee team. We took the field for every game with a scorched earth attitude, a take no prisoners mentality, driven by passions of the disempowered versus the empowered, the disadvantaged versus the advantaged.

Even after winning the peewee championship for Beach School and beating Escatawba in a bowl game for Beach School, I never stepped foot into the school itself. I still haven't been inside Beach School. Nevertheless, I still have the blue letter "B" with a little gold football emblazoned in the middle of the "B" that I earned that year. Instead of being given a jacket or a sweater at our awards banquet, we were given a T-shirt. A football letter and a T-shirt do not go together. A football letter and a jacket go together. A football letter and a sweater go together. A football letter and a T-shirt do not go together. I never knew what to do with the "B" with a little gold football with the little emblazoned football in the middle of the "B." I outgrew the T-shirt before the weather was warm enough to wear it.

Girls

The sixth grade, 1952-53, was the year I discovered girls. I was eleven, then twelve years old, and I suppose my body produced its first hormone and longed to explore girls and their possibilities. Oh, I had earlier liaisons, but these pre-1952 episodes were mere acts of dalliance. For example, in the second grade, I was in love with Janet Gaskin. All second grade boys were in love with Janet Gaskin. One day, I kissed her when our second grade teacher, Miss Olien, was outside the classroom. When Miss Olien returned, the other kids ratted me out. In front of the whole class, Miss Olien rapped my knuckles on both hands with a foot ruler, not with the flat part of the ruler but the edge of the ruler. I dropped to my knees in pain. It was worth the pain to kiss Janet Gaskin.

In the sixth grade, 1952-53, my discovery of girls went beyond the trifling curiosity of the occasional dalliance. The girl was Geraldine, an uncommonly pretty girl with a rare, remarkable, exceptional, wonderful body for her age, whatever her age. She was mysterious. She suddenly appeared as though beamed down from somewhere in Texas. Geraldine was an older girl, already at least thirteen at the beginning of the school year. She moved to Pascagoula to live with her grandfather, who worked with my father at the warehouse. She must be a bad girl, the boys figured. Parents probably couldn't do anything with her, the boys guessed. None of this was true, but of course it nonetheless meant I wanted her for my girl.

Geraldine and I began to meet at the Ritz Theater. We sat in the balcony where we could neck innocently. Everything was great until rival suitors also wanted her for their girl. One of these wannabe swains started something in the Ritz Theater one Saturday when I was minding my own business in the balcony, content to neck my way through the cowboy movie with Geraldine Painter. It was kind of like hockey when a fight breaks out. Mr. Grant, manager of the Ritz Theater, broke up the commotion and threw both of us out. This wannabe swain and I ended up in the alley between the Ritz Theater and Carver's Rexall Drug Store, where we competed like rutting buck deer for Geraldine's affections. Mr. Grant also broke up this ruckus. Mr. Grant banned both of us from the Ritz Theater.

No girl was worth such punishment. Giving up Monte Hale; Alan "Rocky" Lane; Lash LaRue; Charles Starrett, the Durango Kid; Red Ryder and Little Beaver; and Bob Steele; not to mention the girly Hopalong Cassidy and sissy singing cowboys like Roy Rogers and Gene Autry for some girl? I don't think so. No girl was worth it. Canoodling with Geraldine was one thing, but cowboy movies were the thing. Weeks later, Mr. Grant forgave and forgot, letting me back in the Ritz Theater. I stayed away from the balcony and resumed sitting with Billy Hart on the front row, where we could pick up the flattened out popcorn boxes that had been sailed at the movie screen and navigate them back over our shoulders and into the crowd. No girl was worth giving up all that, not even Geraldine and her wonderments.

Then, there was Brenda Bosarge. As the school year ground slowly like the mills of the gods to an end, it also ground ever so finely. Our sixth grade teacher was really excited about the imminent coronation of Queen Elizabeth II. She tried desperately to infect us with her excitement. We were not infected. She tried desperately to convince us that we would remember the coronation the rest of our lives. We were not convinced. Undeterred, she resolutely insisted that we must watch this historic event.

Only four or five kids had a television set in their homes. Our teacher divided the class into four or five groups, and each group went to one of the homes to watch the coronation. I was assigned to the group that went to the home of Jimmy Doescher, who lived behind us on Thirteenth Street. Both of his parents worked. Unless the teacher came to Jimmy Doescher's home to watch the coronation with us, we wouldn't have adults around to ruin everything. Our teacher went to a different home. Brenda Bosarge also was assigned to the home of Jimmy Doescher. At the time, our teacher could not convince us that we would remember the coronation of Queen Elizabeth II for the rest of our lives. The passage of time proved her right. I still remember the day well, although it was not the coronation that made the day memorable.

On June 2, 1953, Brenda Bosarge and I went with a couple of other kids to the home of Jimmy Doescher to watch the coronation of Queen Elizabeth II. I closed the venetian blinds and pulled the curtains shut, cunningly claiming that television reception would be better in the darkened room. Brenda Bosarge and I sat on the sofa in the darkened room. I am sure the other kids must have watched the coronation. On the other hand, maybe they watched Brenda Bosarge and me canoodling on the sofa in the darkened room. Over the years, I convinced myself that Brenda Bosarge probably did not remember our kiss. I remembered. As Anthony Hopkins said in the movie, *Hearts in Atlantis*, we shared a kiss by which all others will be measured.

My high school class of 1959 has had a reunion every five years since graduation. I have attended all of them. In 1989, I attended the reunion of my high school class. I milled around. As usual, I enjoyed seeing my old friends. I looked at some old photographs from high school, including some of me that seemed to focus on my worst side. Suddenly, I looked across the large room and saw Brenda Bosarge.

Once I recognized her, I blurted uncontrollably, "Oh, my God. There's Brenda Bosarge! I haven't seen her in thirty years!"

Brenda Bosarge was beautiful, absolutely gorgeous. She had noticed me. In a slinky dress, she walked sensuously toward me, eyes twinkling, full lips spread in a toothy smile.

"Oh, my God! Brenda Bosarge is walking toward me," I said aloud to no one in particular. Seeing no avenue of escape, I was thinking, the last thing I'm going to bring up is June 2, 1953.

When Brenda Bosarge reached me, she spoke first. With a big smile on her face, she said loudly, "It's the kisser!"

JUNIOR HIGH FOOTBALL: YOU SEE THESE TEETH I AIN'T GOT?

When I was a boy and an adolescent, most of my sports heroes were baseball players. I had heroes like Bob Feller, Al "Flip" Rosen, Larry Doby, and the entire 1954 Cleveland Indians baseball team that won 111 games and lost only 43. A little closer to home, my personal inspiration was Uncle Calvin. He was one of my mother's brothers, Calvin Butler, and he was as big as a silo. In fact, "Silo" was his nickname, the sobriquet because of his prodigious appetite, because he ate enough food to fill a silo.

Uncle Calvin played football for Mississippi Southern College, which is now the University of Southern Mississippi. At the time, Mississippi Southern was a perennial power in the "small college" rankings. Uncle Calvin played the position of center, and he wore number 52 on his jersey. When I played football, I played center to be like Uncle Calvin. I always wore number 52 on my jersey to be like Uncle Calvin. In 1952, Uncle Calvin was the captain of his team at Mississippi Southern. He was Homecoming King, and his wife, Sue, was Homecoming Queen. I saw him play that homecoming game, and I saw him come out at halftime in a dirty uniform to escort his wife to the center of the field where she was presented a bouquet of roses. She was beautiful. He was heroic in his dirty uniform, godlike in his pads.

I also saw him play against Louisville that year in Jackson. Mississippi Southern won, 55-26, despite heroics from a quarterback named Johnny Unitas. He also played defensive back and returned punts and kickoffs. I thought I never would hear of Johnny Unitas again. Mississippi Southern had a regular season record of 13-1, the loss to Alabama, 20-6. In the Sun Bowl played on New Year's Day 1953 in El Paso, Mississippi Southern lost to Pacific, 26-7, thus finishing the 1952 season with a 13-2 record.

In junior high school, I continued to play football. I played both center and linebacker like my Uncle Calvin, "going both ways" as we said in those days. These days, "going both ways" has an altogether different meaning. I wore 52 like my Uncle Calvin. I started on offense and defense in both the eighth and ninth grades. In 1955-56, we won the equivalent of the state junior high school championship for Pascagoula Junior High School.

In those days, football helmets were bare and open in front. No bars, no face masks. A line in one of Hank Williams's old songs went something like, "You see these teeth I ain't got... I've been down that road before." I've been down that road before, too, Hank. These teeth I ain't got are now a bridge permanently cantilevered to some teeth I do got. I was playing linebacker. It was the last play of the first half. A fullback swept to the left, turned to run up field, and lowered his head. I tackled him with my face.

One of my upper front teeth was broken. Alongside the broken tooth was a tooth knocked out even at the gum. The nerve was intact but exposed and dangling like a crimson nematode. The pain was severe, excruciating pain. In those days, we were expected to tough out and play through injuries. I went into the locker room at halftime with a mouthful of blood. Inside my lips were deep, jagged cuts that went almost through to the outside. The coaches were not impressed.

At the beginning of the second half, an assistant coach yelled out, "Davis, what in hell are you doing on the bench? It's the kickoff. Get out there! Go, go, go!"

I went back onto the field and played every down of the entire second half. Every breath, every pulse of my heartbeat sent riveting, excruciating pain throughout my body. In particular, the exposed, dangling nerve was like a quisling within my ranks, a fifth column as treacherous in its willful betrayal as Judas. Instead of a benign presence closeted within my tooth, the pendent neurons used every breath as an excuse to send a sharp, harrowing pain like an icepick pricking and stabbing my brain. During the entire second half, I blew bloody bubbles with every breath, little bloody bubbles and big bloody bubbles that sometimes floated around me like I was a human blood bubble machine.

After the game, I went home and did not sleep whatsoever all night. It never occurred to coaches or parents or me to call a dentist at home at night for immediate emergency treatment for dental trauma. Daddy knew that Dr. Thompson, our family dentist, opened his office at a certain time, and he took me there when his dental office opened the following morning. Dr. Thompson's daughter, Patricia, married Trent Lott, a U.S. Senator from Mississippi. Indeed, Trent once was Majority Leader of the U.S. Senate. More importantly, Trent was the President of our 1959 graduating class.

Dr. Thompson extracted the exposed, dangling nerve with the equivalent of channellock pliers and without any anesthetic. I gasped at the pain, inhaling to the fullest extent of my oxygen uptake, finally exhaling after what seemed like several minutes. Then, Dr. Thompson pulled the tooth. Dr. Thompson told me I would later need a root canal procedure on the broken front tooth to remove dead pulp. He stitched the cuts inside my mouth. Daddy stayed with me, stayed at the side of the dental chair throughout the entire procedure.

Dr. Thompson's office was located downtown in one of the old buildings. It was an upstairs office. From street level, a long, steep flight of stairs led to his office. Afterwards, you had to descend the long flight of stairs to the street level. When Dr. Thompson finally finished his work, I had countless stitches inside my lips, and I had a mouthful of bloody packing to staunch further bleeding from the pulled tooth.

When Daddy and I left Dr. Thompson's office and started to descend the steps of the long flight of stairs, Daddy almost collapsed. I grabbed him by the arm and eased him down to sit on the steps.

He sat there silently for a few moments, and then he said, "I just can't take blood. I knew how much pain you were in. Watching you suffer just about killed me. It was the blood and the pain. I sure hope I don't faint on you."

I managed Daddy back on his feet, and we went a few more steps before I had to ease him back down again. A few steps, and then ease him down again. About an hour later, I finally got him out of the building, got him into the car, and finally drove him home.

Over the years, I kidded Dad about this little vignette. *He laughed soundlessly. His whole face laughed. His eyes were just slits behind his glasses. He took off his glasses and wiped his eyes. He talked between the laughs. I was supposed to be taking care of you, but you had to take care of me. I'd take a step and just about faint. Take a step and have to sit down for a while. I just couldn't take the blood. Never could. Still can't. That's the reason I never killed anything in my life.*

Never went hunting. You were brave, he said. His voice diminished to silence as quiet as a prayer. He had that thousand yard stare, lost and alone in his thoughts, unaccompanied in his exodus unto a good land.

BOXING

I never played organized basketball, only the backyard variety. In the winter, other boys dressed in what looked like their underwear and ran up and down a gym court, sweating and bouncing a ball. I dressed in what looked like my underwear and climbed in the boxing ring, sweating and throwing punches. When I was not boxing in organized matches, I was working out in a boxing ring built in the backyard of the Hicks boys, Burns, Gerald, Darryl, and Duane, who we called Buck. They lived a block behind us.

Mr. Hicks had been a boxer, and he trained his four boys to box. On each of his hands, Mr. Hicks had an extra thumb. These extra thumbs were tiny, perfectly proportioned thumbs but nonetheless grotesque malformations that boys in the neighborhood were afraid to look at. Mr. Hicks also trained me. Once or twice a week, Mr. Hicks organized us into competitive boxing matches of three rounds each, three minutes per round. He timed and refereed these matches. Mr. Hicks and his oldest son, Burns, generally judged these matches, at times joined by Mr. John Evans, the neighborhood postman and later, for a short time, an ill-fated boxing and wrestling promoter in Pascagoula.

Counting these matches, I had well over a hundred fights in the ring including Golden Gloves fights, a few in the novice division but mostly in the open division. We rarely paid attention to weight limits. I just self reported that I was a welterweight, which has a weight limit of 147 pounds, even though I eventually weighed as much as 165 pounds, the weight limit for a middleweight.

I was never afraid in the ring. Never. I was a good boxer with a good left jab that won almost all of my fights on points. My progression in the ring, such as it was, ended in two fights against a Biloxi fighter named Dominic DiCarlo. As I saw him across the ring in his corner before our first fight, he was a skinny, jaundiced-looking kid, but a true welterweight unlike me. I had at least a ten-pound weight advantage, probably more. I thought I was lucky to draw him, and I thought I would keep my left jab in his face all night and score with an occasional right cross. In the first round, however, when I thought about jabbing him, he hit me first with his own left jab. He also had a good left hook and a decent right cross of his own. He threw punches in combination with good hand speed. After three rounds, I was beat up, battered and bloodied. He was unmarked. I did make him sweat.

I then made the worst mistake of my sixteen years. I convinced myself that this loss was a fluke, an outlier widely separated from what should be expected. Weeks later, I had the opportunity to fight Dominic DiCarlo again and redeem myself. This time, I was busted up worse than the first fight. He ripped open a cut over my left eye. By the third round, the blood flowed into my left eye, and I couldn't see out of that eye. I still have the scar tissue to remind me that, for most of us, no matter how good you are at something, there's someone better. The scar tissue still bothers me from time to time. At sixteen, I conveniently concluded my eyesight was bad enough that I couldn't see the punches coming. That was my story, and I was sticking to it. The truth was Dominic DiCarlo. Whatever the reason, I was washed up as a boxer.

Years later, I developed a ganglion cyst on my right wrist attributable to injuries suffered from years of pounding sand-filled canvas bags and soft bodies and hard heads. My right hand was going numb because one of these ganglia grew around a nerve. I had surgery to remove the ganglion. Still later, I had surgery on my left wrist for the same reason. My hands still pop loudly when I draw them into fists. I have lost flexibility in both wrists.

Rocky Marciano

I was a Rocky Marciano fan. When I was in high school, I saw Rocky Marciano and shook his hand. He looked me in the eyes and called me "big guy," which I wasn't. I was merely a middleweight trying to pass as a welterweight.

In those days, wrestling was big in nearby Mobile, Alabama. The local favorite was a wrestler named Lee Fields, who was a Mickey Mantle look alike. His real name was Albert Lee Hatfield. In the ring, he was introduced in a drawn out sing-song voice, "From Paw-HUS-ka, OK-la-HOM-a, Leeeeeeee Fields! FIELDS!" The local villain was a swarthy, gypsy-looking man named Mario Galento. His birth name was Bonnie Lee "Butch" Boyette, hardly a gypsy name, and he was a country boy from Tennessee, hardly an enclave of gypsy culture, and not from New York as he claimed. Lee Fields and Mario Galento staged countless bloody wars in the wrestling ring. Of course, each bloody war was only an exhibition of wrestling. In every state, wrestling is staged and "fake" and thus cannot be promoted as competition, only as exhibition. Otherwise, all parties involved in wrestling could be prosecuted for fixing a wrestling match. To the day she died, Mother in her country innocence thought wrestling was real, and Neil Armstrong's walk on the moon was faked.

Mario Galento had a tag team partner billed as his brother, Al "Spider" Galento. Like wrestling itself, Mario and Spider were fake brothers. Spider was a kind of mentor to Mario. Spider was even swarthier than Mario. He had dark circles under his eyes, and wrestling fans just knew Spider couldn't be trusted. Yet, Spider was comical and could be trusted to provide a little comic relief in his matches. His sneakiness in and around the ring was staged in comical transparency. He was a villain that wrestling goobers could laugh at and even like. Almost always, Spider wrestled only as a tag team when billed as the brother of Mario Galento.

Another tag team twosome called themselves the Smith Brothers. Both Smith Brothers had beards meant to look like the Smith Brothers on the box of cough drops. One of these wrestling Smith Brothers called himself John Smith. One week, the Smith Brothers divested their wrestling brotherhood. The Smith Brother who called himself John Smith shaved his beard, developed an overnight Russian accent, clothed himself in a Russian red satin jacket adorned with hammer and sickle, and miraculously became an overnight Soldat Gorky. One week, John Smith. The next week, a Russian named Soldat Gorky. Only in wrestling.

One night, Spider Galento had his moment of fame and glory. Spider Galento was matched against Soldat Gorky, and they were in the ring awaiting introductions. While Soldat Gorky was strutting around the ring in his communist red satin jacket midst Cold War boos and hisses from the wrestling crowd, Spider stood in his corner and began the signature sneaky convolutions that marked his career, crouching first this way and then that way, apparently looking for some stealthy advantage, his eyes shifting side to side. Of course, Soldat Gorky was scripted to be oblivious of what every half-wit in the wrestling crowd saw. To the uproarious approval of the wrestling crowd, Spider sneaked across the ring and ripped the communist red satin jacket off the back of Soldat Gorky. Then, to the wrestling crowd's delight, Spider ran around the ring with the communist red satin jacket held high, and then tore it into pieces. Soldat Gorky caught up with Spider Galento as scripted and pinned him before the introductions, even before the bell rang. The match was literally over before it began. That's the way it was in those days. Only in wrestling.

One day, a masked man showed himself in Mobile. He called himself "The Mighty Yankee." With a name like that, it goes without saying that he was a villain. A masked man calling himself "The Mighty Yankee" was the end all of villainy in Mobile, Alabama, more villainous than a gypsy from New York, even more villainous than a Russian Soldat Gorky, the commie. The masked Mighty Yankee worked his way through the lesser grapplers week by week and eventually to the pinnacle, Lee Fields. The Mighty Yankee bloodied the beloved Lee Fields and reportedly landed him in the hospital. People began to think that the only person who could stop the Mighty Yankee was Mario Galento, who suddenly became the villain you hate to love. The people's choice, Mario Galento, lost a bloody battle to the Mighty Yankee. He also landed in the hospital. What next? Who next?

One day, I read that Lee Fields was going to wrestle the Mighty Yankee in a rematch. To make sure this masked villain respected a modicum of decorum if not whatever rules wrestling had, Rocky Marciano was being brought in to referee the match.

I had to go. I had to see Rocky Marciano. I scraped together the wherewithal to buy a ringside seat to be close to the champ. I sat at the foot of wooden steps rising into the ring. When the moment came, I saw Rocky Marciano walking from the dressing room, down an aisle, and towards the steps. With respect and reverence, I stood expectantly. When he reached the steps, Rocky Marciano turned to look at me, stopped, and offered his hand. He shook my hand firmly, saying something like, "Yo, big guy." *Big guy!* I still look at my right hand and remember in wonderment that it once shook the hand of Rocky Marciano when he called me big guy.

The match itself went like this. The Mighty Yankee pinned Lee Fields in the first fall. Lee Fields pinned the Mighty Yankee in the second fall. In the third and final fall, the Mighty Yankee was battering the hapless Lee Fields from pillar to post. Poor Lee Fields was bloodied beyond recognition, his face a mask of red and his hands both defenselessly hanging on the ropes to stay upright. The Mighty Yankee could have pinned him at will, but I suppose the script called for giving the impression of punishing Lee Fields. Rocky Marciano tried to separate the Mighty Yankee from Lee Fields, who was helpless against the ropes. The Mighty Yankee brushed Rocky Marciano away with his right hand. Rocky Marciano moved back in and tried again to separate the Mighty Yankee from the helpless Lee Fields, who slumped to the canvas appearing to be unconscious. This time, the Mighty Yankee actually swatted Rocky Marciano with a backhand. Rocky Marciano took a step backwards and then reached out with his left hand, grabbed the Mighty Yankee by the shoulder, and spun the Mighty Yankee around. Rocky Marciano hit the Mighty Yankee with a right, the famous Rocky Marciano right that ended boxing careers such as that of Roland LaStarza. The Mighty Yankee went down in an unconscious heap, flat on his back. Suddenly, the unconscious Lee Fields, battered and bloodied, now lying motionless on the canvas, came barely to life, rolled over, and flopped one arm on top of the knocked-out Mighty Yankee. Rocky Marciano dropped to the canvas, pounding one, two, three, and counted out the Mighty Yankee. The match was over, and Lee Fields was suddenly and unsteadily on his feet, standing nonetheless tall, his right hand held high by Rocky Marciano in the traditional salute of victory.

If a masked man was defeated in wrestling in those days, he had to remove his mask and identify himself. The Mighty Yankee retreated to the dressing room and then returned without his mask and identified himself as Ray Villmer. Some Yankee. Born in St. Louis, his hometown was Tampa, for crying out loud! Ray Villmer, the Mighty Yankee, died in 2005 at the age of 92.

FROM FOOTBALL TO LIFE

When I played football for Pascagoula Junior High, the head coach was Billy Hugh Montgomery. He coached us to play football and taught us boys a lot about how to become men. He taught us lessons about life. After our first football game, which we won handily, he huddled us around him in the locker room. We had won the game, and we were dirty, smelly, noisy, and rowdy.

He quieted us down. He looked around the locker room and began to speak to us while we sat there in our dirty, sweaty uniforms, still in our pads.

"Nothing like the first game of the season, the first win of the season, the first touchdown of the season. Who scored the first touchdown tonight?" he asked in a low, serene voice like an enticing aperitif before the main course.

We roared back the answer in one voice, "Alva Pinson!"

Alva Pinson was our fullback back in the day when fullbacks actually ran the ball. Nowadays, fullbacks are guards and tackles who line up in the backfield as blockers for halfbacks.

Billy Hugh Montgomery quieted us down again. He spoke to us again in a softened tone, subdued and almost muted.

"Let's think about our first touchdown. Let's relive it. We took the kickoff on our own 38. Adams opened up a hole for Larsen, and we picked up five yards. Canty threw a pass to Bishop for fifteen yards. Davis opened up a hole for Pinson, and he ran up the middle for another ten yards."

Billy Hugh Montgomery remembered every play, and he mentioned every name on the team in describing the march down the field to our first touchdown. He mentioned every name on the line and every name in the backfield. Finally, he described how Alva Pinson had plunged off right guard to carry the football across the goal line.

Then, he said in a voice as intimate as lovers swaddled in rustling sheets, "Let me ask you again. Who scored our first touchdown this year?"

We got it right this time, yelling out as one, "We did!"

Billy Hugh Montgomery quieted us down again. He spoke to us again, this time almost in a whisper while he paced up and down. His voice was in taut control like the steady firmness of a cello.

"I want you to remember this. Who scored the touchdown? We did. Every man out there tonight, every man who blocked or tackled or ran or passed, we scored the first touchdown. On a football team, there is no such thing as one man succeeding and the others failing. We succeed or fail together. It takes all of us to move the ball down the field and across the goal line. Each man doing his job, each man relying on others to do their job, and working together as a team. Each man having an interest in doing what is best for the success of the team, each man having an interest in what's best for everybody else on the team. One day, you'll have a job. It's the same thing with a job. On the job, you have to work together as a team. On the job, you either succeed or fail together on the job. There is no such thing as one man on the job succeeding and the others failing. On the job, you all succeed or fail together. That's the way it is with football. That's the way it is with life. It is so in football, and it is so in life."

IT IS SO IN MANAGEMENT CONSULTING

More than thirty years later, I was engaged as a management consultant with a subsidiary of a *Fortune* 500 company. The focus was on improvement in productivity, cost, and profit. Within the subsidiary, units were not working together as a team. The company had phosphate mines in Florida and chemical plants that produced diammonium phosphate fertilizer. One of the mining managers had an idea that dramatically increased throughput in a slurry line. Without changing the horsepower of the pump or the internal diameter of the pipe, the mining manager's idea significantly increased throughput, which meant a lot of money to the bottom line of the company. His idea was simple, dealing with elevation of the pump, and implementation was virtually costless. The idea could be applied in other phosphate mines operated by the company.

The day I learned about this remarkable breakthrough, I asked the mining manager if he had told other mining managers about the improvement.

"Hell, no. Let 'em find out the hard way just like we did."

His response was archetypal of the culture permeating the company at that time. Managers in one chemical plant thought they could succeed while other chemical plants failed. The attitude and behavior was "Let them find out the hard way just like we did." Machine operators thought they could succeed while maintenance mechanics failed. The resounding cacophony was "Let them find out the hard way just like we did." In part, my job was to show them that there is no such thing as one mining operation succeeding and other mining operations failing, or mining operations succeeding and chemical plants failing, or one chemical plant succeeding and other chemical plants failing, or machine operators succeeding and maintenance mechanics failing. Either the company succeeded or the company failed. If the company succeeded, all succeeded with it. If the company failed, all failed with it. My job was to show them that it took every man doing his job, relying on others to do their job, and working together to move the ball down the field and across the goal line. My job was to tell them about Billy Hugh Montgomery. They listened as I had years earlier. They responded appropriately as we had years earlier.

Other Life Lessons

Before our football season even started, Billy Hugh Montgomery sat us down on the first day of football practice. We sat in the shade on the grass of the football field under the relentless August sun. We listened to that remarkable voice.

"Let's talk about our team goals for the season."

The discussion went back and forth in a very democratic way, each player's voice as good as another's. After a half hour or so, we reached a consensus. We unanimously agreed on our team goals for the season.

"Anybody want to change a word?" he asked.

Not a one of us would change a word. We had agreed on our team goals and agreed on the language to articulate those goals. The team goals would be written on a blackboard in the locker as a permanent reminder throughout the season.

"No? Okay, we have team goals. The assistant coaches have cards and pencils to give you. I want each one of you to think about your personal goals that'll help us achieve our team goals. Personal goals are private. After you've thought about it privately, write down your personal goals on the card. Then, place the card in your hat where you'll see your personal goals every day when you put on your hat for practice. You'll see your personal goals before every game when you put on your hat before taking the field."

By hat, Billy Hugh Montgomery was referring to our helmets. As equipment, helmets were as personal and private as personal goals meant to do our part to achieve team goals.

Over the years, I have advised many people to follow the same practice in their families. Before the year begins, have a family discussion about family goals for the year. Then, each member of the family privately writes down his or her personal goals that will contribute to achievement of family goals. Then, the card is placed somewhere it will be seen privately every day. I also have advised many businesses and other organizations to practice the same method. Thank you, Billy Hugh Montgomery. It is so in football. It is so in life.

ATHLETE VERSUS NATURE

Billy Hugh Montgomery forced all football players to turn out for track and field in the spring. He didn't care about or know anything about track and field. He used track and field as a means of keeping us in shape, and keeping us out of trouble. He just made us run and sweat every afternoon. When we had a dual meet against another school, he would pick one of us to compete in each event. At one time or another, I ran the mile, ran a quarter leg on the mile relay, broad jumped (long jumped, as they call it now), high jumped (the first time, I landed on my head in a permanently wet sawdust pit that rivaled asphalt for hardness), put the shot (in other words, competed in the shot put), and once pole vaulted. When I pole vaulted, I had to ask the other school's competitor how to hold the pole, where to place the pole, and how and when to release the pole. We needed the points. We didn't get them. They wouldn't have been enough, anyway. Billy Hugh Montgomery didn't care. He was a football coach just trying to keep us in shape and out of trouble.

By the time I entered the tenth grade at Pascagoula High School in the fall of 1956, I knew that something was fundamentally different about baseball and track and field or football and track and field. At that time, I did not know that in England the term "athlete" is used only in reference to those who compete in track and field and never in reference to those who play, say, soccer or cricket. Those who play a game are, well, they are players. To Americans at the time, anyone who played baseball or football was an athlete. Two countries divided by a common language.

Throughout high school, I knew that baseball and football are contests that pit athlete versus athlete whereas track and field events pit athlete versus nature. From my own first-hand experience, I knew that baseball and football are games with well-known rules and that the games are contested by opposing players within the limiting factor of the rules of the game. From my first-hand experience, I also knew that competitive track and field deals with how fast you can run, how far or how high you can jump, and how far you can throw or put something. As a runner or jumper, I knew my contest was against nature. The measures used in this contest were time or space, the instruments of measurement clock or ruler.

It is so with life. At that time, however, I did not recognize that what I knew about the distinction between baseball or football and track and field could be extended beyond sports and athletics. In life, we are pitted not against others. Instead, we are pitted against who we were meant to be.

FIRST NEGLECT, THEN RUNNING

When I left high school, I neglected my body year after year. With any spare time at my disposal, I certainly didn't use it to exercise. From 1959 to 1971, I led a basically sedentary life as a student and university professor. During those twelve years, I was convinced I didn't have time to be physically active. I was even convinced I didn't need to be physically active. My physical growth was limited to growth that was developed or produced naturally. I had increased in size according to the genes I had inherited and to the food I had assimilated. I invested nothing in physical maintenance, nothing towards my proper physical condition and upkeep. My physical fitness was squandered, frittered away in willful laxity and blithesome insouciance.

A Slow Leak

In 1971, I was not very happy. I didn't realize it at the time, but it was my marriage. The late Methodist minister O. Dean Martin once said, "Most marriages don't go flat from a blowout. Most marriages go flat because of a slow leak." It was the story of my marriage. A slow leak, infinitesimally small leaks that summate ultimately to flatness as surely as microscopically small deposits of limestone skeletons build up ultimately to a massive coral reef. Our marriage was not flat in 1971, but the oxygen that once fueled our marriage was leaking unnoticed. However, I knew my life was dull and insipid, my interests dissipated, my drive enervated.

A change of geography, I thought, is what I need to pump some oxygen back into my life. I resigned my faculty position at Iowa State University and accepted a faculty position at the University of Florida. After four winters in Ames, Iowa, I needed to thaw. I thought Florida would pump some air back into my life, if not my marriage.

When we moved to Gainesville, we bought a house in a subdivision, Oak Crest, which backed up to a large open field of unknown acres, undoubtedly hundreds. Our house had a screened patio. I could sit on the patio and look over a wide expanse of that field. In the spring and summer, the owner of the field raised corn. In the fall and winter, the owner ran cattle. I sat on the patio countless times reading and thinking, often watching a magisterial red tailed hawk soar high in the sky like an airliner in a delay pattern, then suddenly dive like a Douglas SBD Dauntless, then fly nap of the earth over the stalk- and shuck-littered ground, snatch and grab a vulnerable mouse with military precision in its powerful claws, and then fly with swaggering wings to the top of a faraway live oak tree where the prideful hawk or its young would feed on the unfortunate creature. Sometimes, the red-tailed hawks would merely fly high over the field, circling like doom or fate, appearing to fly in judgment, occasionally screaming as though horrified.

Our daughter was age ten, and my wife was back in school to earn a doctorate. I had turned thirty. I felt that my life was not what it ought to be. I felt like I was hungry and had the refrigerator door open but didn't see anything I wanted to eat. I knew the symptoms, but I never thought that slow leaks in a failing marriage might be a contributing cause of the problem.

I kept sitting on the patio, reading and thinking. I probably read too much. In the ten years I lived in Gainesville, I read six hundred books, an average of five per month. I read William Faulkner, John Steinbeck, James Fenimore Cooper, Eudora Welty, Thomas Hardy, Charles Dickens, Iris Murdoch, Muriel Spark, and I read cosmology, biography, philosophy, theology, and history. I also read the occasional mystery or thriller if it was well written, which narrowed the possibilities significantly to Raymond Chandler, Dashiell Hammett, John le Carré, and little more. I know I thought too much. Reading too much, thinking too much, far from the madding crowd's ignoble strife.

After that first year in Gainesville, I still sat alone on the patio much of the time, reading too much, listening to the radio too much, and thinking too much while amidst introspective seclusion. I watched the rapacious red tailed hawks and admired their gift of rapine decisiveness. I watched the patient but persevering lizards that lived on the patio, climbed the screen, and "showed their money" to attract their dinner while accepting delay with equanimity. Sometimes, I had our witless toy poodle, Mimi, to keep me company, sometimes Mimi and Charlie, the intellectual Boston terrier we adopted after his owners divorced, sometimes Mimi, Charlie, and Minkey, a huge, athletic, pugilistic orange-striped cat. He was playfully mischievous like a monkey when he was a kitten, and "minkey" was the pronunciation given to "monkey" by Peter Sellers in his role as Inspector Clouseau in the "Pink Panther" movies.

One day when still forming my sense of personal transformation, a seed planted by W. Edwards Deming, I found myself thinking about when I was last happy. I remembered I had never been happier than when I was a student or when I was hanging around a gym. *You can still be a student! You can still hang around a gym! You work on a university campus, you idiot!*

The University of Florida was on the quarter system in those days and did not convert to the semester system until the fall of 1981. For the next five years, I took a class every quarter. I took a course on the French Revolution from a young historian who specialized in Eastern Europe, particularly specialized in what he called "the potato frontier." He began every class with the French Revolution and finished every class with how the introduction of the potato to the diet of peasants in Eastern Europe added an enormous number of calories and thus added years to their life expectancy. I took a two-quarter course sequence in calculus and relearned trigonometry so I could differentiate and integrate trigonometric functions even though there are few if any applications of trigonometric functions in business or economics. I took courses in American literature and English literature. I took courses in physics and philosophy. I took courses in anything that was scheduled nearby my office in 305 Bryan Hall at either 8:00 a.m. or 12:00 noon. Courses in anything but business or economics. I sat for courses only in the liberal arts and sciences.

Aerobics to Marathons

While I first was sitting for courses, I happened to read a book, *Aerobics*, written by Kenneth H. Cooper, M.D. *Aerobics* included a prescribed program of exercise leading to physical fitness. I assiduously followed the prescribed weekly program that involved walking and eventually jogging. Every week, I diligently did what I was supposed to do. I also began to hang around the gym. The gym on campus at that time was not like these gyms of today. It was not a sissy gym with indoor-outdoor carpet on the floor, potted plants placed strategically for ambiance, and shower rooms outfitted with hair dryers for men. The gym on campus was a manly gym, and it smelled like a manly gym. It smelled like men's sweat as well as the virility and potency of testosterone. Perfect. I loved the smell of manhood because it was exactly the strong odor of the gyms of my adolescence. It was the manful smell of hanging around a gym, altogether offensive to the sensibilities of girls and women, a place perfectly concordant with man's nature effused with the smell of when I was happy.

My journey thus began with a disciplined regime of walking and jogging, gradually adding more jogging, eventually jogging only. For a brief time, I ran two miles a day, four days a week. Jogging took discipline, a lot of discipline, the kind of discipline required of self-denial and mortification. After that brief time, jogging no longer required the dogged, steadfast discipline of a Tibetan monk. I actually began to enjoy the running. I remember the seminal day when it began.

I was driving home from campus on an absolutely beautiful, crisp fall afternoon, and I couldn't wait to go for my run. Like an out-of-body experience, I visualized myself running, and I sensed the forthcoming feeling of endorphin-fed peacefulness and serenity. I doubled my mileage to four miles that day, and I quickened my pace. From that day, I began to enjoy trees and their verdant differences, birds and their different melodies and lyrics, cicadas and their high-pitched drone, and sunsets with their fiery crimson and gold hues like panes of stained glass in an uppity Episcopal Church. The usual two miles a day soon became four miles, then five miles, and then six miles a day. The four days a week became five days, then six days, and then seven days a week. The mileage soon cumulated to more than fifty miles a week. Sunday was the day when I did LSD. Not the hallucinogenic lysergic acid diethylamide, LSD is long, slow distance, meaning longer distance at a slower pace, thus building up the mileage base. Running no longer required pertinacious discipline. I was like Forest Gump. I just liked to run.

I entered local races and placed well, particularly for my age group. Trophies accumulated faster than space to display them. I was invited to join the Florida Track Club, which at the time was represented by a number of track and field competitors who had used up their collegiate eligibility. Roy Benson, the University of Florida track and field coach as well as the Florida Track Club coach, took notice of my performance times and asked me to represent the Florida Track Club in local, regional, and national races. With Roy Benson's guidance, tutelage, and support, the fifty miles eventually became more than a hundred miles a week. Once, on a beautiful, chilly Sunday morning, I went for a long training run of more than forty miles, which I finished under six hours.

Training involved a lot of mileage on the road and on the track, often two-a-day workouts. Distance work on the road in the morning, speed work on the track in the afternoon, distance for endurance, and intervals for speed. We called intervals "speed work." A typical interval workout involved running a quarter mile as fast as I could, then jogging a quarter mile, then again running a quarter mile as fast as I could, then again jogging a quarter mile, and repeating these fast and easy intervals until my legs died and my fast times deteriorated until no training effect was realized. I was on the track with world-class runners who lived and trained in Gainesville, runners who were on Olympic teams and who won Olympic medals.

My favorite training on the track was Indian running. As we practiced it, the idea was to run in single file around the track. Each lap at the starting line, the last place runner had a quarter mile to take the lead. If he couldn't take the lead during that quarter mile, he was forced out. Eventually, after all others had been forced out, the last man running was the winner. I would line up with Frank Shorter, Marty Liquori, Jack Bacheler, Barry Brown, and maybe a couple of others who were world-class runners. I could take the lead two or three times when my turn came, but sooner rather than later I would be the first one forced out when I couldn't take the lead. Frank Shorter was always the last man standing or last man running in this case. The man was a running machine. He won the gold medal in the marathon at the 1972 Munich Olympics, the year that eleven Israeli athletes were held hostage and then murdered by the Palestinian group, Black September, in an unprecedented atrocity. By the late 1970s, I was competing year-round in distance races on the road and on the track. I won countless trophies and plaques for races spanning five kilometers (3.1 miles) to the marathon (26 miles, 385 yards).

Running originated in knowing my life was not what it ought to be, knowing I was not the person I could be and ought to be, and knowing I was not the person I was meant to be. I was not an unhappy person, a person whose human condition is unhappiness, but rather a basically happy person who experienced unhappiness in his life. Sitting on the patio too much, reading too much, listening to the radio too much, thinking too much, watching red tailed hawks prey on field mice too much, and watching lizards show their money too much. Nonetheless, I realized by then that in the case of physical characteristics, choice deals more with development than with growth. At the age of thirty, my physical growth had taken care of itself with a little help from physical activity through the age of eighteen. Now, I wanted to develop my body more fully and maintain a high level of physical fitness. I wanted to make my physical resources more available and usable, and I wanted to bring these latent physical resources to life. I wanted to start taking care of my body. After years of neglect, I turned to running.

As the result of vigorous physical activity, including road races from 5K to marathons, my resting pulse was diminished to forty per minute. When I took a routine physical examination one year, a nurse took my blood pressure three times before asking if I exercised a lot. When I assured her that I did, that I was a marathoner, she was visibly relieved. She exhaled in audible relief with her hand poised over her heart, and said, "I am so glad. I was afraid you were going into cardiac arrest on me."

The Florida Relays Marathon

After I first started running, I visited my younger brother in Athens, Georgia, where Sam was Associate Dean of the University of Georgia Law School. He was lifting weights for his physical activity. I convinced him that he needed cardiovascular exercise. He gave up weightlifting and took up running like his big brother.

Sam called me one day about a year later and told me he wanted to run the marathon in the Florida Relays. It would be his first marathon. Sam finished in about three-and-a-half hours, an eight minute pace.

I never had thought about running a marathon, but I knew I could run the distance easily. To me, the marathon was merely running at a comfortable pace for a long distance. In this sense, it was easier than the 10K (6.2 miles), which required running at an uncomfortable pace for thirty minutes or so to be competitive. I ran my first marathon only months later in 1977. My first marathon was the second annual Marine Corps marathon in Washington, D.C. I finished in a time of 3:14, my slowest time ever. A few years later, I ran the first Navy Marathon at the Jacksonville Air Station. I was a seeded runner and won a nice trophy.

The next year, 1978, Sam and I decided we would run the Florida Relays marathon together. The marathon was an out-and-back course, starting and ending at Percy Beard Field, the track on campus. On our way out, we ran together stride for stride, and we both felt good and strong. On the way back, we kept feeling stronger and stronger. When we entered the University of Florida track for the final lap of the marathon, we were still running together, sprinting the last two hundred meters for the finish line. Many of my running buddies were in the stands. They didn't know my brother from Adam's off ox. They just knew I was running on the final lap stride for stride with some unknown competitor. They began to cheer me on, imploring me by name to kick past this strange dude. With cheers ringing in my ears, I reached out for Sam's hand. Hand in hand and stride for stride, we crossed the finish line together while holding hands, thus signaling that we wished to be recorded as a tie.

The Stress of Life: Philosophic Implications

One Saturday after a long run and my usual trip to do the family grocery shopping while my daughter and wife slept late, I began a book, *The Stress of Life*, written by Hans Selye, M.D. Late afternoon, I reached the penultimate chapter, "Philosophic Implications." I read with heightened interest because I revisited my sophomoric distinction between baseball or football and track and field. I realized that the distinction extended to life. Under sub-headings "Long-range aims" and "The ultimate aim," Selye said,

... [W]hether he puts his faith in God or in creation, man realizes that his ultimate aim must outlast the moment. . . . To achieve our long-range aims we have to act and we must learn how to choose between various optional modes of action. The difficulty here is to formulate these aims precisely and to develop a code of conduct to guide us in the perpetual dilemmas created by the competition between immediate and future happiness. The long-range aims . . . should lead us through a meaningful, happy, active, and long life, steering us clear of the unpleasant and unnecessary stresses of fights, frustrations, and insecurities.

Some people hope to find such aims in the acquisition of wealth, power, and social position; others in religion or philosophy. . . . Others just give up and drift from day to day, trying to divert their attention from the future by some such sedative as compulsive promiscuity, frantic work, or simply alcohol.

That none of these things can assure lasting happiness is self-evident. Of course, there are many better guides to it: love, kindness, or simply the desire to do some good.

I immediately remembered my high school distinction between baseball or football and track and field. Baseball and football games are competitions of athlete versus athlete. Track and field events are competitions of athlete versus nature. Baseball and football involve being as good as the other fellow or being better than the other fellow over the course of a game on a given day. The competition in baseball and football is focused on comparing favorably and beating the opposing players according to the rules of the game. The competition in track and field is focused on nature, against which all competitors are measured.

Baseball and football are finite and discrete, limited respectively by innings and minutes. When the third out of the last inning is made or the last second on the clock expires, the game is over. You win or you lose. You are either better than the other fellows on that given day and win or worse and lose. Track and field competition is infinite and continuous. You may be as good if not better than the other fellow on a given day, but the clock or ruler tells you how well you did in your competition with nature. Your objective is to be as good as you can be in competition with nature. Your contest is against space or time. You can run alone and compete against nature, run alone and see how fast you can run. Your training is not in terms of how can I be as good as the next fellow. Instead, your training is in terms of how you can run faster, and how you can be as fast as you can be. In other words, in track and field, the emphasis is on the man you can be and ought to be, the man you are meant to be.

For most of my life, I thought at the time, I have been competitive. However, I have been competitive against other people, thinking like the baseball and football player that I once was, trying to be a better than the other fellow, settling for being as good as the next fellow, despairing when I was not. I need to think more like a runner, trying to be as good a man as I can be and ought to be, the man I was meant to be.

In Selye's framework, I had no long-range aims and no code of conduct to lead me and steer me. I was probably one of those people who, Selye said, instinctively realize they have been unable to solve this problem. I realized I was drifting from day to day, probably diverting my attention from the past, present, and future by compulsive running. At least it was not compulsive promiscuity or compulsive use of alcohol.

FIRST RUNNING, THEN LIFTING

Years later, I relocated to the University of New Orleans as Dean of the College of Business Administration. I lived in Mandeville, a beautiful little city north of Lake Pontchartrain across a twenty-four mile bridge. At the time, I was reduced to the neighborhood jogger, but I still ran fifty or so miles weekly. On Saturdays, for example, I drove to the westernmost end of the lakefront, and I ran from there to Fontainebleau State Park and back, a run of about sixteen miles on the St. Tammany Trace. Afterwards, I drove to Morning Star Missionary Baptist Church, a black congregation in Old Mandeville, for an hour-long prayer service. Almost always, I was the only white person there. This routine continued off and on for years.

Then, one day, I woke up and discovered that my ears were blocked. A typical man, I didn't go to a doctor, deciding instead that my ears would clear up any day. After a week, my ears were still blocked. Every word I spoke sounded like I was in a cave or a tunnel. After a week or so, I was driving to campus along Lakeshore Drive in New Orleans. Suddenly, I was so dizzy I felt like my head would roll off my shoulders. Of course, I thought I was having a stroke or a heart attack. It was vertigo, the inner ear problem that leads to a sense of imbalance.

After a slow, scary drive to my office a little like O.J. Simpson's slow-speed chase in 1994, I made a phone call to a friend who is a medical doctor. He referred me to an ear and nose specialist who spotted the problem as vertigo. After an office visit, she referred me to an allergist. A patch test on my back showed I was allergic to oak pollen, grass pollen, mold spores, dust mites, and more. The allergist, also a good friend of mine, recommended running on a treadmill at Franco's Athletic Club in Mandeville. I said I didn't think I could do that. He said he thought I could, pointing out that I could run on the treadmill while watching news or a ball game. Eventually, we compromised on one long run a week, all other days on the treadmill at Franco's. So, I joined Franco's, one of America's finest equipped and best managed athletic clubs.

After a couple of years of running on the treadmill at Franco's and continuing my long Saturday run followed by the 9:00 Morning Star prayer service, I took up weightlifting. The impetus was a personal trainer, Kevin Cavaretta, who was always around when I was running on the treadmill. Concerned that my 150-pound runner's frame was losing muscle mass in my upper body, I engaged Kevin for ten one-hour sessions, and then engaged him for another twenty sessions.

Kevin was a strict disciplinarian who imposed his will as surely as a Parris Island Drill Instructor. He taught me proper form on all of the weight machines, but he was irritated that I weighed only 150 pounds. Every day, he put me on the scales, and then he fussed at me. After weighing me a few times, he asked me what I ate for breakfast. Proudly, I told him I ate Post Spoon Size Shredded

Wheat, dried cherries, and a sliced banana topped with whole milk. Sounded to me like a healthy way to start the day.

Kevin yelled at me, "Runners! All you want to eat is carbohydrates! You need to eat 'in the zone,' mixing protein with carbs."

A few days later, Kevin asked me what I had eaten for supper the night before. Proudly, I told him I ate a really good supper. Salad, baked potato, sweet peas, and two pan-broiled pork chops for my protein.

Kevin yelled at me, "Pork! That's poison food! Never tell me again you ate pork."

I obeyed him. I never told him again I ate pork.

Week after week, I was stronger and stronger. As I added muscle mass, I added pounds to my lanky runners frame. When I reached 170 pounds, I still was only thirty-two inches in the waist. The increase in weight was muscle, not fat, particularly not fat around the waist.

By now, I had a new routine. Six days weekly, I ran on the treadmill. One day weekly, I ran a long course outdoors. Three days weekly, I lifted weights. This routine meant that, on Monday, Wednesday, and Friday, I ran over an hour on the treadmill, and then lifted weights for another hour. I had gone from neglecting my body to running and then to running and lifting weights. My physical journey had not reached a destination, but in a sense it was complete, focused on total fitness.

Years later in 2006, I moved from Mandeville to uptown New Orleans. I no longer had Franco's nearby. I joined the Jewish Community Center where I lift weights occasionally. I'm sort of a Jewish wannabe, anyway. However, demand exceeded the supply of treadmills, and time on treadmills was limited to twenty minutes. So, I began to run outdoors again and deal with the allergy symptoms by taking Zyrtec in the morning and Claritin in the evening. From my house on Magazine Street, I run Leontine to Laurel, over to Jefferson Avenue and down to Tchoupitoulas, then to Audubon Park around the 1.8 mile paved concourse, across to Audubon Zoo and through the Fly back to Tchoupitoulas, and backtrack from there. My Garmin GPS watch tells me that the course is more than seven miles, which I cover in about fifty minutes, sometimes less. In other words, I run at a neighborhood jogger pace. So, I run about two thousand miles annually. I go through a pair of Asics GT-1270 shoes every ten weeks, totaling five pairs annually. I buy my shoes only at Phidippides in Metairie. The husband and wife owners are runners themselves and really know feet and shoes. Shirley looked at my narrow heel and high arch and then recommended a shoe that is appropriate for my particular feet. She is the one who put me in the Asics GT-1270 shoes. I don't go to national chains where sales people are college kids working their way through school and know nothing beyond the difference between running shoes and basketball sneakers.

PHYSICAL GROWTH, DEVELOPMENT, AND MAINTENANCE

A sense of genuine integrity, which is to say a strong knowledge and keen awareness of wholeness and fullness, is based in part on physical growth, development, and maintenance. We cannot realize the sense of personal integrity while neglecting our bodies. Each of us has a need to follow a sensible regimen of physical exercise of sufficient intensity and duration for cardiovascular fitness. In addition, each of us must do some form of resistance training to prevent muscle loss. We also must use good sense and good judgment regarding our day-to-day habits; eating sensibly and drinking only in true moderation. No smoking.

NO SMOKING

My father was a smoker. He smoked Camel cigarettes. When I was a boy, I didn't think much about his smoking. Most men smoked, and my father was no different from most men. In the 1960s, he was strongly advised by his physician to quit smoking, and he quit for almost a year. He started back. His health declined still further. Increasingly, he developed the shortness of breath associated with emphysema. Finally, in 1980, he was diagnosed with lung cancer. He still did not quit smoking Camel cigarettes.

After the doctor told Dad he had lung cancer, Dad drove home alone in his

1976 Chevrolet Caprice. On the way home, he stopped at his barbershop and went inside. Dad told his barber that he wanted a flattop haircut.

The barber, who also cut my mother's hair, said, "Mr. Davis, I haven't cut a flattop in a long time, but I'd be happy to give you one. I want to know something. Does Mrs. Davis know about this?"

I looked into Dad's face when he told me this story. He was really laughing. He looked off in the distance, took the glasses off his face, and wiped his eyes. If I had cancer, he said, I might as well have my hair cut my favorite way. I always liked my hair in a flattop.

After Dad died on June 4, 1982, I took a suit to the funeral home, a pewter gray suit I had bought him for Christmas only six months earlier. When I bought it, I had in mind that he would be buried in it. The time had come, and now he would be buried in the suit I bought for him.

When I took the suit to the funeral home, the funeral director pulled me aside and said, "I have taken care of everything, but I have one concern. We can't figure out how your father wore his hair."

I laughed until I thought I would die and be buried with Dad. As I laughed, I had an uncanny feeling of Dad's presence and a feeling that he was there laughing with me. *I might as well have my hair cut my favorite way, he said. I always liked my hair in a flattop, he added. I always liked your pompadour, Daddy. The pompadour you wore when I was a boy.*

Cause of Death: Camel Cigarette Wounds

The morning of the day that Dad died, he was in the hospital. He could not eat anything. With imploring eyes and in a raspy whisper, he said to me, "I think I could eat your mother's chicken and dumplings."

I knew he was speaking in code. Both of us knew he could not eat his favorite meal, Mother's chicken and dumplings. He was telling me that he wanted to go home. He was telling me that he knew he was dying. He was telling me that he did not want to die in a hospital.

"Dad, you want to go home? I can ask Dr. Warren to discharge you forthwith."

In less than an hour, Dr. Warren was holding Dad's hand alongside the bed. All three of us knew that this was a kind of exit interview. All three of us knew what this little dramatic scene was all about.

Dr. Warren held his other hand and said, "Mr. Davis, we've done all we can do for you here. You understand what I'm saying, Mr. Davis? If you want to go home, you can go home. Your son here can settle up later."

Dad looked at him and rasped, "Doctor Warren, I'm not afraid to die. I just hate to put my boy here through all this. You know, my other son and my wife, too. I just hate to put my boys and my wife through all of this. I know it's going to be hard on them."

I cleaned out the closet in his room and the nightstand alongside his bed. In a drawer of the nightstand, I found an open pack of Camel cigarettes. When a man is shot with a bullet through the heart, we do not say he died of heart failure or cardiac arrest. We say he was shot to death by a bullet through the heart. The newspaper account says he died of a gunshot wound. My father did not die of lung cancer any more than a gunshot victim dies of heart failure. He died of Camel cigarette wounds. Camel cigarettes killed my father in 1982 as surely as a bullet killed President John F. Kennedy in 1962.

Stupidity, Not Ignorance

When my father started smoking as a young man, he and others smoked out of ignorance. People at that time didn't know about or fully understand the consequences or harm of cigarette smoking. At that time, Dad didn't know he was ruining his health. No one knew that smoking ruined health. He was ignorant. He and other smokers were ignorant of the ruining, killing effects of smoking.

Nowadays, people do not smoke out of ignorance. They smoke out of *stupidity*. We know and smokers know that smoking causes cancer and that smoking causes lung and heart disease. When highly intelligent people smoke, the smoking is an act of utter stupidity, not an act of uninformed ignorance.

Over the years, I have known many corporate recruiters, the ones who interview graduates for entry-level positions in their corporate hierarchies. Most of them want to meet for dinner or for a cocktail so that they can cajole or otherwise wheedle off-the-record information from me about each of the promising candidates for a position. All of them have told me they would never hire a smoker knowingly. When hiring decisions are made, smokers seemingly are the targets of discrimination more than any other group.

Imitating the Worst Things Adults Do

Smoking holds a curious place in our society. When young people are self-conscious about their immaturity and want to give the impression of being mature and adult-like, when immature young people want to look older, they choose to imitate the worst things that adults do in pathetic attempts to give the appearance of being older and adult-like. Rather than imitate the best things that adults do, they imitate the worst. Among other harmful imitations, they smoke. When women want to be more like men, they do not imitate the best things that men do. They, too, choose the worst things that men do. They smoke. Young women or women of any age will spend hundreds of dollars for a dress and accessories and hundreds of dollars per ounce of perfume so that they smell like an evening in Paris and then smoke a cigarette and smell like a night in a New Orleans pool hall.

In the late 1990s, I was engaged for management consulting with a *Fortune* 500 company. I worked extensively with a particular executive for whom I had great respect. I think the respect was reciprocated. He and I were having lunch at a posh venue. A beautiful day, we had a table outside. As we talked about anything but business, he kept glancing towards another table. Finally, he leaned closer to me over the table. With a discrete whisper, he said, "The young lady at a table behind you is one of the most beautiful women I have ever seen. Don't stare, but look at her. See if you agree with me."

I casually looked at the table behind me. He was right. She was beautiful, gorgeous, dressed in expensive designer clothes. Her male companion was as handsome as she was beautiful, and he too was dressed expensively in what looked like an Italian-cut suit.

However, the executive suddenly blurted in an excited utterance, "Nope. She just ruined it. She lit up a cigarette. She probably doesn't realize how ugly it makes her look and how it makes her designer clothes stink. Her boyfriend is pushing away from the table. He doesn't want her smoke to ruin his Italian suit."

The one in five adults who smoke must realize that the four in five adults who do not smoke feel this way about smoking.

A Physical Issue

I have known many people who smoke. In some cases, these people are food faddists and GNC junkies, taking vitamins and minerals by the handfuls. I think and want to say, *if you are really concerned about your health, you can do far more for your health by quitting smoking than by taking all the vitamins and minerals in the world.* Smoking is not a moral issue. Smoking is a physical issue.

When my daughter was a little girl, I was enmeshed in a conversation with her and heard myself say something she probably thought was just another one of those outlandish utterances her father brought forth now and then.

"Let me give you some lifelong advice. Don't start what other people are trying to quit."

She knew I was advising her not to smoke. She knew her grandfather, my father, was robbed of his health by Camel cigarettes. She knew how many smokers were trying to quit. Don't start what other people are trying to quit.

WELLNESS CENTERS

Most corporations and many other organizations now have wellness centers. In this way, they are investing in the physical health and physical wellbeing of their employees. Of course, these wellness centers center on physical fitness. Treadmills, weight machines, and so forth provide the wherewithal for physical maintenance and development. Some of these wellness centers also deal with proper nutrition and programs dealing with physical issues such as weight loss.

However, the express intent of these wellness centers rarely focuses on intellectual pursuits, emotional stability, or spiritual values. By addressing all-round wellness encompassing physical, intellectual, emotional, and spiritual wellness, these wellness centers would show concern for wellness of the whole person. These businesses and organizations would be investing in personal integrity.

In 2001, I was asked to speak to a large group of executives on the topic of integrity. The previous year, this same group of executives had listened to a retired Marine general speak on the topic of leadership. After my presentation in 2001, my phone never stopped ringing. These executives wanted to engage me to consult with and train managers. They saw a need to have a proper understanding of integrity. They realized that organizational integrity is the outcome of personal integrity taken seriously throughout an organization. Some of these executives wanted me for a morning or an afternoon. Others wanted me for a whole day, some for an entire week.

Human resource managers in particular realized that the focus and objective of their wellness centers were too narrowly conceived. They wanted to find ways to broaden the scope to embrace not only the physical aspect of wellness but also the intellectual, emotional, and spiritual aspects of wellness. Only then would the totality of wellness be addressed. In this sense, personal wellness is the equivalent of personal integrity.

Chapter Three
THE INTELLECTUAL JOURNEY

The word "intellect" comes from a Latin root, "intellectus," which in verb form translates "to understand." The word "intellect" thus deals with the power of understanding, knowing, reasoning, comprehending, and judging. Intellect deals with the ability to perceive relationships. The word "intelligent" implies success in solving problems through the power of understanding, knowing, reasoning, comprehending, and judging. The word "intellectual" refers to belonging, or relating to, or performed by the intellect, which in turn deals with the power of understanding, knowing, and reasoning, comprehending, and judging. To a degree, our intellectual characteristic takes care of itself. Again, to some extent, our intellect is determined genetically, but to another extent is determined by environment and experience. Some of us are more adroit, more alert, more quick-witted, more knowing than others. As in the case of our physical side, however, our intellectual side and our respective intellectual growth and intellectual development also are dependent on choices that we make.

CONTINUAL IMPROVEMENT

At the risk of upholding or otherwise championing "the one great man" interpretation of history, the worldwide quality movement nevertheless can be traced to one man, Walter A. Shewhart. He had a doctorate in physics from Berkeley but worked as an engineer for Bell Laboratories, now Lucent Technologies. Shewhart wrote a one-page memorandum to his boss dated May 16, 1924, proposing that statistical theory could be used to serve the needs of industry. His memorandum included a hand-drawn "control chart." For this seminal memorandum and a lifetime body of related work, Shewhart is regarded as "the father of modern quality control." These principles of quality control were practiced first by Western Electric, the manufacturing arm of AT&T. These practices became known as Western Electric methods.

Later, another man became more famous and certainly more renowned than Shewhart for his contributions to quality. That man was W. Edwards Deming, who also earned a doctorate in physics. Deming is better known than Shewhart, but Deming always referred to Shewhart as "the master." As a devout Episcopalian, Deming's meaning was crystal clear. Deming regarded himself as merely a disciple of the master, Shewhart. By the mid-1980s, the gospel of Shewhart and preachments of Deming were refined by Motorola to embody what we now know as Six Sigma. As Sir Isaac Newton wrote in a letter to one of his scientific rivals, Robert Hooke, "If I have seen further it is by standing on the shoulders of giants," which rather than humility was cruel humor since Hooke was a hunchbacked dwarf. Motorola engineers and others saw further by standing on the shoulders of Shewhart and Deming, the giants. What they saw was Six Sigma. One of the cornerstones of quality and Six Sigma is continual improvement of processes.

In the United States, we sometimes say, "If it ain't broke, don't fix it." A better saying would be, "If it ain't broke, how can we prevent breakage?" Indeed, "if it ain't broke, what can be done to make it better?" This notion brings home the essentiality of continual, never-ending improvement.

Thus, at the heart of the quality movement and Six Sigma is the idea of continual improvement of processes. In addition to originating the control chart as a device to bring processes under statistical control, Shewhart also developed a continual improvement cycle known as the PDCA cycle, often called the Shewhart Cycle. The cycle involves (1) planning a fundamental change in a process; (2) doing it, carrying out the planned change on a small scale or as an experiment; (3) checking results, observing or studying the outcome of the small scale project or experiment; and (4) acting if the results are promising, which means redesigning the process by incorporating the fundamental change. Of course, the cycle does not end here. Another fundamental change in the process is planned, and so forth. In Japan, the Shewhart Cycle was called the Deming Cycle simply because Deming was the one who brought it to Japanese scientists and engineers.

Six Sigma process redesign arose from frustration with the slow if not glacial pace of improvement that often resulted from the basic nature of the PDCA Cycle. PDCA called for making only one fundamental change during each cycle. Near the end of his life, even Deming himself seemed to acknowledge that improvement by one change at a time was too slow. At one of his four-day seminars in the late 1980s, he said, "You can't catch up with something that's going faster than you are." In the context, he seems to have meant that if a company has fallen behind and is trying to catch up, grinding out one change at a time is not likely to close or overcome the gap. Incremental improvements of one change at a time do not allow a company to keep up with the rapid pace of change in technology, customer expectations, and competition. Six Sigma thinking brought together process improvement and process design or redesign. Process design/redesign is effort not only to improve but also at times to replace a process or segment of a process with an altogether new one. Companies stay on top by rethinking key processes on a regular basis.

Ordinarily, Six Sigma utilizes a five-phase process improvement cycle: Define, Measure, Analyze, Improve, and Control. This cycle is known as DMAIC, pronounced "deh-MAY-ick." DMAIC is firmly grounded in Shewhart's PDCA cycle. In other words, DMAIC did not displace or replace PDCA. Indeed, DMAIC is based on PDCA, building on the basic notions inherent in each phase.

The first phase of DMAIC is *Define*. A trained team is formed to work on the process improvement project. One of the first tasks of the team is to identify customers according to their needs and requirements. Critical-to-quality characteristics are defined. Critical needs and requirements are clarified and validated. The extant process is flowcharted, which is a kind of baseline. A "team charter" is articulated. The charter clearly states the problem, goals, and milestones, which is a mission statement, describing what is to be accomplished and how the mission is to be accomplished.

The second phase is *Measure*. Now, the focus turns to identifying key measures and developing a plan for collecting data. A baseline is established for process performance to determine current capability.

The third phase is *Analyze*. Data are analyzed to determine gaps between current performance of the process and performance goals. Possible sources of variation are identified with the intention to unmask root causes. The "vital few" causes of variation are identified and verified.

The fourth phase is *Improve*. Next, possible solutions to the "vital few" causes are developed and tested. Best solutions are chosen based on studies or experiments and analysis of results. The process flowchart is redesigned so that the modification reflects the improvements. An implementation plan is developed.

The fifth phase is *Control*. Finally, a plan to sustain improvements is developed. The improved process steps, process standards, and process documentation are embedded into operations. Ownership and knowledge are transferred to the process "owner" and the process team responsible for sustaining and auditing the redesigned process.

It is so with our minds. Schooling is built on the model of continual improvement. Each year of elementary school, middle school, and high school is meant to improve our intellect, thus continually improving our minds. Continual improvement of our intellect does not end with high school. Colleges and universities offer major programs of study that continue this intellectual development. Advanced studies leading to terminal degrees and professional certification are still further intellectual developments. Sooner or later, however, formal education runs its course. Afterwards, continual intellectual improvement is a matter of choices we make.

Like loss of muscle mass with age if we are physically inactive, loss of mental acumen and its corresponding attributes such as discernment and keenness of insight also diminish with age if we are intellectually inactive. Learning through any informative medium is the equivalent of lifting weights to maintain or add muscle mass. Learning is continual improvement.

NUTRIENTS FOR A CURIOUS MIND

Intellectually, I was born lucky. Perhaps I should say I was blessed with a good mind at birth. My parents were bright people even though they were not highly schooled or educated. Both had high school diplomas. My Davis ancestors in particular were wanderers and seekers, restless and curious people. Eventually, many of us have become teachers, which in a sense fit the mold of curious people. I was exposed to books early in my life. I had access to vast classic literature in the home library of Auntie and Uncle Marion, a great aunt and great uncle who I often visited in summers. By the time I was in the sixth grade, I had read most of these classics.

I always read books in my childhood and adolescence. A lot of my early intellectual growth came through reading. When I was a boy, I routinely rode my bicycle to the Pascagoula Public Library, a large barn-like building at the end of Delmas Avenue where it intersected with Frederick Street. At one time, I believe the old library was a hotel, perhaps the Scranton Hotel. During summers, I rode my bicycle to the library two or three times a week for the loan of a book, particularly history, biography, and science. No Hardy Boys or other juvenile literature for me, although I did read delightedly all of Wilfred McCormick's Bronc Burnett books.

One summer day, I rode to the library but arrived before it opened. I rode my bicycle around to the county courthouse and noticed some old-timers sitting outside on benches. I was curious. I parked my bicycle and sat nearby the old fellows to hear them talking. The topic was fishing, both freshwater fishing and deep-sea fishing in the Gulf of Mexico. I heard one of them say while eliding syllables and dropping some of his letters, "I don't go fishin' out in th' Gulf. I never could catch fish by throwin' up on 'em." I decided to stay for a while. Later, one of them said, "My wife says I'm lazy. I'm not lazy. I just believe in resting before I'm tired." I never made it to the library that day, preferring to be entertained to being informed. As a Southerner, I like a good story and a good aphorism. Southerners also believe that truth should never get in the way of a good story.

Sometimes, my curiosity led me to the courthouse instead of the library. I liked to sit for trials. Argumentation between adversaries and pronouncements from the bench were like a confounding rebus of exotic words and arcane terms. I took notes and ran for the dictionary when I returned home. One day, I sat in the back of the courtroom and listened to testimony in a hearing to determine whether the black maid of a prominent beach family in Pascagoula should be charged in connection with stabbing her common law husband to death.

When she took the stand, the judge himself droned in a monotonous voice, "Tell the court whether you stabbed your common law husband."

The black maid replied in a hushed voice, her eyes downcast, her hands cradled in her lap, her body as limp and droopy as a cooked noodle, "Yes, sir. I stabbed him, stabbed my husband."

The judge scrutinized her from his lofty chair where he seemed to lord over the courtroom scene like a territorial magnate. Presently, his eyes almost closed with evident indifference and detachment, he then asked in a low dull voice like a harmonium, "Tell the court why you stabbed your common law husband."

She answered while glancing to his elevated station, "Yes, sir. I stabbed 'im 'cause they won't sell us no guns."

The judge was not amused. Everyone else in the courtroom laughed. She was not charged. Her late husband was just a man who needed killing. Behind the scenes, the beach family for whom she worked undoubtedly had decided the outcome of the justice system that day.

Another day, Dad and I sat in the back of the courtroom and listened to testimony in a hearing that involved a black man who worked with Dad in the government warehouse on Twelfth Street. Indeed, he was one of Dad's good friends. He was a big man. He had a big frame, and he carried a lot of weight on that big frame. He looked nonetheless solid, suggesting the weight was not to be misinterpreted as fat. He had a gold tooth in front, he smoked cigars in a tortoise shell holder, and he drove a big Buick. On weekends, Dad's coworker and friend was deputized to cruise around and maintain order in the black juke joints and tawdry honkey tonks on the immediate outskirts of Carver Village, federal government-owned housing for black families in the 1950s when segregation of schools and housing was a cruel and unjust foundation of institutionalized racism.

Dad's coworker and friend arrested a black man in one of these beer joints, and he shot and killed the man while in custody. The hearing was intended to determine if he should be charged with any wrongdoing. When he took the stand, the same judge asked him if he shot and killed his prisoner in the barroom while in his custody.

With a strong voice that bordered on a deep base bellow worthy of any pasture bull, he answered, "Yes, sir. I shot and killed him right there in the barroom."

Once again, the judge exuded a sense of indifference without any deference to the seriousness of the matter. With closed eyes, the judge asked why he shot and killed the man in his custody.

Dad's friend and coworker answered in a bold, confident voice, "Well, sir, he kind o' looked like he wanted to escape."

He was not charged. In Pascagoula, we evidently had a lot of men who needed killing. At the time, Pascagoula was a small town set in a highly structured and well-established system of racism that pervaded every social stratum and diffused its injustice to every niche and corner of life. The message seemingly was that black-on-black killings were not worthy of charges. Victims were seen as merely black men who needed killing. I learned a lot hanging around the courthouse. I learned that something was not right. Something didn't pass the smell test.

When I was a boy, we had no television set until Daddy bought one for Christmas midway through my seventh grade. Even after we had our first television set, I listened to the radio, and I read.

I remember knowing a boy who I saw at the movies on Saturdays. I did not see him for a long time, a year or more. One Saturday, I saw him again at the Ritz Theater in Pascagoula. I asked him where he'd been. He told me he and his family had been living in Memphis. At the time, I thought, *I'll never be able to leave this town, never get out of Pascagoula. I'll never have the opportunity to live in Memphis or New Orleans or Mobile or anywhere but here in Pascagoula. I'll never have the opportunity to travel.*

Yet, I read, and I listened to the radio. In my mind, I knew London of the nineteenth century, California of the Great Depression, and Main Street of 1920s Minnesota. Over the years, my understanding and knowing were deepening and widening, springing up and maturing through words I read in books, voices I heard on the radio, and eventually images I saw on television. More often than not, when I heard the name of a town somewhere in America or in the world, I would know something about the town through fiction. Monterey, California: Pacific Ocean and canning, where Doc was a marine biologist, and dogs smiled at him when he walked down the street. The Salinas Valley: a good place to grow vegetables, like the lettuce that spoiled on the way to the East, like the beans that profited Cal Trask during World War I. When I knew nothing of a town or a region through fiction, I knew of it through radio, either through news or sports or drama. I knew about London through Edward R. Morrow, Yankee Stadium through Gordon McClendon, "The Old Scotsman", Cincinnati through Big John and Sparky.

MATHEMATICS, NATURALLY

When I was in elementary school, I took an achievement test each year like every other kid. At the end of the fourth grade, I noticed a mathematics part of the achievement test beyond the questions we were supposed to answer. The section had some odd questions. These questions were strange and mysterious to me, asking questions such as, "If 4X=16, then what is X?" Or, "If 32÷X=4, then what is X?" Or, "If 7+2X=17, then what is X? If 25−X=10, then what is X? I somehow knew the answers, 4, 8, 5, and 15. Although we were not supposed to answer questions in that section, I answered them anyway. Indeed, I answered all of the questions easily.

After the achievement tests were graded, my fifth grade teacher, Mrs. Yawn, asked me to stay after school. She said I had answered all of the questions on the achievement test correctly, including all of the mathematics questions on the achievement test, which we not supposed to answer. She asked where I had learned algebra.

I had no idea what she was talking about. Algebra? What's algebra? Evidently, I had figured out algebra on my own. When I returned home that day, I ran for the dictionary as usual. I learned that algebra was a term derived from an Arabic word, *al-jebr*, meaning "reunion of broken parts." At the time, I thought,

Algebra is a beautiful image, bringing back together and making whole once again parts that had been broken. I didn't think at the time that the image of reuniting broken parts was a kind of metaphor for personal integrity.

When I was in high school, I had a mathematics teacher named Mrs. Mitchell. Mrs. Mitchell was a terrific teacher. As we said in those days, she knew her subject. She knew a lot of mathematics. She did not merely present the mathematics she knew. Mrs. Mitchell could teach the mathematics she knew.

We were lucky if not blessed in those days. Teachers took courses in the subjects they would be teaching rather than courses in education. If someone wanted to teach mathematics in high school, he or she had to major in mathematics rather than education. If someone wanted to teach chemistry in high school, he or she had to major in chemistry rather than education. Mrs. Mitchell, for example, had an undergraduate degree in mathematics, taking only one course in education, viz., a course dealing with methods for teaching mathematics at the secondary school level. Nowadays, young men and women who want to teach at the high school level take too many courses in education, diluting the knowledge of the subject they will be teaching.

In her classroom, Mrs. Mitchell had a blackboard that covered the entire front wall from left to right and almost from floor to ceiling. The blackboard had a low tray for chalk. Mrs. Mitchell had a remarkable, astounding, jaw-dropping skill that never failed to strike us with awe. When Mrs. Mitchell was teaching mathematics, she could stand with her right side to the blackboard and her face turned to us in the classroom, take a piece of chalk in her right hand down at her side in the six o'clock position with the tip of the chalk against the blackboard, then quickly rotate the piece of chalk 360 degrees and draw an absolutely perfect circle on the board! She accomplished this stupid human trick while still facing us in the classroom.

When I was a teenager, I was hard to impress. I was impressed. It was amazing! When I was in high school, I tried a hundred times to draw a circle in this way and failed a hundred times. Years later, when I was a college professor, I tried another hundred times and failed another hundred times. Mrs. Mitchell did it every time.

THE UNDERGRADUATE YEARS

After graduated from high school in 1959, I worked a full year at Coastal Chemical Company, starting as a Kardex clerk in the warehouse but quickly transferring to a better paying job as machine operator in the plant. I saved all the money I could. My only extravagance was the purchase of a Bulova watch for fifty dollars. I still wear it from time to time, no pun intended. In September 1960, savings in hand, I left my job with Coastal Chemical to enter Mississippi Southern College, now the University of Southern Mississippi or just Southern Miss. My only objective was to have a good job when I was graduated, say, a job that paid a hundred dollars a week.

If I had majored in what I liked the most, I would have been an English major, focusing on literature. I still have a passion for reading. At that time, I read what most people would call "classics." However, I had no idea what kind of job other than an English teacher that I could expect with a degree in English. So, I thought I should major in something in the business school and feed my intellectual passions with electives in the liberal arts, particularly literature, history, and philosophy. That was my plan, and I stuck to it. In the end, I received a liberal education as an adjunct to a business major. I completed my undergraduate degree in less than three years.

Spanish, Si; Economics, No

In search of a business major, I perused the university bulletin and thought a major in International Trade looked interesting and closer to the liberal arts than, say, marketing or finance. Actually, International Trade was a contrivance that wangled economics and Spanish into a double major. Before courses in either economics or Spanish, I expected to love economics and hate Spanish, but at the end would be a career in international trade. Wrong. The first two courses in economics were abysmal, limitless in every dimension of boredom and uselessness. Principles of Microeconomics and Principles of Macroeconomics were the two worst courses I took as an undergraduate, each class a microcosm of suffocating, stultifying tedium as dreary as a Russian love story.

On the other hand, Spanish was great, each class an ambrosial delight for the curious intellect.

Mr. Burke taught Spanish. He was a jolly, avuncular Brobdingnagian sort of man. He had a body shaped like a bowling pin, narrow shoulders and wide hips below an abundant girth. Many times in class, I was reminded of the W.C. Fields line directed to Mae West in *My Little Chickadee*, "I have some very definite pear-shaped ideas that I'd like to discuss with thee." Mr. Burke was somewhat pear-shaped, though not as pleasing to the masculine eye as Mae West. I learned more English grammar in his Spanish classes than I ever learned in any English class, and I had thought of myself as already understanding the English language and the intricacies of its arcane rules.

Mr. Burke had a lot of experience teaching English as a second language in New York City. I remember he told us that the most important first word for these foreigners to learn in English was "get." You can "get" almost anything, he said. You can get up, get down, get ahead, get behind, get a beer, get a cocktail, get drunk, get up in the morning, get in bed, get out of bed, get in trouble, get out of trouble, get in a car, get out of a car, get on a bus, get off a bus, get upset, get angry, get frustrated, get religion, get ready, get in the way, get out of the way, get the telephone, get lunch, get a job, get an appointment, get a grade, on and on. Almost always, there is another word for "get," Mr. Burke said to us. I still avoid saying or especially writing the word "get."

Years later, in 1972, I had the opportunity to lecture around Europe one summer. My tour was to begin in Barcelona. On the flight overseas, the plane made a crash landing in Lisbon because of a hydraulic problem, which understandably delayed my arrival in Barcelona. Due to the delay, the driver I had hired to drive me from the Barcelona airport to the hotel gave up and left me abandoned to my own wits. Well, I discovered my Spanish was still good enough to carry on conversation.

After arrival at my hotel, I went to a *tipico* restaurant, Los Caracoles, where I had paella with ghostly white wriggling baby eels atop the mountain of rice and seafood. From the time I arrived in Barcelona until the time I left for Paris, I spoke only Spanish. Poorly perhaps, accented maybe, but I made my way around Barcelona just fine.

Liberal Arts Now, Business Later

As a result of my mind-numbing two courses in the principles of economics, I scheduled mostly electives in the liberal arts each quarter, thus putting off my required business curriculum. Sooner or later, I knew I had to start serious fulfillment of one major or another in the business school. What I dreaded most was still another course in economics, Money and Banking, which was required of all business majors. *Later,* I thought, *after I take more courses in literature, history, and philosophy.*

I completed my first quarter at Southern and earned grades of three A's and two B's. These grades would be the worst that I received while a student at Southern. I finished my undergraduate degree in less than three years with a 3.86 grade point average, graduating with high honors. After staying out of school and working a year before going to college, I was now back on track with members of my high school graduating class who went directly to college.

MY GRANDFATHER, THE COWBOY: DEATH BE NOT PROUD

On January 14, 1961, a Saturday, I was at home in Pascagoula. I was halfway through my second academic year at Mississippi Southern College. My father was with his father, my grandfather the Texas cowboy who homesteaded in the Arizona Territory before Arizona was a state. This robust man suffered a massive and debilitating stroke in 1959. He was placed in a nursing home in Jackson in late 1960. Just before Christmas, he contracted a common cold that progressed into pneumonia. My father, my brother, and I visited him on New Year's Day of 1961. It was hard seeing this cowboy, this once strong, rugged, tough man lying frail and helpless in bed. After we left that day, he lost consciousness.

My father was in Jackson at my grandfather's side on that Saturday, January 14. At 9:00 a.m., I answered the telephone in Pascagoula. The telephone call was my father, who was calling from Jackson. My grandfather the cowboy was dead.

Education of a Different Sort

I had lost my grandfather, the Texas cowboy and Arizona homesteader. Dead. I was very close to him. He taught me to ride. We rode horses together.

He taught me to drive a tractor. We cut clover together on the old John Deere. He taught me how to play poker. Not just the rules, not just the hands. He taught me how . . . to . . . play . . . poker, the art of bluffing and the science of money management. He told me stories about poker games, saloons and cowboys, gamblers and poker. Like the time the "anything girl" shot a gambler in the back of his head while my grandfather was sitting at a saloon table in Tombstone, the county seat of Cochise County when Arizona was still a territory. The gambler was a man who needed killing, my grandfather said. The anything girl was advised to leave the Arizona Territory, and she relocated to New Braunsfel, Texas, where she married a banker and made a good wife and a good mother to his children.

I don't want you sitting around here all the time and playing Parcheesi with those women, he said. He shuffled the cards, put two white clay chips in the middle of the oak table that Auntie and Uncle Marion had bought in Dallas. This is the ante, he said. Seven-card stud. Two cards down, one up. Now, let's think about the probabilities, he said. If my up card beats all three of your cards, you fold. . . .

After he taught me everything he knew about poker, he told me I played the cards as well as cards could be played. When playing against someone who plays as well as I did, the winner would be the one who was dealt the better cards. He said he had just one more lesson to teach me, more important than anything else he had taught me. "Listen to me carefully," he said. "I want you to remember what I tell you the rest of your life."

I waited. I leaned forward. I looked him in the eyes, those remarkable eyes that evidenced intelligence and experience.

He said softly, like a secret, "Never play poker with a stranger. Never gamble with a man who goes by the name of a city."

I was ten years old, long before I ever heard of Minnesota Fats or Amarillo Slim.

I knew a lot of cowboys, he said. I knew all kinds of cowboys coming from all over, some white, some black, some Mexican. Never knew a working cowboy who could play poker. Gamblers took their money. Me, I never believed in gambling. I believed in winning. Cost me a lot of money to learn the game; got it all back and then some. Never knew a working cowboy who could shoot, either. He laughed but no sound came out. I guess that's why we wore six-shooters, he said. Needed to shoot at something six times to hit it once. He laughed again and wheezed a little deep in his throat. He pointed his index finger like a gun and pushed his John B. Stetson hat up in the front to his hairline and looked out the window where pine trees and wisteria and crepe myrtle grew. I knew he didn't see the green of what was there. He saw earth tones, and dust, and mesquite, and home. I was ten years old, and I saw all of it, too.

The Wallet

We left immediately to join Dad in Jackson and to await the funeral and burial in the cemetery at Thompson Chapel outside Wesson, Mississippi. When I arrived at the funeral home in Jackson, my father and I threw our arms around each other, standing chest against chest and man against man, never saying a word. Finally, we released our grips on each other, and then stood at arm's length, each with his hands on the other's shoulders, and we looked at each other. Life was suddenly different, changed. A generation had passed. I had moved up a generation. He had, too.

After several moments, Dad led me away from everyone else, and we were alone together. We sat in plush overstuffed chairs facing each other. He reached for something I hadn't noticed laying on a side table. He carefully, reverently unwrapped some yellowed tissue paper and took out a natural leather wallet, cut long to fit the breast pocket of a man's jacket. It had a leather strap that wrapped around and bound the folds of the wallet. He backed out the strap and opened the folds. Dad began to talk.

"Your great-great grandfather, James Madison Davis, went to California as a young man to prospect for gold in 1849. He was a 49er. He saw the Pacific Ocean. Can you imagine? On his way home, he bought this wallet. You see here where he signed it."

He handed it to me. I had heard of this wallet, but I had never seen it. Now, I held it in my hands like an oblation, and I read in clear handwriting,

James M. Davis

Dec. 5, 1851

He had been thirty-one years old when he signed the wallet. From Mercer County, Kentucky, in 1820 to California in 1849. He saw the Pacific Ocean! After two years in California, he was on his way home in 1851.

James Madison Davis was a wanderer. What was he seeking? What did he expect to find there? Was he content to find gold or something greater than gold? Was he restless? Am I? What am I seeking? What do I expect to find there? Where is there?

I returned the wallet to Dad. He took the invaluable wallet back in his hands, and he talked again.

"When he died, the wallet went to his oldest son, Samuel Godfrey Davis. You can see where he signed it here on the outside of the wallet."

He handed the wallet back to me. Again, I held the wallet in my hands. Below James M. Davis's signature and date, I saw still another handwriting, another signature and date,

Sam G. Davis

Calvert, Texas

1892

Dad's voice became more deliberate, fully aware of the character of his words, saying, "Of course, he was your great grandfather, Samuel Godfrey Davis. When he died, the wallet went to his oldest son, his oldest *living* son, Grover Cleveland Davis, your grandfather."

Dad's eyes misted. He looked away from me with serenity that seemed to draw from something invisible that he saw nevertheless. Grover Cleveland Davis was his father, who now was laid to eternal rest in a wooden casket.

I could not look at Dad. I looked down at the wallet in my hands, my own eyes filling with tears and my sight blurred. I knew where this conversation was going, where it would end.

"Your grandfather," Dad finally managed to say. "My father," he said. "You can see where he signed it."

I looked at the wallet as through a misty darkness, and I saw below Sam

G. Davis's signature and date, still another handwriting, another signature and date,

Grover C. Davis

Bowie, Arizona

1926

Dad's voice deepened, his words spoken in a graveled whisper, saying, "When your grandfather died, the wallet came to me, his oldest son. I thought you might want to be here when I sign it."

He took the wallet back from my hands, took a pen in his hand, and wrote on the wallet. He handed it back to me without a word. I thought I could hear the silence of the Earth at that moment. I took the revered wallet in my hands like a precious stone. With blurred eyes and constricted throat, I read where he had written just below his own father's signature,

Marion F. Davis

Pascagoula, Miss.

January 14, 1961

He and I knew what he must say next. He didn't want to say it, and I didn't want to hear it. Yet, it had to be said. He said it haltingly in a low rustling voice, like the whisper of wind soughing through limbs and branches in a pine forest.

"When I die, the wallet will go to you. You'll sign it."

Father and son were bonded as one flesh and as one mind. I rose and walked across the room to look out a window at nothingness. I cried. I could not look at my father. I knew he could not look at his son. He cried.

On June 4, 1982, the wallet came to me. One hundred and thirty-one years old, the wallet had passed from great-great grandfather down to me. I signed it just below my father's signature,

J. Ronnie Davis

Jackson, Miss.

June 4, 1982

I have no son, but I will leave the wallet to my daughter, Amanda Lee Davis. In the wallet, she will find a letter, written in pencil in a boy's handwriting on lined paper, trying his hardest but failing to spell all words correctly,

Calvert Tex,

Feb. 10, 1888

Dear Aunt:—

I will write to you as I promised you. I have been sick all this week but I am getting alright now and I have been very lonely since Monday. I am still going to school and I am getting along very well. Mr. Johnson hasent whipped me yet. I will be glad when I can get back to school again. Miss Melisa has had a bad spell of sickness the last few days. And Mama was the only woman to take care of her. We all had a fine time staying by ourselves sister cried a rite smart. It has been drizzling rain all morning and I have not been out of the house very much. I read your last letter to Mama. I got me a yoke but I traded my steers off for a colt. I will have a fine time when my colt gettes big enough for me to ride him. . . .

Now I will close.

Write soon to me.

Your Nephew

Earl.

Earl was my grandfather's brother, his older brother. Earl wrote this letter in 1888. He wrote the letter in February 1888 when he was eleven years old. He had a yoke, and he had some calf steers. He traded these calf steers for a colt. In May 1888, three months after writing this sweet letter to his aunt, Earl was dead of a heat stroke. Earl never rode his colt. My grandfather placed his brother's letter in the wallet. Earl was the oldest son. If he had lived, the wallet would have gone to him and then to his oldest son. Instead, the wallet went to my grandfather, then to my father, and then to me.

Amanda Lee

On January 14, 1961, at 9:00 AM, the telephone rang. At exactly the same moment, my wife returned from a doctor's appointment. I answered the phone. While I learned that my grandfather had died, my wife mouthed to me, "I'm pregnant." It was the best of times and the worst of times. One generation passes and another begins. Life on this Earth continued the regularity of its inexorable design. On July 18, 1961, Amanda Lee was born. Amanda Lee, Amanda Lee, girl with golden hair. Her nose a wrinkle, her laugh a tinkle, tinkle, tinkle. And from her tiniest of hearts, she gave me a King's share. It was a poem I wrote when she was a little girl, a daddy's girl, a poem we have shared through her adulthood.

PI KAPPA ALPHA

When I was an undergraduate student at the University of Southern Mississippi, I made good grades. I finished with a 3.86 grade point average. I knew a lot of the social fraternity boys because I drank beer with them now and then at Jerry's Drive In, which had cold beer in longneck bottles, good country cooking served as lunch specials every day, the best steak sandwiches on the planet Earth as I knew the planet Earth at that time, and habituated by wonderful characters with nicknames like Hamburger and Stainless Steel.

I knew the Pikes, members of the Pi Kappa Alpha fraternity, better than other fraternity boys. As young people say now, I hung with the Pikes, usually the bad boys on any campus. One night, I was sitting at the counter of Jerry's Drive In, quietly drinking a cold beer or two and awaiting a steak sandwich. The Pike president, Don Renegar, and three of his fraternity brothers came in, all of them gesturing loudly and wildly to bring a round for everyone, including one for me.

They bought me another beer and then another. I was highly suspicious but grateful for the beer. I accepted the gifts graciously without voicing my dubiety.

Finally, Don Renegar began to unsnarl his agenda. He looked straight ahead, thus avoiding any eye contact at the moment.

"You ever think about being a Pike?"

"Well, yes. You know I don't have that kind of money. I couldn't pay the initiation fee."

Don said, "We've already talked about it. We could waive the initiation fee, you know."

There was murmuring and nodding along the counter where the other fraternity boys sat with expectant looks on each face, all eyes suddenly on me. Even Don now faced me.

"Okay," I said, "but you know I don't have the kind of money it takes to pay the monthly dues and assessments."

Undeterred, Don said, "We talked about that, too. What if you won't have to pay dues or assessments? No monthly dues, no special assessments, no fees of any kind. Ever."

There was more murmuring, more nodding down the counter. Eyes were glimmering with hope. I sensed a confidence that swelled in them like leavened bread. I also sensed an excitement that comes with anticipation of pleasure.

"Well, I appreciate that," I said. "I don't want to go though pledging. I don't think I could put up with the hazing."

Don swung his body around the stool, crossed his legs importantly, leaned back with the posture of authority, hooked his thumbs in the belt loops of his fraternity khakis, and then looked at me with piercing eyes. The other Pikes followed suit.

"We talked about it this afternoon back at the fraternity house. We voted to make you a member by special dispensation. You don't have to pledge. We'll dispense with pledging. You'll be initiated directly into the fraternity. Initiated by special dispensation."

Still more murmuring, still more nodding down the counter. The eagerness on their faces was transparent. After an abundance of pause, I finally replied.

"Don, what's this all about? I'm not going to agree to anything that seems good for me until I know what's in it for you."

Disappointed that I didn't immediately cave to his generous offer, Don began to explain. "Our fraternity grade point average is so low it's going to dip below the average required by the Dean of Students to remain socially active. Unless we do something, Pikes are going to be placed on social probation. The Pikes would not be able to host parties or any other social functions until our grades improve. Once placed on social probation, that means at least two consecutive academic quarters without any social functions whatsoever. You have to understand that social probation is the equivalent of the death penalty for a social fraternity."

"So," I said, "what does social probation have to do with me?"

Don cleared his throat, a little uncertain about how his answer would be received. There was conspiratorial murmuring along the counter, indicating deepness of thought and seriousness of mind.

"You have a high grade point average, almost straight A's. If your grades are included with ours, our fraternity grade point average will be over the minimum required. We won't be put on social probation. What do you think? Will you help us?"

His tone was like a fundamentalist preacher just before taking up a collection. For where two or three are gathered together in my name, take up a collection. I liked these guys. They were a lot of fun.

"Okay," I said. "When?"

Jerry's Drive In erupted with an joyful uproar, legs along the counter standing on tiptoes like ballet dancers *en pointe*, arms reaching for the vault of heaven like offerings of thanksgiving by elders of ancientry, lungs emptying with whoops and hollers like the outcries of warriors as they dash bravely into battle.

Don yelled for all to hear, "Tonight! Now! We have to report our grades tomorrow morning. The whole fraternity is waiting for us at the house. We have the initiation paraphernalia ready. Let's go!"

We went. I became a fraternity man. A Pike. My grades kept the Pikes off social probation. Who says good grades don't pay?

THE HUMBLE SUMMER

I continued in school at the University of Southern Mississippi. The name of the school was changed from Mississippi Southern College to the University of Southern Mississippi on February 27, 1962, when infamous, opprobrious Governor Ross Barnett signed the law. Nowadays, it is often called Southern Miss, particularly on sports pages and on ESPN. School officials wanted the name changed to Mississippi Southern University. Sports writers objected, saying the state already had a MSU, Mississippi State University, and it would be confusing to have two MSUs in sports section headlines. These flatulent knuckleheads had their way, and USM was birthed.

I continued to make good grades, all A's every quarter. The summer of 1962 was the summer before I had enough credits to be classified as a senior. I was going to complete my undergraduate degree in ten quarters, entering in September 1960 and graduating in June 1963, a four-year degree in less than three years. I finally had taken the required course in economics, Money and Banking. The professor, Jim McQuiston, was the best teacher I ever had. He interested me in economics, which was not so labored and dull after all. The spark he ignited was fueled into a white-hot flame of fervor and zeal. As electives, I took courses in mathematical economics and microeconomic theory under a man who became a lifelong friend and mentor, Coldwell Daniel, III.

Mr. McQuiston and Dr. Daniel used their influence to arrange a really good summer job with Humble Oil, later consolidated with Standard Oil of New Jersey before renamed Exxon. I worked at a production office in Harvey, Louisiana, on the West Bank across the Mississippi River from New Orleans. I roomed with an engineering student from Mississippi State University named Don Unland from Darling, Mississippi, who also worked for Humble that summer.

Don Unland and I rented a garage apartment in Westwego. Our landlady was Cajun and spoke no English whatsoever, only French. She was good to us, inviting us to Cajun wakes and weddings. I often confused Cajun wakes and weddings, the only difference being one drinker. Occasionally, we dropped by a place called the Twilight Inn on the West Bank, and at times drove to Boutte, Louisiana, to a place called Betty's Music Box. At times, we crossed the Huey P. Long Bridge to New Orleans itself. We liked a place called Ched's 1-2-3 Lounge across from the Roosevelt Hotel because it had a lot of big band music on the jukebox. There, we listened to Glenn Miller, Benny Goodman, Tommy Dorsey, Artie Shaw, Duke Ellington, and Count Basie.

Sometimes, Don and I wandered into the French Quarter. One day, Don and I were walking on Royal Street towards Jackson Square. As we crossed St. Louis

Street, we walked in front of the Napoleon House. A thin, gaunt, tense young man with thinning dark hair was passing out leaflets. Don and I took one of the leaflets and kept walking. I looked at mine and was startled as a sun-struck vampire.

"Don, you see this? I think it's communist literature!"

Don looked intently at his leaflet.

"This is pro-Cuba stuff! You're right."

We turned and looked back. The man was still standing there with his back to us, still passing out his scurrilous leaflet. We began to drift back in his direction, readying ourselves to say something when an older man stormed out the Napoleon House, walked to the gutter for a wadded up leaflet where he had thrown it earlier, picked it up, opened it, and read it.

He shouted at the lanky man who was now half a block away, "You communist son-of-a-bitch! Get the hell out of here!"

He ran the man off. The pro-Cuba commie actually jogged a block or so, then disappeared walking towards Canal Street.

That night, Don and I were watching the evening news on WWLTV and saw footage of this thin, gaunt, tense young man with thinning dark hair, now standing on Canal Street, handing out his leaflets. He was interviewed. He was identified as Lee Harvey Oswald.

Later in the week, Don and I heard a rumor that a group of some ilk was recruiting a kind of private army to invade Cuba. We had an address and a man's name. Don was a former Marine pilot. Feeling adventurous, we went to the address and walked down a long hallway. I don't remember the building itself, but I remember a long hallway with offices, perhaps with glass panels and signage painted on the glass. We found the man in a spare office strewn thick with papers and other debris. We listened to him talk about his grand plan and his dubious resources. While he talked and we listened, a number of outlandish, freaky oddballs drifted in and out. These wackos seemed absurd at best if not downright crazy. Don and I left and laughed about how crazy these people were. They had no apparent resources.

ECONOMICS MAJOR

By the end of the summer of work with Humble Oil, any doubts about majoring in economics evanesced. I wanted to be an economist. When I arrived back in Hattiesburg, I was excited about my decision and called Mr. McQuiston at home to ask if I could talk to him as soon as possible. He invited me to come immediately to his apartment. We sat in his kitchen, and I told him about my decision. I could tell he was pleased. He placed a bottle of scotch whiskey on his kitchen table.

"I want to be like you," I said. "I want to earn my Ph.D. in economics. I want to go to the University of Virginia like you did. I want to study under Buchanan like you did. I want to be a professor like you are."

At the time, Mr. McQuiston was ABD, all but dissertation. He had completed all of the doctoral course requirements, and he had passed his comprehensive qualifying exams. All he needed for his doctorate was completion of his dissertation.

I talked to Dr. Daniel later that week. He advised me to apply for admission to the University of Virginia, University of Chicago, Rochester, and UCLA, all doctoral programs noted for their "conservative" points of view. Economists at these universities were free market adherents who believed in small government with limited intrusion into our private lives and limited intervention in markets. These beliefs were mine at the time, and these beliefs are mine today.

In the fall of that year, I took a course in public finance from Mr. McQuiston. The textbook was written by James M. Buchanan, who was on the economics faculty of the University of Virginia and who was the man under whom Mr. McQuiston had studied. My first choice of Virginia was strongly reinforced. I absolutely longed to go to the University of Virginia and study under Buchanan.

After finishing my undergraduate degree in the spring of 1963, I stayed another year at the University of Southern Mississippi to earn a master's degree in economics. Dr. Daniel awarded me a graduate assistantship. In addition to working with Dr. Daniel on his research, I taught a class each quarter and took graduate courses in economics, mathematics, and econometrics. I applied for admission to Virginia, Chicago, Rochester, and UCLA. I was admitted to all four doctoral programs. Dr. Daniel, Mr. McQuiston, and Dr. Joseph A. Greene, Dean of the College of Business Administration at the University of Southern Mississippi, were former students in the economics program at the University of Virginia. They wrote letters of recommendation and used their influence behind the scenes on my behalf.

I was admitted to Virginia, and I was offered a fellowship. I was given a very generous grant as a fellow of the Thomas Jefferson Center for the Study of Political Economy, founded by Warren Nutter and James Buchanan himself. I was going to the University of Virginia in the fall of 1964 to study under James Buchanan. I was going to live and study in Mr. Jefferson's "academical village."

MR. JEFFERSON'S ACADEMICAL VILLAGE: THE GRADUATE YEARS

In the fall of 1964, my wife and I moved with our daughter to Charlottesville into a nice apartment on Appletree Road near the football stadium, Scott Field, nicknamed the "Toilet Bowl" in honor of the donors, the Scott Paper Company. Our landlord was a man named John Cockcroft, who seemed to forget his last name each time he introduced himself. He would say, "I'm John Cock, uh, uh, uh, croft." Later, we moved into University Gardens, married student housing.

My first year at Virginia was very difficult. I took graduate-level courses in mathematics and economics. At Virginia, academic titles were disdained so that all male faculty members with doctorates were known by the courtesy title of Mr., *e.g.,* Mr. Buchanan and Mr. Nutter. Moreover, students in the classroom were called upon by the same title of courtesy. So, *Mr.* Davis took *Mr.* Buchanan's course in public finance the first semester.

Mr. Buchanan came to class once a week, gave us a topic on which to write a two-thousand-word paper due the next week, and returned the graded two-thousand-word paper we submitted the week before. During the semester, I wrote sixteen two-thousand-word papers, each one on an original topic, not the sort you could go to the library and look up the answer or go to the computer center and calculate a solution. It was before Al Gore invented the Internet.

Each week, Mr. Buchanan's class began with turning in our papers, followed by discussion of the topic of our papers. At times, the discourse strayed briefly from the narrow topic of our papers. One day, Mr. Buchanan raised an esoteric, arcane question concerned with optimal income taxation of a perfect monopoly, a question of interest and relevance only to the most cultic rituals of academic economics. I knew the answer! I did not volunteer. Indeed, no one ever volunteered. We waited for Mr. Buchanan to call on us, usually hoping he called on someone else. Since I knew the answer, I hoped he called on me. Be careful what you pray for.

Mr. Buchanan called on Mark Pauly. Mr. Pauly did not know the answer, which surprised me because Mr. Pauly knew everything. Then, he called on Tom Willett. Mr. Willett did not know the answer, which surprised me because Mr. Willett knew everything. I sat in back, knowing the answer, and a golden auroral glow began to form around me like a halo in an Orthodox icon. Next, he called on Tom Ireland. Mr. Ireland did not know the answer, which surprised me because Mr. Ireland knew everything.

The golden glow now diffused throughout the entire room as I began to think that Mr. Buchanan might not elicit an answer from anyone until he got around to calling on me. Finally, the soft golden glow diffused around me, and Mr. Buchanan called on me, the golden boy. I answered the question!

Mr. Buchanan lit up like an incandescent bulb. I think he did not expect anyone to be able to answer his question. He responded with approval and a modicum of praise.

"Very good, Mr. Davis," he said. He paused momentarily before continuing, "Explain it to the class."

Every word coming from my mouth made no sense whatsoever. The golden glow imploded to occupy only point space, a singularity in time and space. I couldn't explain it. I knew the answer, but I couldn't explain it.

After listening to my unintelligible inanity for several minutes, during which I knew, Mr. Buchanan knew, and everyone in the class knew I couldn't explain the correct answer to the class; Mr. Buchanan gave up on me. Every other doctoral student in the class was delighted to see and hear Mr. Know-It-All Davis founder like a ship that strikes a reef.

"Well, Mr. Davis," Mr. Buchanan said while smiling like the wolf who dwells with the lamb, making the lamb nervous. I was the lamb. "Since you couldn't explain it to the class, I guess I'll just have to give you a zero for today."

This one comment was public humiliation from the man under whom I hoped to study. I knew the answer. I just couldn't explain it. Mr. Pauly, Mr. Willett, Mr. Ireland, and others didn't know the answer. Why not give them a zero for today? What was the message? Perhaps the message was that if you invest in knowing the answer to a question or go to the trouble of calculating the solution to a problem and then cannot explain the answer or interpret the calculation, then that wasteful endeavor is worse than not knowing the answer in the first place, worse than not being able to calculate the solution in the first place. All these years later, on any exam on which a calculation is involved, I always ask students to write a narrative interpretation of the calculation. I tell my students not to blame me. Blame Buchanan.

At the University of Virginia at the time, letter grades with pluses and minuses were given. At the end of the course in public finance, I was given a grade of B+. I felt I had disappointed Mr. Buchanan. My first semester, my first course under Mr. Buchanan, and I had failed to earn an A. I asked for an appointment to see him, not to argue about the grade but rather to express the depth of my regret and the range of my anguish. Betty Tillman, his secretary, scheduled a meeting.

I sat down in Mr. Buchanan's office, woebegone, wretched, and downtrodden from my own doing. I explained how I had come to Virginia to be one of his students. I began to apologize to Mr. Buchanan, but he stopped me.

"Are you trying to apologize for making a B+?" Mr. Buchanan asked. "Do you think you have let me down by making a B+? Do you think you have disappointed me because you didn't make an A?"

"Yes, sir," I answered honestly, almost in tears. I am sure that my dejection and downheartedness were palpable.

Mr. Buchanan actually laughed at me, worsening the measure of my despair to the unfathomable depths of whale excrement before finally saying, "I've never given an A for the course. That's the first B+ I've given in years!"

Suddenly, I was enraptured, transported to a place beyond space and time, my chest swelling with jaunty esteem. I was elated immeasurably with exultant joyfulness. When I entered Mr. Buchanan's office, I didn't feel worth two cents. When I left his office, I felt like a million bucks. The first B+ that Mr. Buchanan had given in years!

I also took a course supposed to be taught by G. Warren Nutter. However, Mr. Buchanan taught the course. Mr. Nutter was on leave with the Goldwater campaign. He traveled with Goldwater. Mr. Nutter was a man's man. He was a highly decorated World War II infantryman, served in the CIA, and spoke German fluently. He was recognized as an expert, the expert on the Soviet economy.

While Mr. Nutter was on leave with the Goldwater campaign, I met his wife, Jane. I saw her regularly because she and Mr. Nutter lived next door to the Montessori School where our daughter went to school as a three-year-old. Mrs. Nutter liked me, and she pressed me into the Goldwater campaign locally. I didn't mind. I had heard Barry Goldwater speak in Hattiesburg and had read his book, *Conscience of a Conservative*. I considered myself a Goldwater Republican and still do. Even if I had minded, I would have worked on the Goldwater campaign. After all, Mr. Nutter was chair of the economics department.

YEAR ONE

The first year at Virginia was demanding and challenging, thus requiring great diligence and perseverance. When I played football in Pascagoula, I weighed about 165 pounds. When I finished high school and when I finished my degrees at the University of Southern Mississippi, I weighed about 165 pounds. After my first year at Virginia, I weighed less than 150 pounds. At Virginia, we had a backbreaking, punishing schedule of study. Classes during the day, study in the library when not in class, study in the library at night. From daylight to midnight and beyond, we were reading, computing, writing, and studying. The pace and the intensity of study were highly stressful, requiring obstinate perseverance that would have challenged even the most devout, most pious cloistered monk.

Throughout the second semester, I sometimes wanted to quit and go home. I called my father every week and asked him to talk to Francis Lundy to inquire if the offer of a job with Southern Bell was still good. Every week, Dad told me that he would call Mr. Lundy. He never did. In addition to being my father, Dad was the village wise man. He was wise enough to know that I was not a quitter.

The Seminar from Hell

On Friday afternoons at 4:00 PM, the economics department held a weekly seminar. Faculty members and visiting scholars presented papers. All graduate students were expected to attend. No attendance was taken, but about five minutes after each seminar started, Mr. Buchanan would turn around slowly and deliberately in his front row seat and simply look around the room. No graduate student dared to be absent when Mr. Buchanan looked around the room. We knew our absence would be noted. We were convinced that if absent, we would bear the wrath appropriate to an exalted personage.

At times, one of the graduate students presented a paper, usually a paper dealing with his dissertation. These presentations were bloody, merciless in the brutality of criticism. Graduate students attacked graduate students, probing for soft spots where wounds could be inflicted, fatal wounds where possible. Judgments were made about us based on the penetrating, cutting keenness of our criticism. Criticism was consequently merciless to a superior quality and degree appropriate to a momentous occasion. The hypothesis had to be exacting. The mathematics had to be flawless. The statistics had to be perfect. Any miscues made the presenter look bad, the faultfinder look good. I knew my day would come. I hoped I would survive it. I did. I not only survived, I flourished with more than a little panache.

One graduate student in my class was interested in economic history. His dissertation research dealt with trade of commodities among the original thirteen colonies with focus on Virginia and nearby colonies. He had collected some really interesting data. Indeed, he derived a lot of data from original sources, which enabled him to develop and discern definitive patterns of trade. Graduate students were impressed, finding his presentation interesting and compelling. We admired his diligence in tracking down original documents that when analyzed showed colonial trade patterns conclusively. After thirty minutes or so into his presentation, Mr. Buchanan suddenly interrupted him.

Buchanan asked in a curt, impatient tone, "I don't hear a hypothesis. What is your hypothesis?"

In response to this laconic demand, he made a mistake, answering the question without thought, "Mr. Buchanan, I don't have one."

Mr. Buchanan snapped back at him, "If you don't have a hypothesis, how will you know when you're through?"

To avoid this circumstance from which escape or relief would be difficult, he should have responded, "You're right, Mr. Buchanan. It was foolish of me to say I have no hypothesis. Of course, I have a hypothesis."

Instead, he made another mistake, falling victim to this clever *coup de main*. He began to argue that he didn't need a hypothesis. It was bloody, and he exsanguinated. The seminar presentation was terminated with extreme prejudice. Mr. Buchanan told him to come back when he had a hypothesis. When he made still another presentation weeks later, he opened with his hypothesis as though nothing had happened weeks earlier. His presentation was as interesting and compelling as before.

When the seminar was over each week, our grueling week was over. We immediately herded ourselves like a rabble of ragtag pensioners pursuant to a rumor of free bread, hastening for the graduate student lounge at the south end of West Lawn. Beer, wine, and liquor were cheap, sold at cost. Many arrived early and stayed late. Not me.

The Poker Game

Friday night was poker night. A doctoral student from Toronto, Canada, John Ridpath, was quite wealthy and leased an estate in Albemarle County. He and his wife had been Olympic swimmers for Canada and had competed in the 1956 Olympic games in Melbourne, Australia. He was an Ayn Rand fanatic, an Objectivist as fervent and dogmatic in his beliefs as any Christian energumen. He hosted the poker game. In addition to John and me, another doctoral student in the class ahead of the two of us, Charlie Plott, also played in this game. The others were businessmen and townspeople. The game was table stakes, pot limit. If you are a poker player, it doesn't get any better. It was not a game for the timid or the uninitiated. I played with my checkbook in front of me, meaning I would cover any bet. We played all night. In three years, I never lost money in the poker game. The least I ever won was sixty-seven dollars.

You taught me well, Papaw. You taught me there is no such thing as an original hand. You taught me the principles, and you gave me the practice, the curriculum and the practicum. I never lost, Papaw. As you said, I didn't believe in gambling. I believed in winning.

Dr. Knapp

During my first year at Virginia, I once went to the Student Health Service because I seemed to have recurring sinus problems. The doctor told me that sinuses were stress areas, and he told me a lot of his practice dealt with treating symptoms of stress. Later that year, my lower back was bothering me. I went back to the Student Health Service. The same doctor told me that I had a sore back.

"Yes, Doctor. I know I have a sore back. That's why I'm here."

He told me it was stress. Both my sinus problems and now my back problems were attributable to stress. I began to think of him as Doctor Stress. Towards the end of my first year, however, I became highly concerned about an irregularity in my *modus vivendi*. I would be walking, say, to the Alderman Library and would walk right by it and end up somewhere else without any recollection of having walked by my intended destination. I would be driving home and find myself a mile or so beyond my intended turn without any recollection of driving, including driving through a number of traffic lights past my planned turn.

I went back to Doctor Stress, who seemed to think stress explained every-thing. He said it was nothing to worry about. It was stress. As Frank Knight once said, "Any theory that explains everything explains nothing." Rather than stress, he might as well have said that the cause of everything is God's will. After pushing him hard for a theory that explained my sinuses and my back and my blackouts, he finally relented and agreed to refer me to a neurologist.

The neurologist conducted a number of tests, and everything was perfectly normal. He shrugged off my symptom as a benign, idiopathic occurrence. His assurances did not dispel my concern. When I expressed a strong interest in pursuing the matter further, he suggested I discuss the matter with a friend of his. He didn't tell me his friend was a psychiatrist. I didn't realize he was a psychiatrist until I made an appointment. Now, I was really scared. I was seeing a psychiatrist!

Dr. John Knapp was a kind man, avuncular if not grandfatherly, a pipe smoker, and an archetypal psychiatrist sent from central casting. He was gener-ous with his time. We talked for about two hours.

I told him about my family, talked about my interests and plans. The talk was friendly and informal. I told him about my concern. I told him I was walking or driving at times and not recollecting these experiences. Finally, Dr. Knapp asked me to tell him about my schedule.

"Let's start with today," he said, "and then work backwards as far back as you can remember. Tell me as much detail as you can. Tell me times as far as you can recall."

I began to tell him about what I had done that day and at what time I had done those things, and what I had done the day before and the times I had done these things, and the day before that, and the day before that. He stopped me.

"Wait a minute," he said. "Let me interrupt. When are you sleeping?"

"When I'm not doing these things I'm telling you about."

Now, Dr. Knapp looked concerned. He peered at me over his glasses, looking the part of a Viennese psychoanalyst, seemingly in deep thought while puffing on his pipe.

"Are these days typical? You're telling me you sleep only two or three hours a night, at times not at all. You're not getting enough sleep. Your body will sleep one way or another. You've been living on two or three hours of sleep a night. Your brain will sleep. It may be when you're walking across the grounds or when you're driving your car. Your brain is sleeping, but you're still functioning. I think if you get more sleep, your problem will go away."

He also told me something else. He told me he thought my spiritual growth had lagged behind my other growth. "Just listening to you, I think your spiritual growth has lagged behind your other growth."

That's strange, I thought. *Listening to you, he said. I could not imagine what I said in our friendly, casual conversation that led him to this conclusion.*

"You might want to think about it and work on it."

That was all he said. I did not think about it, and I did not work on it. I was so relieved that there was nothing wrong with me other than lack of sleep. I went home, slept, and I never had a recurrence of the problem, no more walking or driving while my brain slept. I did not heed his call to think about and work on my spiritual growth, which he thought lagged behind my other growth, particularly intellectual growth.

YEAR TWO

My second year at Virginia was fun, breezy and carefree. We moved into University Gardens, university-owned apartments for married students. I took more classes in economics, more classes in mathematics. I found a topic for my dissertation. I applied for a Ford Foundation Doctoral Dissertation Fellowship. The Ford Foundation competition was national in scope and thus really intense. Doctoral students from every doctoral program in the country, including Harvard, Yale, Stanford, Chicago, MIT, Virginia, and other truly great schools applied for a Ford Foundation Doctoral Dissertation Fellowship and competed for the honor, not to mention the money. Being a Ford Foundation Fellow was a great honor, carrying with it great prestige and great recognition, not to mention the money. I won one of about twenty awarded that year. I was a Ford Foundation Doctoral Dissertation Fellow.

Year two of the program was all coursework taught by Jim Buchanan, Gordon Tullock, Warren Nutter, Rutledge Vining, Andy Whinston, Hal Hochman, Leland Yeager, Bill Breit, Alan Walters, Clarence Morrison, all stars of the discipline. More important than the courses were the people. I did not merely take this course or that. I took Buchanan or Tullock or Nutter or whoever, each a study in and of himself.

At the end of the year, however, faculty threw down the gauntlet challenging our abilities and resources. This demand for justification was comprehensive qualifying exams, the bugaboo of doctoral students. We studied in groups, dividing the vast literature of economics into distinct areas for each of us to read and report back to the group. By the time we took our comprehensive exams over a three-day period, we were understandably exhausted. All of us who had survived two years of demanding courses passed the comprehensive exams. All we wanted was a grade of Satisfactory. Any higher grade would have meant we studied too much, studied unnecessarily. Passing with a grade of Satisfactory made us a candidate for the degree. I passed with a grade of Satisfactory and became a candidate for the Ph.D.

YEAR THREE

My third year was even more fun, exciting, electrifying, and intoxicating. Well, most of it was fun, mitigated with annoyances that stood in the way of our doctorate. Regardless of discipline, all doctoral students at the University of Virginia had to pass examinations demonstrating competence in *two* foreign languages. *Two!* Thanks to Mr. Burke, I knew Spanish well enough to pass the Spanish exam. When I took the exam in Spanish, I saw the format. A passage was given in Spanish, and then a series of multiple choice questions and answers were given in *English*. Upon reflection, it seemed to me that each passage had one and only one set of mutually consistent answers, and the answers were written in English. I thought I should be able to take an exam in any other language and game the exam.

I chose German. All I needed was a score of 435 on the standardized exam. My score was close, so close to 435, but no cigar. Next, I bought a box of a thousand flash cards in French, memorized them easily, sat for the exam, and scored 450. Although I was hardly competent in French, I fulfilled the requirement. I was so pleased. I needed 435, scored 450. I didn't waste any time memorizing.

For a time, I researched my dissertation topic in the Alderman Library every day. After I completed my basic research, I stayed home every day to write. Gordon Tullock worked closely with Mr. Buchanan in the Thomas Jefferson Center. He provided invaluable help and advice. In December, I took a copy of my first draft to Mr. Tullock. He read it. A few days later, I met with him again.

"It's okay, but you have plenty of time. Rewrite it. I don't mean edit it. I mean set this draft aside and write it again."

Privately, I whined and complained, murmured and grumbled. However, I set the draft aside and wrote it again. Four months later, I had the rewritten, final draft ready for my final defense before the faculty. On April 28, 1967, I defended my dissertation before the entire economics faculty. The director of the doctoral program was Leland Yeager. From him, I learned the number of the room in which I would defend my dissertation. Beforehand, I went into the classroom and stole all the chalk.

I had two strategies when I planned ahead to defend my dissertation. First, start an argument among the faculty. I succeeded. I brought up the gold standard. Faculty who favored freely floating exchange rates began to argue with faculty who favored the gold standard. Tempus did fugit. Time flew while the faculty argued, and we had only so much time. Every minute they argued was a minute I did not have to answer questions. Second, steal the chalk so I couldn't be asked to prove anything on the blackboard. Surely enough, one of the faculty members asked me to go to the board and derive the Kuhn-Tucker conditions. I looked innocently at the chalk tray. Sorry, no chalk. The discussion limped to the finish line. Finally, it was over. Mr. Yeager asked me to step outside the room while the faculty consulted. Afterwards, Mr. Yeager congratulated me, offering a lot of nice comments about how well I had done.

Then, he added, "We were pleased you had enough sense to steal the chalk. If you had been dumb enough to leave chalk in the room, we probably would have flunked you. Starting an argument among the faculty is always a good idea."

I passed. I was Dr. Davis. I was the first in my class to finish the doctoral program. I entered in September 1964 and took my degree in June 1967. I earned my undergraduate degree in less than three years, my master's degree in less than a year, and now took my doctorate in less than three years. I weighed 139 pounds, looking like a prisoner of war who built the bridge on the River Kwai.

FINAL EXERCISES

The University of Virginia did not have a campus. The University of Virginia had grounds. At Virginia, we spoke of "the grounds" in the same way that other college students speak of "the campus." The University of Virginia did not have graduation or commencement. The University of Virginia had "Final Exercises." After the procession of all graduates from the Rotunda down The Lawn, I sat outdoors on the concrete of the McIntire Amphitheater with other graduates who would receive the terminal degree in their respective discipline. I sat next to Louis H. "Buddy" Zincone, who was in the class ahead of me. Buddy was a neighbor in University Gardens and would be a lifelong friend. We sat on the top row of the Amphitheater.

Sitting there obliviously, I was startled by an unexpected tap on my shoulder. It was Mr. Nutter.

"When this is over," Mr. Nutter said, "come to my house, and we'll drink some champagne."

Buddy Zincone and I received our diplomas. My father and mother were there to see their son take his degree. That day, I believed I had made someone of myself. I know that Dad and Mother were proud of me. I was proud of myself. I had persevered. I had survived. I had endured. I had prevailed.

He's an egghead, Dad told his buddies about me. Educated beyond his intelligence, he said. He would grin so broadly that his eyes would squint shut. He was proud of me.

Buddy and I went to Mr. Nutter's house. Another Ph.D. graduate was already there. He had taken his classes well ahead of us but finally had taken his degree that day. I didn't know him and never saw him afterwards.

Mr. Nutter escorted all of us to a sunroom that was shaded by large, perfectly green trees. We were indoors, but we seemed to be outdoors. Mr. Nutter pointed to a washtub icing down bottles of champagne, grinned, and said, "Let's celebrate, doctors."

When he opened the first of the bottles we drank, Mr. Nutter proposed an odd toast.

"Until you men take your degree, I keep you at arm's length. I'm Warren, now. No more Mr. Nutter." He looked at me and added, "You're Ronnie, now. No more Mr. Davis."

He held his glass high, and we held our glasses high. It was a peculiar form of congratulations. He was telling us we now had the privilege to call him Warren! I was stunned. Over several hours of genuine camaraderie, the four of us eventually drank all of the champagne. I could have listened to Warren's stories all day and all night. Maybe it was the champagne, but I finally felt like an economist. An economist!

THE SNAVELY PRIZE

In 1971, I returned to the University of Virginia and again sat in the McIntire Amphitheater. At Final Exercises, I was awarded the Tipton R. Snavely Prize for the best dissertation presented to the economics faculty for the three-year period, 1967 to 1970. All of the dissertations from that period were read and judged by Ronald H. Coase of the University of Chicago, who later won the Nobel Prize in economics in 1991. Coase chose my dissertation as the best. My brother, Sam, received his LL.M. in law from the University of Virginia at the same Final Exercises. Once again, Dad and Mother were in attendance. They must have thought that their two boys had indeed made something of themselves.

AFTERWORD

Mr. Nutter wore a Greek fisherman's cap. He looked a little like Humphrey Bogart and talked a little like Humphrey Bogart without the lisp. I had total respect for Warren Nutter. A few years later in 1979, he died of cancer. I never saw him after we drank the champagne.

Mr. Buchanan received the Nobel Prize in Economics in 1986, but by then he had moved from the University of Virginia to George Mason University. He was a truly great man who had highest expectations for his students. I strove mightily to exceed his expectations.

Mr. Tullock was disappointed about not sharing the Nobel Prize with Mr. Buchanan, and he left George Mason University for the University of Arizona. Eventually, he rejoined Mr. Buchanan at George Mason University although Mr. Tullock's faculty position was in the Law School.

I never saw Dr. Knapp after our two-hour session. I heard him, but I should have listened to him. My spiritual growth lagged behind my other growth, he told me, lagged behind my intellectual growth. Just listening to me, he said, my spiritual growth had lagged behind my other growth. You might want to think about it, he said, might want to work on it. I did think about it from time to time. *What did I say? What did he hear me say? What did he mean?* The 1960s ended, and the 1970s began. I thought about it from time to time. Eventually, I saw it, saw it clearly, saw what Dr. Knapp had seen, and I understood. The vision and understanding were years away.

OLD DOGS, NEW TRICKS

Intellectual growth always came easily for me. Intellectual development always came easily. It still does. I read a lot of science because I want to advance and to further my understanding of the world around me. I read cosmology because I want to have a basic understanding of the universe. I know something about quantum physics, something about chaos and fractals. I know the First Law of Thermodynamics and the Second Law of Thermodynamics. I know who Maxwell was. The late Richard Feynman is my favorite physicist and remains a man who thoroughly entertains me through books written by him and books written about him.

I realize that intellectual growth and development come less easily for others. Yet, if intellectual growth is left behind, we become smaller people. If we want the sense of integrity we are seeking, we must grow and develop intellectually, exercise the muscles of the mind along with the muscles of the body. The old saying "Use it or lose it" probably was meant in reference to the body, but it also applies to the mind.

Dad once asked me, "Did you ever hear an old saying? You can't teach an old dog new tricks?" Of course, I had heard it. "Well," Dad said, "as long as you are learning new tricks, you will never be an old dog."

Dad, the village wise man, had it right. Learning new tricks is simply intellectual growth and development, another component of the four-legged stool of personal integrity. Intellectual growth should be balanced with physical, emotional, and spiritual growth and development.

After taking the doctorate at the University of Virginia, I systematically studied a number of topics. I returned to my passion for literature and became somewhat of an authority on William Faulkner, frequently giving lectures to high school and university classes. I took a class every academic quarter at the University of Florida for five years, almost all of which were classes in the liberal arts. On my own a bit later, I studied World War II submarine history, again becoming somewhat of an authority. I gave frequent talks and presentations about submarine warfare; torpedo failures and development; submarine skippers such as Mush Morton, Dick O'Kane, and Eugene "Lucky" Fluckey; specific submarines such as the U.S.S. Wahoo, the U.S.S. Tang, and the U.S.S. Barb; specific submarine patrols; and more. I learned that Mike Gannon, who I had known as Father Gannon when he was on the history faculty at the Florida, had become the authority on World War II German submarines. I ravished his books, *Operation Drumbeat* and *Black May*. So, I kept learning new tricks and thus put off becoming an old dog.

Right after the millennium, I thought about some kind of organized, programmatic study. I wanted to be a student again, enrolled in organized study under the tutelage of authentic scholars. I enrolled in Education for Ministry, a four-year program of study offered by extension through the School of Theology, University of the South, Sewanee. Every Monday night, I joined another six or so students at St. Michael's Episcopal Church in Mandeville for our weekly three hours of class under the tutelage of a certified, trained "mentor." The first year was Old Testament; the second, New Testament; the third, Church History; and the fourth, Theology. The reading requirements were highly demanding but rigorously stimulating and provoking.

Two years into the Education for Ministry study, I also was admitted to the School for Ministry, a program of study offered by the Episcopal Diocese of Louisiana mainly for local formation of men and women seeking ordination. The first year covered the Old Testament and the New Testament. The classes were taught by Chris Brady, professor of Old Testament and Old Testament Hebrew at Tulane University, and by Demetrius Williams, professor of New Testament and New Testament Greek at Tulane University. Both were superb. The second year was church history, ethics, and theology taught by a succession of Episcopal priests in the Diocese.

In May 2005, only a couple of months before Katrina, I was graduated from both programs. I was not seeking ordination. I was learning new tricks. My purpose was to be a student again, a student in organized study with authorities as teachers and mentors. In other words, I undertook these studies for intellectual growth, perhaps also contributing to my spiritual growth.

EDUCATION IN THE ORGANIZATION

Since the late 1980s, the quality movement has settled into Six Sigma, widely adopted business methods and practices dealing with continual improvement. One of the tenets is that both managers and workers alike must be educated in new methods. The forebear of Six Sigma, W. Edwards Deming, often said that a man should rejoice in his work. This joy, he believed, comes from self-improvement, and he also believed the company's obligation is to offer opportunities for continuous education. Clearly, Deming believed something is inherently good about education. For its own sake, education is good for people and eventually will add something positive to an organization and society. In his book, *Out of the Crisis,* Deming said, "What an organization needs is not just good people; it needs people that are improving with education."

Everyone in an organization needs to be encouraged to pursue knowledge. Each person in the organization needs to think of ways to apply new knowledge to their work. Continual improvement applies to people as well as to processes and systems. Yet, education is not necessarily job related. When we learn about anything, it stimulates thinking. Learning helps us make new connections between and among even familiar ideas. It prepares us for change and readies us for the future. This sort of stimulation can produce creative ideas about products, services, processes, and systems. Invention and innovation are important to our future, long-term success. If people in an organization continue to educate themselves, they will be more ready to thrive in an innovative work environment.

Many companies say their people are their greatest asset. Actions tell a different story. Companies invest huge sums in equipment and new technology as well as resources needed to maintain these investments. On the other hand, employees and their education and training are considered expenses rather than investments. These companies have much to learn themselves.

Chapter Four
THE EMOTIONAL JOURNEY

The word "emotion" comes from a Latin root, "emovere," which in turn comes from "e-," meaning "out," and "-movere," meaning "to move." Emotion deals with feelings such as fear, anger, disgust, grief, joy, surprise, and yearning. Emotion means to move out, which is to say to move out feelings. When we say that we are moved, we literally mean it. In general, feelings and emotions are responses that are partly physical and partly mental. Emotion generally refers to a departure from calm, a departure that includes strong feeling and an impulse toward open action. This departure from calm involves certain internal physical reactions. All of us have an emotional side to our individualities. As children, this emotional characteristic is undeveloped and immature. As we grow toward adulthood, our emotional characteristic should grow, develop, and mature. Otherwise, we remain emotionally as children.

BENCHMARKS

In business practice, firms often send teams of engineers and technicians to visit other firms for the purpose of obtaining information concerning best-practice methods and procedures. The idea is to learn these best practices and then adapt them to your own processes and systems. This practice is known as benchmarking, and the practice has produced valuable, breakthrough results for many companies.

As far as I know, benchmarking was undertaken first by Xerox in 1979, when the company realized Japanese manufacturers were selling photocopiers for less than Xerox's own production costs. At first, Xerox management thought the Japanese were dumping, perhaps selling copiers in the United States at prices below their production costs to establish a foothold in the American market.

However, a mission to Japan led Xerox engineers to the astonishing conclusion that Japanese production costs in fact were much lower than Xerox's costs. Confronted with the threatening double whammy of falling market share and declining profitability in its core photocopier business, Xerox began a serious examination of its methods and corresponding cost implications.

Someone at Xerox suggested the company could learn a great deal from other firms, even firms in seemingly unrelated fields. For example, intent on improving their warehousing operations, Xerox managers and engineers searched for a firm with exemplary warehousing operations to study. After reading trade journals and discussing warehousing systems with consultants, Xerox decided to visit L.L. Bean, the Maine apparel and footwear seller, which had distribution problems similar to those of Xerox. Based on study of L.L. Bean warehousing methods, Xerox modernized and improved its own warehousing operations.

As companies strive to improve their practices, they often turn to benchmarks in seemingly farfetched industries. For example, when Southwest Airlines wanted to improve its turnaround of aircraft at airports, it did not study other airline practices but instead went to the Indianapolis 500 to watch how pit crews fuel and service race cars in a matter of seconds. After adapting Indy 500 methods to its own business, Southwest was able to cut its turnaround time by fifty percent.

It is so in life. People come into our lives, and we can learn from these people by adapting their best attributes of character to our own situation. These benchmark people might be family members or teachers, coaches, mentors, or others outside the family. Benchmarks are particularly influential in emotional growth and development. Watching or otherwise observing how benchmarks conduct themselves and how they handle adversity, tragedy, and even atrocity leads to adaptive attitudes and behaviors that are fit for our own emotional requirements. In this way, emotional maturity hinges critically on those in our lives who show us the way.

KEEPING THE LITTLE BOY (OR LITTLE GIRL) HAPPY

We are every person we ever have been. I am still the little boy I once was. I am still the adolescent I once was. Each of us is still the little boy or little girl that he or she once was. Each of us is still the adolescent that he or she once was. Each of us must find a way to keep the little boy or little girl in us happy. I have found that one way to keep the little boy in me happy is baseball.

When I was a boy, I played baseball. It was a childhood passion for which I had boundless enthusiasm that filled me with ardor and zeal. Now, years later in adulthood, baseball still keeps the little boy in me interested, excited, thrilled, involved, and engaged. When the little boy in me is interested, excited, thrilled, involved, and engaged, the little boy in me is happy and does not run my life. I go to baseball games, I follow the standings of major league baseball, and I follow the statistics of major league baseball players. I am a Cubs fan. The Cubs won the World Series back to back in 1907 and 1908. Some people have a bad hair day. The Cubs have had a bad century.

Baseball Cards

I have a lot of baseball cards from the 1950s. However, I acquired these baseball cards in the 1970s. My father threw out the baseball cards I acquired in the 1950s after I went to college. My mother inveigled him to clean out the closet in my old room at home, and he threw out my baseball cards, a whole box filled with baseball cards. He thought I had outgrown them and wouldn't want them now that I was a grown man and living away from home. Not. I could retire now on the money for which I could have sold those 1950s baseball cards in the 2010s. Not that I would have sold them.

In the 1970s, I regularly visited a coin and card shop in Gainesville, undoubtedly to recreate a part of my lost childhood baseball cards. I always asked the crosspatch who owned the shop to let me take a look at his baseball cards from the 1950s. I generally bought one card every week.

One day after I had been going to the shop over several months, I was looking at his 1950s baseball cards, and the grump of the shop came over to keep an eye on me. In his unmistakable New York accent and Yiddish chutzpa, he asked, "What you collecting? Guys collect a team, a player. You, I can't figure out. What you collecting, you?"

I kept looking at his 1950s cards, ignoring him for a moment. I was creating dramatic tension. The little boy in me wanted to have some fun. I wanted to make the little boy happy.

"Well, my collection makes sense to me. The Don Mossi card I bought? I bought it because Don Mossi was ugly, the ugliest man who ever played major league baseball. You ever see his ears? He could have played Dumbo in the Disney movie. Remember the George Zuverink card? I bought the George Zuverink because alphabetically he's listed last among former major league baseball players. You know in lexicographic order from Aaron to Zuverink. He's the last. I bought the Spook Jacobs because I saw him in the minor leagues at Hartwell Field in Mobile when he played for the Mobile Bears. One night, he took a high, inside pitch that brushed him off the plate. I mean he bailed out. He flopped down in the dirt at home plate and wallowed around in it for a minute. Spook stood up, reached in his back pocket, and then pulled out a compact mirror. He stood there outside the batter's box, looked into the compact mirror, primped his hair, touched up his eyebrows, puckered his lips, and then dusted off his uniform while looking into the compact mirror before stepping back in the batter's box. You remember Spook. Played with the A's, the old Kansas City A's. And the Phils."

I put on my best show, country accent and animated theatrics. He was from New York City, probably Brooklyn. I had him going. The old crank's jaw slacked, his mouth agape in astonishment. His eyes bulged like a balloon. His eyebrows lifted like an elevator. His brow wrinkled like a Shar Pei. I knew I had him going. I kept talking.

"Well, let me see. I bought a Milt Bolling and a Frank Bolling because they were brothers who grew up in Mobile and ended up playing short and second for the Tigers together. Frank never could make the All Star team in the American League because of Nellie Fox. He made the All Star team in the National League after he was traded to the Braves. His last year in the majors was the last year the Braves were in Milwaukee."

Now, I really had him going. Going, going. . . .

"I bought the Al Worthington because, when I was a little boy, I listened on the radio to the first game he ever pitched for the Giants. It was a two-hit shutout over the Phils. I listened to his second game, which was a four-hitter against Brooklyn. I bought a Walt Moryn because he played right field for the Mobile Bears, and I went to the ballpark early so I could talk to him. Do you know that, when he was playing right field for the Cubs, he led the league in assists? I think it was '56. Called him 'Moose,' a big, red-faced guy. I bought a Joey Jay because he was the first Little League player ever to play in the major leagues. I played on the first Little League team in the town where I grew up. Bought a Clint Courtney, the catcher, because when I was a little boy, he was the only baseball player I knew of who wore glasses. Course, I wore glasses, too. Bought a Paul Giel, the pitcher, because he was an All-American football player at Minnesota. Bought an Elroy Face, the relief pitcher for the Pirates, because he won seventeen games in a row in relief and finished 18-1 in 1959, the year I finished high school. I bought a Pete Whisenant because his card says Cincinnati Redlegs. You know, people forget they were the Redlegs. They just think of them as the Reds. Oh, yes. I bought a George 'Shotgun' Shuba because I saw him play for the old Mobile Bears. I can tell you all his superstitions. Did you know he ran to left field every inning and touched the same sign on the left field wall?"

I had the grouch going. Going, going, GONE!

The kvetch just gawked at me with undisguised insolence. When he realized that was it, he looked from side to side, and then looked at me with his hands extended to the side, palms up.

"Such megillah, that. Like a yenta, that. Know what you got? Nothing, you got. Cats and dogs, you got. What you doing? You out of your mind! What, I care? You want? I sell. Mobile Bears? I sell you Mobile Bears. Yosemite bears. Grizzly bears. I sell you any kind of bears."

He laughed, again looking from side to side. He had reopened the door to opportunity.

"Hey! Come to think about it, how about Wayne Belardi? First baseman. Went up with the Tigers about the same time that Moryn went up with the

Dodgers before he was traded over to the Cubs."

The curmudgeon shrugged, gestured with his hands that he was through with me, and walked to the other end of the shop. He mumbled and muttered to himself for a while, and then couldn't contain himself.

"What a business, this! Daddy Claxton, he should be so jammy. Fruitcakes like you walk in from the street like manna from heaven, he wouldn't have to bake them little brick doorstops."

Those baseball cards kept the little boy in me very happy. They still do.

EMOTIONAL TAPES

I have a very good memory. Not quite eidetic, but a very good memory. Somewhere in my boundless memory are numbers, names, dates, words, paragraphs, sentences, pages, phrases, quotations, and more. I also retain and recall past sensations and thoughts. These recollections are strikingly sharp and accurate, as alive and vital and sensitive as first experienced. Many times, memory tapes play back from my childhood or my adolescence. I find myself engaged in an experience, and the circumstances of the experience are so similar to a childhood or adolescent or adult experience that memory tapes start playing. These tapes play in my mind and replay emotions of earlier experiences. The tapes play, and my feelings and my emotions are replayed. Any of the senses can push the play button. I smell something, and tapes play. I see something, and tapes play. I hear something, and tapes play. I taste something, and tapes play.

I suppose emotions are recorded somewhere within us. The intense mental state is still there in our profound core, dormant and awaiting stimulation. When spurred, the mental state leaps to the surface, emotions revivified from their dormancy. Once again, we must remind ourselves to control our emotions rather than to be controlled by our emotions, thus letting feelings run our lives.

The First of Many Who Died in My Arms

When we speak of a "calling," we usually mean an inspired urge or impulse to pursue a particular occupation, vocation, profession, or career. A calling often implies that the causative source of the inner urge or impulse is God. At times, I have thought that I have a calling. I have thought that I have been called to a kind of ministry of death, men and one woman to die in my arms. It is a direful, awful, fearful calling, but it is an emotionally difficult burden that I have shouldered like a rough beast.

When I was a boy, I delivered newspapers. I had a morning route and an afternoon route. Each of these routes involved riding a lot of miles on my bicycle. In those days, we rolled our own newspapers, we filled a canvas bag with these rolled papers, we tied the canvas bag to our handlebars, and we rode our bikes while throwing these rolled papers on the lawns or steps of our customers. We collected door-to-door on Saturdays. *Paperboy! Collllllectttttt!*

One weekday afternoon after school, I was riding my bike along my route, and I suddenly heard a startling noise. It was a scary noise, loud and crackling, crepitating like hands clapped sharply together. I immediately brought my bicycle to rest and looked up a nearby telephone pole only a few feet away. A telephone lineman had been electrocuted and was bent backwards, dangling halfway down the pole, held there by his leather belt.

I was a boy. I didn't know what to do. At first, I was petrified. After a moment, I climbed up the pole and somehow managed to get the electrocuted man to the ground. I looked into the man's face, which was turning blue, already trending towards black. I started artificial respiration, and then mouth-to-mouth resuscitation I had learned in scouting. Nothing was doing any good. I gave up. I held him in my arms. I knew he was dead. He died in my arms.

Grown men materialized from neighborhood houses. They were running, shouting, and gesturing. One of them took the man from my arms. He tried artificial respiration. After a few minutes, he also accepted the grim reality.

I stood there, holding my bike to the side and looking at the man's face. I knew he was dead. He had died in my arms. It seemed to me that he died on my watch, that I was somehow responsible. I never had seen a dead person before. He was blue, now almost black, and he was not breathing, and he was not moving.

The grown men were shouting again, and they were gesturing again, and one of them gave the electrocuted man mouth-to-mouth resuscitation. After a while, he also surrendered to the finality of death.

As I watched, I had an out-of-body experience. I was behind me. I was watching me. I saw myself from behind. I saw the bicycle I held to the side. I saw the back of my head. I turned around to look behind me. When I turned, I saw myself turn, and I saw my face, and I saw my eyes. I saw the man beyond me, the man with the blue face that was now almost black. I saw me, I saw the bike, and I saw the man with the blue face that was black. Then, it was over. The men took him away. I finished my paper route. I went home. As a boy, I never dealt with the experience, my first witness to death, the first man who died in my arms.

The memory tape plays from time to time. I don't talk about the feelings that I relive. I have internalized the experience totally. It was one of the most traumatic experiences of my life. I don't like to ride bicycles. I relive as a boy the death of an electrocuted lineman each time I ride a bike. I see his blue face, and I see the back of my head. I see myself turning around, and I see my face and my eyes. I see the bike. When the memory tape plays, I cannot let the relived immature feelings and emotions of a boy control an adult experience. I do not always succeed.

I struggle with periodic nightmares. For a week or more, I have nightmares every night, and then the nightmares stop. I see faces, the faces of men and one woman who died in my arms. The nightmares arouse fear, horror, and distress. I see faces, the telephone lineman; two men whose wartime deaths are too horrible to write about, talk about, or even think about; Gilda Tomasso, the Republic Steel nurse once handpicked by Jonas Salk to administer his polio vaccine; and Dad cradled in my arms taking his last low-pitched rattling breath. The nightmares of faces are emotional responses of my mind. Recalled emotions range from distress to thoughtful sadness as the mare demon torments me. I am cursed with reliving each death in my arms, undergoing each death in every sensate dimension as real as first experienced.

Mother's Glasses

When we lived on Twelfth Street, we had a long yard on the Wilson Avenue side. The yard was good for pitch and catch, and it was good for pitch and hit. If you really tagged a ball solidly, it would fly beyond the yard, sail over Twelfth Street, and thud against the warehouse wall like the ivied brick wall of Wrigley Field.

One day, I was playing pitch and hit with a neighborhood friend, Bobby Goodgame. He lobbed the ball to me, and I made solid contact with the bat and hit a screaming line drive. I hit the screaming line drive just as my mother walked around the corner of the house. It hit her right between the eyes and knocked her flat. I broke her glasses and badly bruised her face. I was only nine years old, and I felt a strong, overwhelming sense of guilt and remorse. I knew I had hurt my mother. I knew I had cost the family a lot of money we didn't have for new glasses, and I felt guilty about that, too.

Twenty years later when I was on the economics faculty of Iowa State University, Mother and Dad visited us in Ames. We all went out in the car one day. When I drove home, I pulled the car into the garage. I stepped out of the car and walked ahead of others to unlock the front door, leaving the manual garage door open as usual. A moment later, Mother hobbled inside while holding her hand, dripping blood with every halting step. She had tried to close the garage door. With her bad eyesight, she didn't realize there was a garage door handle. She pulled the garage door down by one of the folds and didn't realize the fold would close shut on her fingers. The middle finger of her hand was caught in the garage door and smashed.

The memory tape began to play. Emotionally, I was nine years old again. I felt a strong sense of guilt, the same guilt as a twenty-nine-year-old man I felt as a nine-year-old boy. I felt I had hurt my mother, and I felt personal guilt.

When I watch sports on television, I gasp in anticipation of only one peril. It's not a vicious overhead right thrown by a heavyweight boxer. It's not a murderous hit on a wide receiver going across the middle in a football game. I gasp at only one hazard. I audibly gasp every time I see a pitched baseball heading for a batter's body. A memory tape plays. I see my mother hit by a baseball. My baseball, hit off my bat.

SHIRKING RESPONSIBILITY

Usually, when we say that someone needs to grow up, we refer to the emotional aspect of the person. He or she is behaving childishly or adolescently, shirking responsibly for the consequences of one's own choices and actions, blaming others or thinking that things just happen.

When I was on the faculty at the University of Florida, I taught Principles of Microeconomics on television. During the fall and spring quarters, I taught in a television facility in Bryan Hall that once had been the moot court for the law school. I had 250 or so students sitting in the live television classroom. The lectures were taped. Another thousand or more students attended hourly classes throughout the day and evening in Matherly Hall where classrooms were outfitted with television monitors. A certain number of these students would come to my office with their personal problems. Some of these problems were related directly to the course itself. Others were related to boyfriend problems, girlfriend problems, parent problems, financial problems, legal problems, social problems, or just miscellaneous problems.

When these students came to my office, they closed the door, sat down, and usually said, "Something tells me I can talk to you."

Next, many of them cried. I kept a supply of Kleenex tissues on my desk at all times. Most of these students were wonderful kids with real problems, and they had real needs for understanding, help, advice, and care. Students wanted someone they trusted and respected to recognize and acknowledge the problem and someone they trusted and respected to comfort them or advise them.

One day, a young man who probably was a sophomore came into my office, noisily closed the door, and immediately evidenced trembling agitation.

"I am so angry! Over the weekend, I got drunk and totaled my car. Cops gave me a ticket for DWI. Now, my car is totaled, and I've got a ticket that'll cost me $500 and probably my license. I don't have the money. My folks cut me off because of low grades. Then, on top of all that, I find out my girlfriend is pregnant."

He was misty-eyed. He looked at me with red-faced anger, and he raised his voice in an obnoxious dither. "Why does this stuff have to happen to me? Everything was going pretty good, and then all this stuff has to happen. Anything you can do to get me out of all this?"

He didn't really say "stuff." The word he used was a little more scatological than "stuff."

I leaned forward over my desk. I was dismayed about his attitude and his display of irresponsible, childish, adolescent behavior.

"Listen to me. Look at me, and listen to me. All this stuff didn't just happen to you. Let me tell you about 'happen.' When you walk across campus and a bird flies over and drops stuff on your head, that's something that just happens to you."

Although I am not given to vulgarity or profanity, I didn't really say "stuff." Following his lead, I was also a little scatological in my choice of language. I kept talking to him.

"You were drunk because of a choice you made. Totaling your car was a consequence of your choice, a consequence for which you were responsible. The cops were not responsible for the ticket they gave you. The ticket was a consequence of your choice. You and you alone are responsible for the consequences of your behavior. I assume you got your girlfriend pregnant. If she's pregnant, she's pregnant because it's a consequence of your decision. Both of you are responsible. These things didn't just happen to you. These things aren't like walking along and having something happen like bird droppings on your head. Grow up! You can't go through life thinking things just happen. You have a childlike problem with accepting responsibility. You're irresponsible and dismiss your irresponsibility by saying, 'Things happen to you.' The easiest person in the world to fool is yourself, and you have succeeded fully."

Raymond Massey. I could see him. James Dean as Caleb Trask. Steinbeck was retelling the story of Cain and Abel. Raymond Massey saying, "Cal, man has a choice. There's where he's different from an animal."

I was hard on the kid, perhaps too hard. I regretted lowering myself to the use of scatological vulgarity.

He cried. He told me I was absolutely right. He said he didn't know what to do. He told me if he could just get out of this mess he would never get into another mess as long as he lived.

This little scene was scripted from his childhood. These words were the words that worked for him when he got in trouble as a child, juvenile, or an adolescent. These words were words he used with his parents. When he was a child, he would cry, and he would tell his parents that he had learned his lesson and would never do it again. I never saw him again. I suppose he dropped out of school. Wherever he is, I suppose pigeons and seagulls use him for target practice and hit the bull's-eye every time. Maybe he'll remember. Maybe he grew up.

Profanity and Vulgarity

I am not a man who uses profanity or vulgarity. I believe use of profanity and vulgarity is an emotional weakness of character, unworthy of a gentleman or lady. As a Southern gentleman, I certainly don't use profane or vulgar locker room language around women.

Recently, my daughter, Amanda, sent me a text that she and her husband were watching *To Kill a Mockingbird* on television. She texted that she and her husband, Brian, agreed that I reminded them of Atticus Finch. I was so touched to be likened to Atticus Finch, the highest honor bestowed on a father. I turned to the channel and watched the remainder of the movie. For some reason, I thought it was unimaginable that Atticus Finch ever used profanity or vulgarity. My wife, Arthurine, was in New York City. I sent her a text, asking if I had ever used profanity or vulgarity in her presence. Her text reply was "Absolutely not! Never! Who accused you of that?"

I suppose I am just "old school." I don't use profanity or vulgarity around women. I open doors for women. I believe a lady should never pick up something she has dropped. A gentleman should pick it up for her. I always stay on the street side of my wife when we walk together on a sidewalk. I don't believe a lady should ever buy her own fragrance. A gentleman should buy the fragrance for her. Sorry, ladies. I'm taken.

EMOTIONS, SENTIMENTS, AND PASSIONS

Emotions arise subjectively rather than through conscious effort. Yet, emotions are the part of consciousness that involves feelings and sensibilities, *i.e.*, the ability to feel or perceive. Often, feeling and emotion are used interchangeably in ordinary conversation, but feeling is more general than emotion. Emotion is stronger, implying excitement of agitation. Sentiment is a thought arising from emotion or perhaps influenced by emotion. Passion is an intense, compelling emotion. Thus, emotions, sentiments, and passions are intertwined into a common fabric with feelings and sensibilities at its center.

As we mature, our emotions, sentiments, and passions should mature with us. Our perceptions and receptiveness cannot remain unchanged since childhood or adolescence. We cannot pout or throw a fit when we don't get our way. We cannot behave as though we are not responsible for consequences of our behavior. As we mature, we must learn to control our emotions rather than be controlled by them. This need for governance of our emotions does not mean, however, that something is wrong with being emotional, sentimental, or passionate.

A Sentimental Old Fool

I often describe myself somewhat derisively as a "sentimental old fool." What seriousness lies in this self-mocking description is that I am a man with feelings so that my intellectual perceptions are colored at times by emotion rather than reason. I am particularly sentimental in my mental or emotional responsiveness toward the feelings of others. Being sentimental is healthy when authentic and bounded. When healthy, sentimental does not mean bathetic, which is insincere or grossly sentimental; does not mean mawkish, which is excessively and objectionably sentimental; does not mean maudlin, mushy, schmaltzy, or soppy, all of which are terms meaning excessively or insincerely emotional. When healthy, sentimental implies sincere responsiveness based on the ability or capacity to feel, having thoughts or ideas or attitudes shaped by emotions.

Of course, sentimental also can refer to our susceptibility to tender or romantic feeling, perhaps to nostalgia, perhaps to delicate, sensitive feeling as in responsiveness to art and literature. Particularly in this sense, I am a sentimental old fool. Inside, I have a vast empathy, always vulnerable to identification with and understanding another's circumstances, feelings, or motives. This empathy is no less an experience when the people involved are fictional, whether embedded in a novel or a movie. I cried when I read the ending of *The Grapes of Wrath,* and I cry every time I watch the ending of my favorite movie, *Shane.* It's the sentimental little boy in me.

Mistrusting Feelings

I know I cannot trust my feelings. I do not believe that any of us can go through life using our feelings as our guide to direction. We cannot rely on our feelings to tell us what to do. Our feelings change too much. One day, we feel like doing this, and the next day, we feel like doing that. We cannot trust our feelings to run our lives. How we behave is a matter of how we act or change in relation to an environment. How we respond in relation to an environment has its physical, intellectual, and emotional aspects.

Behavior implies a standard of what is proper. In terms of emotional maturity and growth, behavior implies that adults mature and grow emotionally to the extent that our actions and behavior show our own power to direct or control our lives. We mature and grow to the extent that as adults we direct and control our emotions rather than be directed and controlled by our emotions, as we were when we were juveniles and adolescents. This kind of emotional growth and maturity does not just happen. Directing and controlling our emotions rather than being directed and controlled by them must be made to happen.

When we grow and develop physically and intellectually but not emotionally, we don't have the sense of integrity, the sense that the parts add up to make and complete the whole. When we leave emotional growth behind, our actions and behavior are often childish responses in relation to situations. Often, these situations are parallax in our minds to those of childhood, and our actions and behavior are childhood responses repeated over and over again to these situations. Grow up usually means grow up emotionally.

Sentimental or not, I have matured emotionally. I have emotional struggles from time to time, but I deal with these struggles in a mature way. As we say these days, I have learned to keep my emotions under control. I was taught well, and I learned well on my own.

FROM SICKNESS UNTO DEATH

Sometimes, I have thought that I am one of the most flawed people anyone will ever know. At such times, I have been struggling emotionally. At those times, I have felt alone, the consequence of actual abandonment sometimes coupled with unquestionable betrayal. If not feeling alone due to abandonment and betrayal, then just simple rejection. After all I have done for so many other people in my life, I have found it hard to accept the isolation and solitude offered in return from a few of these same people. Such struggles bring to the surface in every grinding and frightening detail other adverse experiences of my life. Hence, images are renewed, and nightmares are vivified. Hurt from every wound penetrates the surface to the core.

I am a reader. When I struggle emotionally, I usually try to read my way through such difficult times. I often reread what has helped before. In particular, I go back to sources such as Kierkegaard, as far as I know the father of existentialism. I find an inexplicable solace in his philosophical treatment of despair, "the sickness unto death." Conscious despair, from which he thought we all suffer, is of two kinds: despair of not willing to be oneself, and despair of willing to be oneself. Despair of not willing to be oneself is weakness. Despair of willing to be oneself is defiance.

Since Kierkegaard believed all of us suffer at one time or another from conscious despair, I suppose I'm included. He gave a name and an understanding to the kinds of distress I have felt. Weakness is self-explanatory. At times, I have not been strong enough to confront my fears and demons, not strong enough or willing enough to be the man I was meant to be. Defiance is more daunting to explain, more complex. At times, my defiance is looking too intently into the rearview mirror, focusing on paths not taken, roads not traveled, promises squandered, all of which are unrealized potential. It is the defiance of thinking I could have done it on my own without any help from anyone else.

Who I Was Meant to Be

In 2004-05, I was a student in the School for Ministry, a two-year program of the Episcopal Diocese of Louisiana. We met once a month on Friday and Saturday. One Saturday, our teacher was John Bauerschmidt, at that time Rector of Christ Church of Covington, Louisiana, now Bishop of the Episcopal Diocese of Tennessee. I was listening intently as usual as I heard words that materialized in my mind as palpable as a river rock. Some force directed me to write them down. *"Refocus on who you are meant to be."* Whether spoken by Fr. Bauerschmidt or not, I cannot say. Nevertheless, I found my own voice. *Refocus.* When you lose your focus, regain it. Both focus and refocus are aimed at being who we are meant to be. I first heard this signification from W. Edwards Deming in 1975. I needed to hear it again.

Remember Who You Are, and Remember Whose You Are

A month later, again on a Saturday, this time on one of our breaks, I heard a voice so real I looked around to see who had uttered them. No one was to be found. I was alone, separate from all others. The disembodied, incorporeal voice said, "Remember who you are, and remember whose you are." I know this kind of sensate anomaly must sound mysterious at best, crazy at worst to others who never have had any such eerie experiences that baffle us in any attempt to explain rationally. The experience was nonetheless real to me.

Remember whose you are. The meaning bewildered me and churned my emotions like a storm convulsing waves. Who could lay claim to me? God? Nature? Humankind? Family? Somehow, I knew the question was more important than the answer. I realized I was not alone in this world, not in and of myself. I understood I was an embodiment belonging to something bigger. In this sense, I am always in the company of others.

Remember who you are. Refocus on who you were meant to be. Remember who you are, and remember whose you are. These are words that can overcome weakness and defiance, words that bolster language to a listening heart. Anyone who thinks we cannot have listening hearts is not listening.

ACCORDING TO YOUR OWN LIGHTS

I keep a copy of Hans Selye's book, *The Stress of Life,* on the bookshelf in our formal home library. I reread parts of it as much as once a month. What he offers as philosophical implications underscores what Kierkegaard said much earlier. Selye certainly underscores a focus, if not a refocus.

"As I see it," Selye says, "man's ultimate aim is *to express himself as fully as possible, according to his own lights.*" Emphasis is mine.

I read this sentence often, thinking and pondering its meaning and significance. *That's all I want to do, express myself as fully as possible, be the best me that I can be rather than settling for being as good as the next fellow or despairing for not being as good as the next fellow.*

"Whether he seeks this by establishing harmony and communion with his Maker or with nature," Selye said, "he can do so only by finding that balance between long- and short-range aims, between sowing and harvesting, which best fits his own individuality."

Which best fits my own individuality. Back to the parts that make up my own individuality, viz., the physical, intellectual, emotional, and spiritual components that make up "me."

When I first read Selye many years ago, I kept returning to the words, "according to his own lights." I knew that Selye probably did not mean what these words meant to me then or now. What are my own lights? Who are my own lights? Who were the lights of my life? Who were the benchmarks? Who were the lodestars? Who were the ones who showed me the way?

MAMAW

My mother was a Butler. She was born Ida Belle Butler, one of eleven children of Ed and Sally Butler. My grandfather was a common, simple dirt farmer who along with my grandmother raised a large family in the piney woods of Mississippi. The two of them settled in the pine forests outside Wesson, Mississippi, between Beaver Dam Creek and Little Bahala Creek, near the communities of Strong Hope and Sandhill and Thompson Chapel.

My grandparents had an unpainted house with a tin roof, no plumbing, and no electricity. They had an outhouse. They had a smokehouse. They had a well. They had a wood-burning stove. They had a big fireplace in the front room where two beds were located and a small fireplace in the bedroom across the breezeway hall that ran from front to back of the house. They had lanterns that burned kerosene, which they called "coal oil." They had no fans except funeral parlor fans. They had an icebox with a fifty-pound block of ice in it. They had a sixth grade education, just enough to read and write, just enough learning for ordinary subsistence farmers. I knew the two of them as Mamaw and Poppa.

Mamaw and Poppa rose long before dawn every morning. Mamaw prepared coffee and a breakfast of eggs, bacon or ham or sausage, biscuits, and grits. Poppa ate a prodigious breakfast every morning. He sipped his black coffee from a saucer. He liked sorghum syrup on his biscuits. Poppa left for the fields at daybreak when there was just enough light to see what he was doing. He returned at dusk just when there was no longer enough light to see what he was doing. In the country, this work schedule was known as working from "can see" to "can't see." At the end of work, Mamaw had supper prepared. A supper of tomatoes, peas, beans, rutabagas, greens, okra, corn, potatoes, or whatever Mamaw had fresh in her vegetable garden or had put up in Mason jars. A supper of pork or chicken grown on the farm or squirrel, rabbit, possum, coon, bird, or other small game killed by Poppa. There was always cornbread. There was a cobbler or a pie made from fruit or berries growing wild around the farm. The milk came from their cow, and it was raw milk.

We milked the cow. Mamaw walked ahead of me. I walked behind her, carry-

ing the galvanized bucket filled with warm milk. I wanted the milk while it was
still warm. In the house, she strained out the black things and the hairs through
a cloth. I drank the warm milk. It was like drinking the milk of human kindness.
Rose of Sharon nursed a starving man with her own milk of human kindness.

Mr. Ed

Poppa didn't like people very much. He liked dogs. He had some good ones. They were mostly hounds with names like "Trailer" and "Thumper." Poppa raised dogs. He trained dogs. He raised dogs and trained dogs because he enjoyed their company. He didn't enjoy the company of people. In fairness, many people didn't enjoy his company any more than he enjoyed theirs. He was hard to get along with, a cantankerous old coot, an irascible codger who looked as old as Methuselah.

People who knew Poppa told a story about him. Mr. Ed, they called him. Mr. Ed was so good at training dogs, the story went, if he wanted to hunt coons, he would take his dogs to the smokehouse where he had a coonskin tacked to the wall, let them smell the coonskin. The dogs were so well trained they knew they were supposed to hunt coons. Then they went out and treed coons. If he wanted to hunt possums, he took the dogs to let them smell a possum skin nailed to the smokehouse. The dogs were so well trained they knew they were supposed to hunt possums. Then they went out and treed possums. One day, Mr. Ed decided to play a trick on the dogs. He had a skunk skin tacked to the smokehouse wall and let them smell it. The dogs went out and treed Mr. Ed.

Poppa cussed. He pretty much cussed all the time. In his *Leather Stocking Tales,* James Fenimore Cooper said through the central character, Nathaniel Bumppo, that scalping was a gift given to Indians. It would be wrong for a white man to scalp another man, but it was not wrong for them to scalp another of their own kind. In after-dinner speeches, I once joked that buses are a gift given to Baptists. It would be wrong for a Methodist church to have a fleet of buses, but buses are a gift given to Baptists, and it is not wrong for a Baptist church to have a fleet of buses. I also joked that there are more Baptists in Alabama than there are people. Poppa was given the gift of cussing. It would have been wrong for another man to cuss like he did, but cussing was a gift given to Poppa, and it was not wrong for him to cuss. It was just natural for Poppa. It was his gift.

Poppa also liked the occasional tall tale, both listening to one and telling one. Two Hamilton brothers, Walt and Bill, were accommodative. Poppa referred to both Walt Hamilton and Bill Hamilton as the biggest liars in Copiah County. One time, I asked Poppa whether Walt or Bill was the biggest liar.

Poppa leaned forward in the handmade chair on the front porch of his house, spit his tobacco juice into the front yard, which scattered the white leghorn chickens, wiped his mouth with the back of his hand, and said, "Just whichever one you seen the last."

I was sitting on the front porch with Poppa one time when Walt Hamilton came walking down the gravel road in front of Poppa's house.

Poppa said to me, "Here comes ol' Walt Hamilton. I'll get 'im to tell a lie right off."

Walt Hamilton walked up to the front steps. He took the hat off his head and mopped sweat from his forehead with the long sleeve of his shirt.

Poppa said to him, "Walt, you don't look too good. You ain't been sick, have you?"

Walt put his hat back on and looked off in the distance and said, "Sick! Just got back from the doctor. One kidney gone, and just half a heart."

He backed off the steps, turned around, walked back to the gravel road, and then moseyed down the gravel road towards Little Bahala Creek.

I could tell Poppa was pleased with himself. Poppa finally turned to me and grinned. His eyes didn't seem as old as the rest of him. His grin seemed bigger than it really was because he had no teeth.

After Walt Hamilton was out of sight, Poppa leaned his chair back against the wall. The chair had a cowhide seat, held to the frame by cowhide thongs.

"One time," Poppa said, "Walt and Bill, they was lying to each other 'bout how old they was when they began to walk. Bill, he said he started walking when he was six months old. Walt, he says, 'Well, that ain't nothing.' He says, 'I was only five months old. So I says to both of 'em, 'Hell, I run away from home when I was only four months old.'"

Poppa leaned forward and spit. It was a hot July day, and the Garrett sweet snuff juice seemed to sizzle when it hit the scorched dirt in the Mississippi heat. He tilted the chair back against the wall.

"Walt Hamilton. He'd tell a lie when the truth would make a better story."

He wiped his mouth with the back of his hand, peering over the field of corn across the road. Jim, his mule, stood motionless at the edge of the field staring at the black dirt beneath him as though reverenced in prayer for deliverance.

"Bill Hamilton. If you was to order a liar from Sears Roebuck, they'd send you a rail carload of Bill Hamiltons."

Poppa made moonshine whiskey in an underground still. The still was cut into the side of an embankment like a cave with a chimney pipe terminating at ground level to vent smoke from the fire that heated the boiler. He liked to burn ash logs because he said ash did not make smoke. He even had a charred oak barrel that he used to age some of the whiskey. It didn't age long, but it had a little amber color to it. He never worried about local law enforcement officials. The local sheriff provided him with sugar in exchange for a share of the whiskey. He didn't worry too much about the feds because they were not as smart as he was.

I stayed a lot of summers on Beaver Dam with Poppa and Mamaw. When members of his own family visited home, Poppa usually disappeared into the woods or fields to avoid being around them. He seemed no crazier about his children and grandchildren than he was about anyone else. On the other hand, Poppa seemed to like me, and he didn't mind if I was around him. I never expected to be entertained by him. I just wanted to do what he was doing. When he was digging potatoes, I dug potatoes with him.

One day, Poppa and I were digging potatoes near the fence along the gravel road. A car stopped abruptly on the gravel road alongside the field. Not just any car, it was a Kaiser Manhattan as big as a Mississippi River barge. Poppa and I kept digging potatoes. Poppa didn't even look up. Both he and I kept our heads down, continuing to dig potatoes as though they were gold nuggets. After letting the dust settle for a moment, a large, beefy man emerged from the car like a whale breaching the surface from the fathoms. He stood hunched on the driver's side, wiping his forehead with a handkerchief and leaning an arm on top of his car. He had jowls like a Poland China hog. He wore a suit, but the jacket was thrown in the back seat. His collar was loose, and the knot of his tie was midway to his waist. His shirt was stained dark with sweat. The big man put the handkerchief away and finally yelled at us.

"Hey! Got a question for you."

Poppa looked up. He was not one to feel like he had to please anybody else. He was not one to be at the beck and call of another. He was not one to respond to demands made by anyone.

"Know where a man can get a drink 'round here?" the thickset, obese man asked, his fleshy jowls jiggling like gelatin.

"Water?" Poppa said. "Got plenty of water. Glad to oblige."

The man laughed, and then smirked. He looked side to side as though checking to see whether anyone was listening. His handkerchief was back out. He was sweating faster than he could mop it from his face.

"No, sir. No water, thank you. Talking 'bout whiskey! Know where a man could get a drink o' whiskey 'round here? Pay good money! Got plenty o' money."

Poppa leaned on his shovel. He spit. He wiped his mouth with the back of his hand. Finally, after a dramatic pause, he yelled back across the fence.

"No, sir. Can't say I do. Don't know a thing 'bout whiskey 'round here. It's against the law, you know."

The man pulled out his handkerchief again, wiped his forehead, patted his whole face, and then the back of his neck. His jowls wiggled from side to side and jiggled up and down. He looked at the barren stretch of gravel road behind him, and then the empty expanse of gravel road ahead of him. Heat waves from the road seemed so palpable you could touch them.

The man yelled, "Say, what's your name?"

Poppa yelled back, "Eisenhower."

The man looked right at Poppa, paused and then looked from side to side again.

"Eisenhower! Any relation to the President?"

"Same fam'ly," Poppa said.

"Well, you must have a good job, then," the man said.

"Best job in the world," Poppa said.

The man scratched his head and asked, "What would that be?"

Poppa yelled back, "I'm a holiness preacher!"

The man just stepped back in his car, started the engine, and drove away slowly on the gravel road towards Little Bahala Creek, Thompson Chapel, and beyond.

Poppa laughed silently as he watched the clay dust rise in the wake of the car and then settle back down on the road after the car was out of sight. Then, he took out a brown jar of Garrett sweet snuff, removed the cork, tilted the jar while he pulled out his lower lip, and filled it with an exorbitant dip from the jar. With the jar still in his hands, his eyes still peering menacingly down the road, he murmured something under his breath to no one in particular.

"Revenuer."

When he said it, a little cloud of dry Garrett sweet snuff billowed around his face. He wiped his mouth with the back of his hand. I could hear his whiskers when he wiped. I liked the old man. I liked him a lot.

Poppa died when he was ninety years old. By then, he was almost blind with cataracts. The family had moved him and my grandmother to a farm near the Mississippi Gulf Coast in a rural community called Hurley. Even though he was practically blind, he walked around the yard in his sock feet trying to beat the squirrels to pecans. He would feel the pecans with his feet and pick them up.

Suddenly, he had blood in his urine and needed to see a doctor. He had never been to a doctor in his life.

One of my aunts came to me and said, "Poppa needs to see a doctor. We talked it over. You're the only one who might be able to do anything with him."

Indeed, I was the only one who could do anything with him. For some reason, Poppa liked me. I took Poppa to see a doctor. He had cancer. I also was the one who admitted him to the hospital where he had surgery. He did not last long after he returned home.

Opposites Must Attract

My grandmother, Mamaw, was a soft-spoken woman. She had a soft voice and a soft manner, a gentlewoman with a kindly character, never harsh or severe. She was slow and deliberate in everything she did. Mamaw had long, straight, coal-black hair that she brushed every morning before she knotted it into a bun. If she had been highborn of noble birth or as fashionable as a vamp, her knotted bun at the neck would have been called *chignon du cou*. Her hair was fine as gossamer, soft and shiny even in the low light of the coal oil lamps. She wore glasses. When she laughed, she laughed soundlessly. Her voice was low and quiet.

Mamaw stayed busy every day, all day. If she heard Poppa cuss around me, she would say softly, "Aw, Ed, don't talk like that 'round that boy." I never heard her complain about anything. I never heard her say anything stronger than "Thunderation!" Whatever thunderation meant. I heard her say thunderation only once. I never heard her raise her voice. She was the sweetest person I ever knew. It was as though she never lost her innocence, somehow born not guilty of original sin.

When we visited Mamaw and Poppa or stayed with them, I always took chewing gum for Mamaw. I never gave anyone a gift with more love in my heart than when I placed chewing gum in her hands. No one ever appreciated a gift any more than she did when she looked in her hands and saw the chewing gum there. I also took toilet paper, a luxuriant upgrade from pages torn from a Sears Roebuck catalog. Chewing gum and toilet paper were gifts that surpassed all others in her mind.

My grandmother was a Christian woman. She was not a student of the Bible, and she did not make a public or pious display of her faith. Her faith was total but reductionist in its simplicity. She went to church when she could, which was not often. When she could go, she went to Thompson Chapel, a Methodist church in the piney woods at an intersection of two gravel roads. A small cemetery was situated next to the church itself, and she had an unnamed, stillborn daughter buried there. That infant would have been her twelfth child. When she could go to Thompson Chapel, she did go, but she worshiped in her own way every day. I never heard her say an unkind word about another person. I never knew her do an unkind deed. She had the simplest faith I ever have known. If ever there was a saint on the planet Earth, she was one.

After my grandfather died, Mamaw began a long, slow slide downward. The family eventually placed her in the old Singing River Hospital, a nursing home located between Pascagoula and Moss Point. The last time I saw Mamaw was a year before she died, when she was ninety-three years old. She was bed-ridden. She had her good days and her good minutes during the day, and she had her bad minutes and bad days when she didn't recognize even her own children. My Aunt Madalyn drove from Mobile, Alabama, almost every day to feed her and take care of her. She would sob when her mother, my grandmother, did not recognize her.

One weekend, I visited my Aunt Willie Mae in Pascagoula. Her sister, my Aunt Madalyn, drove from Mobile. After a huge Sunday dinner at Aunt Willie Mae's home on Grant Circle, Aunt Madalyn took me to see Mamaw. On the way, Aunt Madalyn warned me that her mother's mind had failed and that she did not always recognize Aunt Madalyn herself even though my grandmother saw her almost every day.

"You haven't seen her in a long time," Aunt Madalyn said, "and she hasn't seen you. Don't be upset if she doesn't remember you."

I was upset already. I knew this time would be the last I ever would see Mamaw, that wonderful woman who was always kind to all, who was soft in all that she said and did, who never did any harm to anyone in her life, who loved chewing gum and appreciated toilet paper, who put up with Poppa all his life without complaint and somehow found a way to care for him unconditionally. We were not even there at the nursing home, and I already was choking back tears.

We arrived and parked. I had a conscious grip on myself. We walked slowly and deliberately and silently up the sidewalk to the front door of the nursing home. I held open the door for Aunt Madalyn, and then followed her inside. I almost ran into Miss Olien! Miss Olien, my second grade teacher who once rapped my knuckles for trying to kiss Janet Gaskin while Miss Olien was out of the room. Miss Olien had been shuffling down the hall, and I knew immediately that she was a resident of the nursing home. She was dressed well enough to attend any Baptist church on any Sunday. She had not seen me since the second grade. Yet, she looked up, immediately recognized me, greeted me by name as though she saw me every day, looked down, and then continued to shuffle along the hall. I fell apart, my steely resolve dissipated to nothingness. Emotionally, I was suddenly a second grader again. The little boy in me couldn't cope with the sudden emotional overload. The steel grip that I had on my emotions loosened and went limp like a dishrag.

Now, we were walking down the hall to my grandmother's room. The smell. I hated the smell. The air was stuffy, heavy and old and stale and rotten as if it had been sealed in a cornerstone for a hundred years and then unsealed. The odor of ether remained from the days when the nursing home was still a hospital.

This is not a nursing home, I thought, it is a dying home. They are exhaling life and as life leaves their bodies with every breath, the very air of life itself leaves them and hangs about like a shroud of ghastly fabric, a cerement, graveclothes for the end game.

We entered an open door, and my grandmother was there in bed. Mamaw was lying on her back, her long, fine, luxurious, still coal-black hair loose around her shoulders and spilling over her pillow like oil over water. *Rose water*, I thought, *she made rose water from the petals of her roses. Glycerin, water, and rose petals in that little depression glass bottle, and she would dab a little on her finger, then rub her finger behind her ear, then behind the other ear, then the back of one hand, then the other hand.*

She was not the robust, strong woman of my childhood, but rather the frail, vulnerable figure of my adulthood. She weighed a fraction of her lifetime setpoint weight. She was not moving, and I feared we arrived an instant too late.

Aunt Madalyn whispered to me, "She's just asleep."

I said nothing in return. I was utterly silent, utterly motionless, standing there like a totem. We waited. My mind was vacuous. The intermission of body and mind was like a moratorium pending some obligation that must be discharged.

Finally, she stirred from her stillness. Her head turned a little toward us. She opened her eyes, blinked, and then struggled to focus.

As Aunt Madalyn moved silently to her side, I stood like a sympathetic observer.

"Mama, it's Madalyn. Are you awake?"

Mamaw did not say a word. She slowly and slightly nodded to indicate that yes, she was awake.

A washtub, I remembered. I was a little boy, and she would wring the solid white chicken's head, and the headless chicken would fall to the grass and flop with red blood squirting in pulses out its severed neck, and I would throw the tub over the chicken to keep it from flopping off the grass into the dirt. Then, I listened to the headless chicken thump inside the tub. Thump, thump, and then thump no more.

"Mama, see who's here. It's Ronnie. You remember Ronnie, don't you, Mama?"

Suddenly, I was by her side. Somehow, I had moved there timelessly as though through a rip in the fabric of space.

She looked up at me and said, "Oh, yes. I remember Ronnie. He was such a pretty little boy."

I reached for her hand and held it in mine. My hands felt coarse in the softness of hers, and I saw the dark purple veins in the dappled porcelain skin of her hands. My eyes were moist and misty. The tears came next. The tears ran down my cheeks in rills and runnels, and then fell from my face. I was afraid the tears would fall on her hand.

I didn't feel very pretty. She was the woman she was meant to be. I was not the man I was meant to be. I had a meaningless, aimless, directionless, purposeless life at the time. I was not very pretty.

We are every person we ever have been, I thought. I want to say something to her. If I say something, it'll be the little boy in me, speaking as the little boy, and I can be the pretty little boy for this moment, at least.

My throat was completely constricted. I could not speak, could not say anything. I could only think the words. I held her hand for a long time. I was the pretty little boy renewed and restored. She looked at me with eyes that penetrated to my innermost self where the pretty little boy still resided. Finally, still as death, she slept.

Tenderness, Patience, and Forbearance

From my grandmother, I learned so much. I learned tenderness, characterized by gentle emotions. Not tenderness in the sense of weakness or fragility that ensues from easily bruised or easily crushed feelings. Instead, I learned tenderness in the sense of sympathy. Also, I learned patience, characterized by calmness and self-control, willingness to tolerate waiting until things can be worked out in their own time. I learned forbearance characterized by restraint in retaliating, demanding what is due, or giving voice to condemnation. Tenderness, patience, and forbearance are attributes of character, all attitudes and behaviors arising from emotional maturity.

AUNTIE

My father was a Davis. He was the son of Grover Cleveland Davis, who in turn was the son of Samuel Godfrey Davis and Susan Belle Logan. Sam and Sue Davis had three children, my grandfather, Grover Cleveland, Lucie Mae, and Earl, who died of a heat stroke when he was eleven years old. Lucie Mae and Grover were raised in Calvert, Texas, where Lucie Mae met Marion Douglas Fuller. Lucie Mae and Marion married, lived in various places including uptown New Orleans on Calhoun Street near Audubon Park and Tulane University, and finally settled in a beautiful white frame house on hundreds of acres outside Wesson, Mississippi. They had a large lake stocked with bass, and they raised Beef Master Cattle. I knew Lucie Mae as Auntie, Marion as Uncle Marion.

Uncle Marion

Uncle Marion had a business he operated from a large office building in the backyard of the house. He always had five or six salesmen covering the mid-south states and selling his lines of electrical bench tools. Throughout the

1930s, 1940s, and 1950s, he ran his business from this site. When he held semi-annual sales meetings, everyone including factory representatives stayed in the house. With help from black women and their girls who lived on the grounds of their property, Auntie prepared all the meals.

My grandfather, Grover, loved and respected his brother-in-law so much that he named his first child after him. Marion Fuller Davis, my father. To my father, Marion and Lucie Mae were Uncle Marion and Auntie. Though they were my great aunt and great uncle, they were Auntie and Uncle Marion to me, too. Uncle Marion, who was definitely a wide-body type, always said he received his doctor's degree at birth, since his initials were M.D. Fuller or Fuller, M.D., when asked for last name first. Indeed, his salesmen and factory reps called him "Doc." He was highly intelligent and elegantly refined. He also was just about stone deaf. He was daring at times. He drove a Hudson Commodore four-door sedan.

Uncle Marion had a round face, and he had wrinkles that looked like folds in his face. One day, I rode with him to town to pick up mail. On the way back, I began to look at him with familiarity and recognition.

Finally, I said, "Uncle Marion, you look just like a bulldog."

He was a jolly, roly-poly man with a hairless pate as slick as a peeled onion. He laughed, and his whole body seemed to laugh with him as it bounced with the laughter and with the ruts and holes of the gravel road. After we arrived home, he disappeared, and then suddenly materialized again.

"You're right. I do look like a bulldog!" He had looked at himself in the mirror. He told the story the rest of his life.

Auntie and Uncle Marion had a large house. The upstairs had a bed in a large room that ran almost the entire length and width of the house. In this room, they also had a library, a formal library with stacks and books in the stacks. The books were classics. In this library, I learned early in my childhood to love books, and I had read all of these classic books by the time I was graduated from high school.

Meals were formal. Manners were not an option. Manners were mandatory. At each meal, we stood behind our chairs and waited for Uncle Marion to make his grand entrance into the dining room. When he entered, he paused in the doorway to survey those who were dining and the meal that had been prepared, always scratched his stomach and chest with both hands, and then approached the oak table. When he sat, only then we sat. No sooner. I still have the oak table in our dining room. I now eat meals at the table where I learned formal table manners.

The Nash-Davis Reunion

By the time I knew and visited Auntie and Uncle Marion, Auntie was a little white-haired lady who wore rimless glasses with gold wire temples. She was bright and feminine and natural. I never saw her with makeup. Her hands were always busy, if not productively, then twisting and turning an apron string or a kerchief. She had a soft-toned voice and spoke in articulate but measured words and sentences and paragraphs. She knew things, knew facts. She was a thinker and acted on her thoughts. With her, the past, present, and future were one. There was no arrow of time pointing in one direction, forward. Time went forwards, backwards. We were connected timelessly with the Reverend W.W. Nash and with his daughter, Camilla Jane born in 1834, and with James Madison Davis born in 1820, who married Camilla Jane in 1852. We were reunited timelessly each year in Calvert, Texas, where the Nash-Davis family celebrated its oneness. When I was a little boy, she let me know wordlessly that I was the future, she was the present, and James Madison Davis and Camilla Jane were the past, and that we were timelessly one.

Auntie had a piano. It was a modest box piano, plain and simple, unadorned and unpretentious. She could and would play it. The sound was a little thin and tinny like a saloon piano, like a Storyville whorehouse piano played by a professor. When she played the piano, she used a lot of left hand. Indeed, she had a very active left hand like Duke Jordan, and I always suspected she was not playing the notes exactly as she read them in front of her. Maybe played correctly with her right hand, but not with her left hand, the effect a little jazzy. She sang. Her voice was high, though not really a soprano. It was a little girl's voice, immature, innocent, and sweet. It was a little girl's voice I heard, but quivering with the vibrato of age, remarkably and startlingly loud from such a demure and seasoned body.

I stood behind her as she sat on the bench stool and played the music, at times placing my hands on her delicate shoulders as she played the music from an old, worn Cokesbury Worship Hymnal. She taught me the parts. I learned the tenor part and the bass part to most of the old Methodist hymns. When she and I sang, I was the bass.

I just memorized the parts, Auntie. I remember the bass to Amazing Grace, and I remember the bass to Faith of our Fathers. You taught the parts to me, and I memorized them, and I remember them, Auntie. I sang the bass on Lookout Rock and in the church at Fontana Village when I went back and found the people and their voices. I sang the parts, Auntie. My voice and their voices lifted up the songs for ears to hear.

When I was a boy, Auntie and Uncle Marion and my grandfather, Papaw, took me to the Nash-Davis reunion. The reunion started in 1939, and from the beginning it was highly formal. Officers were elected. President, vice president, secretary, and treasurer. Minutes were recorded, and an annual scrapbook of photographs was pieced together. The reunion has been held every year since 1939 except one year during World War II. Almost always, it has been held in Calvert, Texas. The reunion is basically the descendants of James Madison Davis and Camilla Jane Nash. When I was a boy, the reunion was held south of Calvert in the community of Elmo under a large walnut tree standing in the front yard of Cousin Cleveland Nash. At one time, it was held on the fourth Sunday in July, but now it is held on the second Sunday in June.

When I was boy at the reunion, I played with my Nash cousins, Weldon, Johnny, Tommy, and Pat. Whatever we were told not to do, we did. "Whatever you do," Cousin Cleveland would say, "don't play in the hayloft." Like heat-seeking missiles, we headed for the hayloft. Pat would wheeze with asthma, but he and the rest of us would play in that hayloft as long as life and limb held together.

In 1957 when I was sixteen, I was asked to drive everyone to the reunion.

Everyone meant Auntie, my grandfather, my brother, and me. My brother was still Sammy Davis, not yet Sam. We left from Auntie and Uncle Marion's home, and I drove to Palestine, Texas, where we stayed with Cousin Polly and Cousin Katherine, an elderly aunt and niece who lived together. That night, Polly and Katherine brought out a new game to play. Scrabble. I was good at the game. I still am. Katherine, a retired schoolteacher, eventually gave me the Scrabble tiles. I bought a black cowboy hat, a John B. Stetson, while I was in Palestine. Then, we went on to Calvert for the reunion, then on to west Texas, to Haskell, where we picked up Cousin Louise Green, who was recently widowed. She was coming back to Wesson with us for an extended visit with Auntie.

At every stop and stay over along the way, my brother and I found horned toads everywhere. We picked out the best ones and put them into a box. If we found a better one, we would exchange him (or her) for one we had in the box. We brought the box of horned toads back to Pascagoula and played with them for a time. One by one, they would get away. Then, there was none. One day, we picked up the *Chronicle-Star,* the local Pascagoula newspaper, and saw a front-page story about horned toads discovered locally. Speculation was that a population of horned toads was migrating from Texas, through Louisiana, and into Mississippi. Now, there are no horned toads, none to speak of even in Texas. I hope that Sammy and I were not responsible.

O Shame, Where Is Thy Blush

The 1957 reunion was my last for a number of years. When I was a junior and senior in high school, I was too busy rebelling. When I was a college student, undergraduate at the University of Southern Mississippi and graduate at the University of Virginia, I was too engrossed in studying. When I was on the faculty at Iowa State University, then the University of Florida, then Western Washington University as Dean, I was too rapt in single-minded career advancement. From 1958 to 1982, I stayed away for one reason or another.

I did see Auntie after the 1957 reunion. I saw her at the wonderful house outside Wesson, and I saw her in the small house in Hazlehurst where she and

Uncle Marion lived after giving up the big house and the acreage. When I was a high school senior, I bleached my hair blond and wore ducktails. She saw me looking like a Bourbon Street barker, and I was embarrassed in her presence. The insubordinate, mutinous statement of my hair was only temporary unlike the permanency of self-mutilation and disfigurement such as tattoos. Even then, I knew that tattoos and body piercing were prohibited in Leviticus 19:28. Being reversible, I immediately let my hair begin to grow back to its natural color, and I belayed the ducktails.

Auntie never lectured me or preached to me. She just lived her life every day as a witness to her aim, a testimonial to her grail. She was kind to all people, her ministry that of helping any person in whatever way she could. She loved in an intelligent way. The love and care she had for her family, all of her family of any time or of any place, were soft and gentle and refined. She was a lady, a true lady without pretense or affectation, genuine and real. She had wholeness and fullness. Her married name was Fuller, a name apt for her even though its origin was a person who "fulls" wool to prepare it for spinning and weaving, treading the wool in stale urine for an entire day. The last time I saw her, she had lost both breasts because of cancer surgery. She was still standing there like a lady, wearing her signature rimless, gold-wire temple glasses, looking me in my eyes with her own eyes wet with tears, mouth quivering, chin trembling, just looking at me wordlessly, speaking to me silently, saying, *This is the last time.*

I knew it was the last time I ever would see her. It was. I had taken my coarseness to her each year, each summer, and she had transmuted coarseness to refinement, genteelness, and smoothness. Like clay in the hands of the potter, culture was in her hands, and I was shaped and molded like fine art. Like a Jesuit or Sacred Heart nun, she shaped and molded me to inquire, to pry, and to snoop with my mind. She had the mildness, graciousness, and mercifulness of a holy and godly person, and the intellect, curiosity, and creativity of a literate person. She was a saint and a scholar. *Those quivering lips, that trembling chin, I thought, and those words, always the right words, the intelligent words, the kind words, the soft words, as though she was reading cue cards prepared as the benignant act of inerrant gods.*

I never saw Auntie again. Her hopes for me set high standards, but they were expectations I knew I could fulfill. When she last looked at me with those wet eyes behind those rimless, gold-wire temple glasses, I think she saw me, the man I was meant to be. She wasn't disappointed. That would have been like Janus facing only the past. She was saying wordlessly, *I am here. Soon, I will be there. Here, there. You will not only endure, you will prevail. I remember, Auntie. I read your books. Prevail. I remember my Faulkner, Auntie.*

Refinement and Kindness

Indeed, I prevailed and fulfilled. She gave me gifts. Refinement, an aversion to coarseness in conduct or demeanor, an appreciation of the best and highest level of civilization, expressing the good breeding within me through good manners, poise, and sensitivity to the feelings of others. Kindness characterized by a tender, considerate, and helpful nature, a disposition of generosity and warm-hearted charity. Refinement and kindness are attributes of character and emotional maturity.

DADDY

Grover Cleveland Davis and Ina Warren had a whirlwind courtship, married, and homesteaded in the Arizona Territory before statehood in 1914. Their homestead was 640 acres of land about six miles north of Bowie. Grover was a cowboy and at one time a car inspector for Southern Pacific. In the railroad strike of 1923, he was terminated from Southern Pacific for an incident that involved a "scab" worker who was tarred, feathered, and ridden out of town on a rail. After holding jobs in the copper smelters in Globe and Bisbee, he moved his family into the town of Bowie but got back into the cattle business. His cattle brand was S Bar S for his father and mother, Sam and Sue.

Grover and Ina had three children, Marion Fuller, Warren Samuel, and Billie Joy. Marion Fuller Davis was my father. Dad grew up in Bowie. Bowie was the site of old Fort Bowie, a bastion against the Apaches. The Dos Cabezas Mountains were in plain view, and Cochise Stronghold in the Dragoon Mountains was nearby.

The cattle ranch outside Bowie had a windmill, and my father and grandfather built a corral for the cattle and horses. The corral still stands, the wooden posts free of rot and the barbed wire free of rust. The windmill is still there, but it has fallen into a monumental heap, seemingly venerated for some notable past civilization. At one time or another, Dad lived or went to school in Bowie, Globe, Bisbee, Dos Cabezas, and Willcox. For a time, he went to school with Rex Allen, the "Arizona Cowboy" as they called him when he was a singing cowboy in western movies of the 1950s.

In 1931, my grandfather was involved in mining again. He formed a partnership with Bill Dorsey and his brother, Chet, and they prospected in several localities in Arizona. In the summer of 1931, Bill Dorsey and my father, who was only sixteen years old at the time, prospected together at one of these locations. Dad and Bill Dorsey spent the entire summer of 1931 in Paradise, Arizona, living in a one-room cabin. The work was laborious. Dad manned a jackhammer and a star drill.

While Dad was prospecting, he met the famous Lee brothers. Dale Lee and his brothers were notorious lion hunters who first became known as predator-control hunters working for ranchers. Dale and his brother, Clell Lee, and their brother-in-law, Fred Bendele became famous in Texas, New Mexico, and Arizona for their lion hunting and eventually in South America for their jaguar hunting. Dad was raised with Fred Bendele, who was born and raised in Bowie. Fred, or "Slim" as he was known in Bowie, died at an early age. He was so tall that his feet and part of his legs had to be removed to fit him into a conventional coffin. Dad was no wimp.

In 1932 when my father was not quite seventeen years old, he and my grandfather drove from Arizona to Mississippi. They settled in Copiah County where Auntie, Uncle Marion, Papaw, and John Riley, a childhood friend, had decided was the best place to cope with the Great Depression. Dad finished his high school education at Copiah-Lincoln Agricultural High School. At Co-Lin, as it was called, Dad was an athlete, particularly in the pole vault. He vaulted thirteen feet on a bamboo pole. Many years later, he told me no one would ever vault more than fifteen feet on a bamboo pole. To date, no one ever has. Nowadays, he said, the pole vault is merely gymnasts hanging onto a slingshot.

The farm in Copiah County was six miles east of Wesson, Mississippi, between the communities of Thompson Chapel and Sandhill. There, he met my mother, Ida Belle Butler, one of five daughters of Ed and Sally Butler. They married and had two children, James Ronnie (not Ronald, Ronnie), born in 1941, and my brother, Samuel Marion, born in 1944.

Days after America's entry into World War II, Dad joined the U.S. Navy but never saw sea duty. He never served further than San Diego and Pearl Harbor. When he enlisted, the Navy discovered my father was smart and could do almost anything, carpentry, welding, plumbing, typing, or whatever. Easily, he could have been a yeoman, the Navy's secretary and record keeper. Instead, they put him to work in San Diego and Pearl Harbor where he repaired ships and refitted submarines. Once, he installed an ice cream machine on the U.S.S. Barb for its skipper, Eugene "Lucky" Fluckey, a Medal of Honor recipient.

Pascagoula

My mother was very close to her older sister Willie Mae. Her husband went to Pascagoula during World War II in search of work. There was no vacant housing during the war. He stayed in an exhibition booth on the county fairgrounds until he eventually found shelter for himself, his wife, and son. He convinced my father and mother to come to Pascagoula after my father was honorably discharged from the Navy, and my brother was born there.

My earliest recollection was in Pascagoula. Mother was bathing me outdoors in a galvanized tub. I looked up, and a dirigible hovered silently and motionless about three hundred feet above us, then slowly and silently drifted away. It seemed threatening, like a nimbus cloud of doom and the fate of inevitable destruction and ruin. It scared the bejabbers out of me.

During the War, my Aunt Willie Mae worked in the shipyard as a welder like Rosie the Riveter, and my mother worked in the shipyard canteen. At the time, we lived in a house on Admiral Dewey Street across from my Aunt Willie Mae and Uncle Jim.

Mother as Teacher

After the war, my father and my grandfather decided to go into the pulp-wood business. Daddy moved us to Union Church where we lived in a farm-house, and then to Fayette where we lived in a house immediately across a dirt road from a black family with a boy my age named Woody, who was one of the dearest friends and playmates I ever had.

I started school in a one-room schoolhouse as the only student in the first grade. Being the only first grader was actually an advantage. I learned to read long before I started school. I learned my letters when I was very young. I spelled words from the newspaper to my mother while she ironed or cooked. She would tell me what word the letters spelled. By the time I was in the first grade, I read well enough to read any newspaper, magazine, or book. Indeed, by then, I read the newspaper to my mother every day. To this day, I am a news zealot, and I believe this fanaticism was impressed upon me in early childhood. When I was the only student in the first grade, I finished my own work quickly and was able to learn as the teacher worked with, say, the sixth grade boys and girls.

In addition to teaching me how to read, my mother also taught me the Pledge of Allegiance and the Lord's Prayer. The schoolhouse teacher began every day with the Pledge, followed each day with the Lord's Prayer. I was the only kid in class who had memorized either one. From the first day of school and continuing the entire year, I led the class each morning in reciting the Pledge of Allegiance and the Lord's Prayer. Nowadays, the teacher probably would be incarcerated in a penitentiary for such lawless shenanigans as saying the Lord's Prayer in a public school. Moreover, I probably would have been thrown in a juvenile detention facility for being an accessory to this crime.

Back to Pascagoula

We moved back to Pascagoula where my father at first worked for Ingalls Shipyard and then for the federal government running a warehouse for maintenance of federal-owned housing in the Pascagoula area. When we first moved back to Pascagoula, I attended South Elementary School. At the time, elementary schools in Pascagoula operated on shifts. Some kids went to school in the morning, others in the afternoon. The same teacher had both shifts, but different kids in the morning and afternoon. I was a morning kid. Later, I attended Central Elementary School through the fifth grade and then ersatz knockoff Eastlawn Elementary School for the sixth grade.

Daddy was active in city politics, using a true gift for organizing and delivering votes on behalf of his candidates. His candidates won. Because his candidates won, he had a succession of fairly high-level but somewhat invisible city jobs. Pascagoula had a commissioner type of government, and Daddy basically ran the public works department for the public works commissioner, Shorty Ezell. Eventually, his mayoral candidate, Ben L. Briggs, also won, and his county commissioner candidate, Joe V. Krebs, won. Daddy was a delegate to Democratic Party conventions in the state, but he never could afford attendance at national conventions. Later in life, because of his respect for Senator Thad Cochran, Dad switched to a Republican. Afterwards, he never voted for a Democrat for national office. From the beginning, neither did his son.

The city jobs led to a job as a residential housing inspector with the Federal Housing Authority (FHA). In 1967, he was made Chief Inspector of single- and multiple-dwelling construction for the entire state of Mississippi. Dad and Mother moved to Jackson, Mississippi, where he lived for the rest of his life. My mother remained in Jackson until her own death.

Politics

I learned politics from Dad. He not only worked actively on political campaigns from the local level up through the state level, he also was the official in charge of the voting precinct in the old government warehouse across the street from our house on Twelfth Street. I learned every detail of political campaigns from him. Years later, I have done everything in politics except run for political office. I have been a campaign manager, a campaign finance chairman, a speechwriter, a pollster, and a get-out-the-vote manager, everything in politics except run for office. Never.

When we lived on Twelfth Street, Daddy campaigned as usual for several candidates. On election night, he was in charge of the hand-counted vote tally. As usual, I was there in the warehouse where the votes were cast and counted after the polls closed. I never thought much about opposing candidates. In the middle of the vote count, one of the candidates who Daddy had not supported, Hollis Temple, came in to check on the vote tally. I looked into his face as he saw the disappointing and unfavorable vote count. It was the face of a shattered, distressed loser. That night, I kept seeing his sorrowful, desolate face in the dark, feeling the excrucation as he did. *I still see his face. I see it now. I never could run for political office because of Hollis Temple's face.*

When I was in the fourth grade, my teacher was Mrs. Yawn. Her husband was active in politics. On election night that year, Daddy asked if I wanted to go with him. I did. After the votes were counted and his candidate won, he took me to an election party. I was totally shocked when Mrs. Yawn answered the door that night. It never occurred to me that schoolteachers had any life apart from the classroom. Worse, I had been in trouble that day, a lot of trouble in Mrs. Yawn's classroom. Like Poppa, I just had to say something.

Earlier that day in school, Patricia Ann wet her pants while sitting at her desk. She sat two rows from me. I saw the puddle under her desk, and I knew what had happened. I couldn't let it go. I couldn't leave it alone. Like Poppa, I had to say something.

"Mrs. Yawn," I said, "is it raining outside?"

She looked at me like I was crazy. The sun was shining brightly through the open windows. By now in the school year, she knew me pretty well. She knew I was up to no good.

"Ronnie, you can see for yourself that it isn't raining outside."

She knitted her brow, peered at me minaciously and forbiddenly through her schoolmarm glasses. Her teacher's instinct forewarned her a punch line was coming.

"Well, if it's not raining outside, how come there's a puddle under Patricia Ann's desk?"

Yes, my insensitivity had led to a heap of trouble that day in Mrs. Yawn's room. Now, I was in her home that night with my father. When you are a boy in the fourth grade and you've been in trouble, the two people you never want to see in the same room together are your teacher and your father.

On the way home that night, Daddy said, "I guess you better tell me about Patricia Ann."

I squirmed in my seat, which was suddenly hot. I had dreaded this moment. I needed time to make up my story. In more than politics, when you're explaining, you're losing.

"Patricia Ann? Let me think. Patricia Ann. Oh, yes. I remember. She's a girl in my room at school."

Daddy drove along. He was quiet for a moment. The tension tightened up a notch or two, like frapping a rope.

He said, "That would be the one, alright. Tell me about her."

I looked off in the dark distance, as dark as chaos ere the infant sun. I found no comfort there in the impenetrable darkness. The world was suddenly a dark place. Finding no solace in the void, I knew I had to confess, but confess with my own spin.

"She was the girl who wet her britches today. I saw a puddle on the floor, and I thought it was raining. But Mrs. Yawn found out it was just Patricia Ann. It was her puddle. It wasn't raining like I thought. It was just Patricia Ann peed in her pants."

Daddy drove ahead. He looked off to the left so I couldn't see his face. I think he was trying not to laugh out loud.

I remember three comments in particular that Dad made about politics. Once, he said, "In politics, you can't beat somebody with nobody." Over the years, this adage has proved true about politics and even other domains. Another time, he told me, "In politics, don't ever take it personally." At still another time, he told me, "In politics, when you're explaining, you're losing."

Runt and Sambo Caesar

Someone once said you can judge a man by his heroes. When I was a little boy growing up in Pascagoula, Daddy was my hero. Daddy was a likeable man.

Whatever your age, his company was enjoyable. My brother and I certainly enjoyed being in his company.

When we were little boys, he called me "Runt." I never asked for an explanation. He just called me Runt. He called my brother "Sambo Caesar." My brother never asked for an explanation. He just called him Sambo Caesar. As we grew up, he gradually stopped calling me Runt, and he gradually shortened Sambo Caesar to just Sambo.

One year in the 1980s, I sent a package of Christmas presents to my brother and his family. He and I like to have a little fun now and then at the other's expense. I addressed the package to Mr. Sambo Caesar Davis. When the package was delivered, no one was home. Sam had to go to the post office to pick up the package. He was asked to identify himself as Sambo Caesar Davis. When he convinced the postal employee of his identity, all other postal employees poured out the back rooms *en masse* to have an amused look at this man called Sambo Caesar Davis. I could not have scripted it any better. I just wish I had been there to see it.

Saturday Coffee and the Occasional Toot

Every Saturday morning, Daddy would disappear early to drink coffee with his buddies. I always wanted to go with him. I could go with him if I got up in time to leave with him. Daddy never would wake me to go with him. I had to wake up on my own. Most of the time, I would wake up too late because he left the house at daybreak. Sometimes, however, I would wake up in the pitch black of night and hear him in the bathroom or in the kitchen, and I would leap out of bed like a startled gazelle.

We would leave the house and drive to Mac's drug store where we would sit at the counter and drink coffee. He would smoke his Camel cigarettes, and I would listen to the political talk with his buddies and listen to the stories and jokes they told. Then, we would go to Shorty's service station. Shorty would join us, and we would go somewhere for coffee. Daddy and Shorty would meet up with some more of their buddies to talk politics and tell stories and jokes. After

Shorty was driven back to the service station, Daddy and I would go to the B.F. Goodrich store, where we would get together with Alan Atchison, the general manager, and the three of us would go next door to Peale's Drug Store to drink coffee. Daddy would run into still other buddies there and talk politics and tell stories and jokes.

Maybe twice a year on a Saturday, Daddy would disappear from the house for a couple of hours, and he would come home smelling a little like bourbon whiskey. Daddy knew he would be the object of the mopes. He endured in silence and acquiesced in Mother's melancholic mood. He was just being a man, and he did not have a drinking problem. Letting him have an occasional drink at home might have kept him from an occasional drink at Alvis's Bar on Lincoln Avenue. Daddy did not drink often, but when he did, he was fated for sulky, gloomy disposition.

One time over several weeks, Mother chivvied Daddy to clean out the clutter under our house. Our house was built up on concrete blocks, and there was crawl space under the entire house. One Saturday, Daddy put on some old coveralls, crawled under the house, and began to haul things out and throw things away. He must have had a bottle under the house. As the day wore on, Daddy was dirtier and dirtier, his unshaved face grittier and grittier, and he drank his half pint of Early Times. Mother was oblivious.

Midday, Mother suddenly remembered we needed to go to Foodtown, where she did her grocery shopping. There was a drawing for a new wringer washing machine. You had to be present to win. Mother had been stuffing the box with her name, Daddy's name, my name, and my brother's name for a month. All of us had to go to the drawing to be present. By now, Mother suspected that something was amiss. She wasn't certain because the smell of sweat and grime overwhelmed the smell of bourbon whiskey on his breath. Oh, if only Altoids had been available in the 1950s. Unless something unforeseen happened, Dad must have known he had a rebuke coming later in the day. Daddy was a good sport, and he drove us the short distance to the store.

Daddy wore filthy coveralls. His unshaved face was a mask of dark unwashed stubble streaked with grit and grime, and he was sweaty and dirty on his arms and hands. He also had the distracted attention of a half pint of Early Times.

Hundreds of people were gathered at the grocery store, crowded together, milling around and jockeying for position. The moment came to call out the name of the lucky winner of the wringer washing machine. The store manager talked too much, but he built a little excitement, leading climatically to the name itself, pausing, drawing the name from a bin, and then finally announcing the winner dramatically, "Marion F. Davis."

I looked up at Daddy. He didn't move. I looked at my brother, Sammy. He was looking up at Daddy. I looked back at Daddy. He still hadn't moved.

The Foodtown manager cried out Marion F. Davis again, this time louder to be heard over the murmur of the hundreds crowded together, all hoping Marion F. Davis was not present to win the fine new wringer washing machine.

"Marion F. Davis! Is Marion F. Davis present?"

Suddenly, I was aware of Mother. She was agitated, punching Daddy on the arm, trying to coax some life from him.

"Mar'n, that's you! Mar'n, that's you! Say something, Mar'n!"

Daddy did not move. He did not say something.

"Here!" Mother yelled. "He's here! Mar'n F. Davis! He's here!"

The store manager yelled back, "Come on up here, Mr. Davis, and get your brand-new wringer washing machine!"

Mother pushed Daddy forward, now imploring him.

"Get yourself up there, Mar'n. You won that washing machine!"

Daddy worked his way through the crowd, and he finally stood triumphantly before the hundreds collected there. He stood there in his dirty coveralls, sweaty streaks of under-the-house filth on his unshaven face and his arms and his hands. He was grinning, his eyes mere slits. By God, he won that brand-new wringer washing machine!

Mother and Daddy kept the washing machine on the screened front porch a few days while it was advertised in the newspaper. Eventually, it was sold for cash to a young black woman, who was thrilled to have her first washing machine.

Mother never fussed at Daddy about the half pint of Early Times that comforted him as he drudged under the house. She never rebuked him. How could you fault a man who won a brand-new wringer washing machine?

The Last Minute

Daddy was the kind of man who had a tendency to wait till the last minute to do anything. Every year, he would wait until the morning of Christmas Eve even to think about what to give Mother for Christmas. He was not a procrastinator. The man simply had no sense of urgency.

On the morning of Christmas Eve, he and I would alight in the car, riding aimlessly around town, drinking coffee here and there.

"What do you think we ought to get your mother for Christmas? Got any ideas?" I never did.

"Know anything she wants?" I never knew anything she wanted.

"Can you think of anything she needs?" I could never think of anything she needed.

"Well, let's get some coffee. Maybe we'll think of something."

We made the same rounds we always made. At times, we were blessed with luck that seemed as heaven-sent as divine intervention. One Christmas Eve, we were drinking coffee at Mac's drug store and decided to look around. Daddy found a lazy Susan with four or five brownish ceramic dishes. We would have made Marty, the main character in the eponymous movie, seem decisive by comparison.

"Do you think she'd like it?" one of us would ask the other. "I don't know. What do you think?" the other would answer. "I don't know. What do you think?" the other would say. Then, one of us would say, "You have any other ideas?"

Countless repetitions followed. Mother liked the lazy Susan. She used the lazy Susan till the day she died. Now, I have it. I treasure it.

Another Christmas Eve, we drank coffee all day, looked leisurely here and there and ended up after dark without a clue. Somehow, we meandered into a railroad salvage place where neither of us ever had gone before and where neither of us ever would go afterwards. It was our last chance since everything else was closed. We saw a large, framed print of a painting called "Sunday Morning."

One of us would say, "What do you think?" The other would answer, "I don't know. What do you think?" Then, one of us would say, "Do you think she'll like it?" The other would say, "I don't know. What do you think?" After innumerable repetitions, we bought the painting. Mother liked it. She always had it hanging in her dining room. Now, I have it. I treasure it.

Hard to Motivate

When I was playing junior high school football, Daddy had a contract for carpentry work at the complex that housed the U.S. Army Corps of Engineers in Mobile, Alabama. This work was done at night after office hours. As a result, he never was able to attend any of the junior high football games and see me play. All of our home games were played at night. He never said anything about it, and I supposed he was indifferent. Of course, he was not indifferent.

One time, we had an afternoon game at home. After the opening series of downs on offense where I played center, I took my position at linebacker on defense. For some reason, I looked up into the stands and saw my father sitting there close to the field.

The coaches always said that I was hard to motivate. I played hard, but I did not play emotionally. Billy Hugh Montgomery once said, "Davis will play for me till he pukes." I would. Maybe I got it from my mother. My grandfather, Poppa, always said, "She was my best worker. But I had to watch 'er. She'd stay in the sun too long. I was afraid she'd have a sunstroke."

Ordinarily, I played hard, but I played under control. The coaches were right. I was hard to motivate. When I saw Daddy sitting there and watching me play, my heart pounded and all of my emotions suddenly were engaged. I just wanted him to be proud of me. I played with abandonment, reckless and ferocious. I forced a fumble and Frankie Larson recovered it. Forced another fumble and recovered it myself in mid-air. I intercepted a pass and ran it back until I took a terrible hit to the quadriceps of my right leg. I regained my feet with the ball still in my hands, but I had the worst charley horse of my life. It was severely painful, but my threshold for pain was that of a man possessed, which I was. I played with what my mind told me was merely a little hurt, played with un-diminished savagery and violence, played through and transcended the pain because I played to a higher calling.

I stopped everything that day. The other team tried to run away from me, but I got there anyway. They were shut down by a linebacker who they must have suspected of being Faust reincarnated after still another deal with the devil. After each play, I glanced up in the stands to see some sign, some indication. He sat alone in the stands, motionless. Late in the game, I looked up one more time, and he was gone. Waited until the last minute, I suppose, and then had to leave for Mobile.

That day, we won a game we probably should not have won. After the game, the coaches were saying to everyone, "We don't know what got into Davis to-day! We didn't know what he'd do next! Man! Looked like another Ed Beatty out there."

Ed Beatty played center and linebacker for Ole Miss. He was drafted tenth overall in the 1954 NFL draft by the Los Angeles Rams. He had a seven-year playing career in the NFL, playing both center and linebacker. Later, I knew Ed Beatty. After football, "Big Ed" was a dentist. We both were parishioners of St. Michael's Episcopal Church in Mandeville, Louisiana. His wife, Joy, was the best-dressed woman in the congregation. I attended his funeral in June 2008.

Daddy never said a word, never said he'd been there and never said he'd seen me play. Undoubtedly, he wanted me to be proud of myself. *Daddy, tell me you saw me. Tell me I had a good game, Daddy. I played for you, Daddy. I played hurt. It was a gift to you, Daddy. Tell me the gift pleased you, Daddy. Tell me you were proud of me, Daddy.*

Hurricanes

My father had a fascination with hurricanes. He followed a hurricane zest-fully if not vigorously enjoyable from the first time it was mentioned. When a hurricane headed even remotely close to the Mississippi Gulf Coast, he followed it with special excitement. When we were under the infinitesimally slightest influence of hurricane weather, he would look at me with a big grin on his face and say, "Let's go and see what it's doing." We would drive to the beach and drive the entire length of Beach Boulevard from the Surf Grill to the Coast Guard Station and back to the Surf Grill and then to the Coast Guard Station again, from one end of the beach to the other over and over again. I suppose he just liked to see nature doing something, liked to see the waves flopping in. *One-Eyed Jacks. Ben Johnson saying to Marlon Brando. Nothing to do but sit and watch the damn waves flop in all day.*

In the 1940s and 1950s, hurricanes were unnamed. Moreover, the location, path, and intensity of hurricanes were relatively unknown and uncertain until landfall. When a hurricane headed for the Gulf Coast, Daddy would stay up all night listening to the radio. Even when I was a little boy, I would stay up with him, but I would fall asleep. Later, I stayed up with him, and I stayed awake with him. He and I rode out a number of hurricanes together.

When I moved away from home as an undergraduate student, I often came home on weekends. I was home once when a hurricane headed our way. When 10:00 rolled around, Dad said, "I think I'll let you handle it tonight. I'm going to bed." He did. *Now, I'm the one,* I thought, *I'm the man, no longer the boy.*

Overnight, direction of the hurricane became difficult to predict. Local television stations had signed off the air. I was listening to a battery-operated radio. Evidently, radar could not pinpoint the eye and its movement. It was out there, and they thought it would make landfall in Biloxi or Gulfport. The weather went from bad to worse in Pascagoula. The wind howled as though in pain, and I could hear pine trees grumble in resentment.

I kept looking outside at pine trees bent over from force and pinecones and small pine branches being blown along the ground. Then, suddenly it was still. The wind was still, but I heard sounds that astounded me. Birds, hundreds of birds, thousands of birds, each bird making the sound of its kind, its noise, perhaps its cry of alarm. The birds were caught in the eye of the hurricane and moving along with it. We were in the eye of the hurricane!

Finally, I heard on the radio that Keesler Field in Biloxi was reporting the eye of the hurricane had made landfall in Pascagoula. It was almost dawn. I knew the backside of the eye would be worse. Minutes passed, several minutes passed, more minutes passed. The wind came back up.

Dad was at my side, waking at dawn as usual. He looked worried and distressed. He had slept but had not rested. I told him about the night. We had lost electricity. He made coffee on the gas stove. We drank coffee, and we listened and watched. We talked in hushed tones, whispered with tenseness, paced, sat, imagined, dreaded.

When it was over, he said nothing to me about my staying up all night. Later, however, when he talked to family and friends by telephone, however, I overheard him. "I went to bed. Ronnie stayed up all night. He stayed on top of it for us."

During that particular hurricane, I was reminded of the subtle racism of Pascagoula, at that time probably neither more nor less than the racism of any other town of its size in the South or, for that matter, in the North, East, or West. When the hurricane weather was bad enough to affect schools and businesses in the late 1950s and early 1960s, local radio stations would announce school closings, business closings, meeting cancellations, and so forth.

I was listening to the local Pascagoula radio station during the early morning, and the announcer periodically was giving out information.

"Classes have been cancelled in the Pascagoula Public School System," he would say. "The day shift at Coastal Chemical Company should not report to work today," he would continue. "All maintenance personnel at H.K. Porter should report immediately," he would say.

In the background, I could hear someone occasionally bringing in messages and whispering in the announcer's ear. Then, the announcer would pass the information along to his listeners.

"All electricians at Ingalls need not report to work until further notice," he said.

I heard whispering to the announcer followed by, "Negroes should not report to Ingalls until further notice."

Negroes, I thought. *Negroes? Negroes! Negroes should not report? What? Why Negroes?*

I bent forward, listening, expecting some explanation. I once again heard whispering to the announcer.

"I have a correction," the announcer said. "That's all *riggers* should not report to Ingalls until further notice. Repeating, riggers should not report to Ingalls until further notice."

It was just one of those moments when at a time of institutionalized racism and racial slurs I could laugh at the attempt to be what we now call politically correct. For whatever it is worth, I never heard my parents use a racial slur, and I think they would have skinned my brother and me alive if we had ever referred to black people with anything less than the courtesy, respect, and dignity that any person deserves.

Dad was a wise man, and he was a teacher of wisdom. Once, he summarized his beliefs regarding other people in a few wise words. He said, "Treat all people with courtesy, respect, and dignity regardless of their circumstances." Skin color is a circumstance. Gender is a circumstance. Age is a circumstance. Income is a circumstance. Religion is a circumstance.

Sixteen: When Assets Become Liabilities

My father was a nice man. To borrow from Steinbeck's Cannery Row, Dad was so nice that, when he walked down the street, dogs would smile at him. He had a hushed but masculine voice, a deep but soft voice. His voice suited him. He was that kind of man; Quiet but manly, deep but gentle. When I was sixteen, I mistook his gentleness for weakness. I took the softness of his voice as lack of intensity and forcefulness, and softness of voice as softness of manhood.

The assets of being soft-spoken and mild-mannered and being soothing and agreeable became the liabilities of manhood. At sixteen, I understood manhood as a process of maturity culminating in the practice of harshness, roughness, and even violence. Like James Dean in *Rebel Without A Cause,* I wanted Dad to stand up for something. Having a quiet but strong nature like Shane was okay if, like Shane, you were dangerous, capable at any time of walking into a saloon and taking the place apart or taking on Wilson in a gunfight. *It was Wilson, alright. He was fast, fast with a gun.* My father was not dangerous. If he walked into a saloon, the saloon dog wouldn't sense danger and slink away on tiptoes the way the dog did in the movie, *Shane*. The dog would have smiled at Dad and gone back to sleep.

Dad had many friends, close friends in the black community in Pascagoula. These black men and women knew that Dad was their genuine and true friend. When they had problems, they often came to our house for solutions. When they had needs, they often came to our house for help. When they wanted the company of their friend, they often came to our house to visit. They came to our front door, knocked, and were invited inside, invited to have a cup of coffee or a glass of iced tea, invited to have a slice of pie or a piece of cake. Dad was liked, appreciated, and respected in the black community.

One Sunday afternoon, a loud knock was heard at the front door. It was a group of white neighbors. I was in my bedroom, and I heard the spokesman of the group tell Dad they were upset about "niggers" coming to our house and coming to the front door. The spokesman said if "niggers" insisted on coming to our house, they should go to the back door and certainly should not to be invited to come inside the house.

I wanted Dad to take the place apart, stand up, and kill if he must. Instead, he merely thanked them for coming. I hated him at that moment, and I hoped I never would be like him. Of course, Dad never changed anything. When black people came to our home afterwards, they knocked at the front door and were invited in for coffee or tea, pie or cake. Daddy just ignored the ignorant.

The Dark Side

In high school, I was a member of a harmless gang we called the "Gamblers." We played poker now and then. The other Gamblers were Ronnie "Baby Huey" Dossett, called Baby Huey because he looked just like the cartoon character, Baby Huey; Carl "Pig" Nulta; Jimmy "Poopie" Green, and Jesse "No Nickname"

Grizzard. I was Mogey, pronounced MO-gee. It's a long story.

One night, grown men beat up a poolroom friend our age. He came into the Palace Pool Hall where the Gamblers were playing snooker for a dollar a game. He had broken ribs, and he was a bloody mess. He told us the thugs worked him over for no reason. They were just looking for someone to beat up, and he was available. He told us the men stayed in flats over the Lucky Strike Bar on Delmas Avenue. They couldn't do that to one of us. They couldn't get away with beating up one of us.

We jumped into a car and went looking for revenge. Three of us jumped from the car alongside the Lucky Strike Bar while the other one stayed with the car. We were ready. There was only one way down from the second floor, which had a gallery completely around the living quarters above the Lucky Strike. The one way down from the gallery was a narrow enclosed stairway. We knew an advantage when we saw one. When these men came pouring down the stairway, we picked them off one at a time, doubling them over. They just piled up. We were taking the place apart.

We miscounted their numbers and overplayed our advantage. There were too many of them. They started beating us back in strategic retreat. We fought them off as we backed our way to the car and jumped in one at a time. One slight, jaundiced-looking man was animated outside the car next to the open back window. I was sitting in the back seat away from the open window and away from this swarthy man. Poopie Green had jumped into the car next to me, near the window, near the jaundiced, swarthy, mustachioed man. The man looked like he was trying to hit Poopie inside the car. Poopie instinctively put up his right arm to ward off the blow, and a knife was buried in the fleshy part of his forearm. If he had not taken the knife in his arm, it was headed for his chest.

I was never afraid during the fight, but I shook uncontrollably with fear and dread after Poopie was stabbed. I was materially unharmed and unmarked, but I recognized that potential danger had materialized this time. I was harmed and marked in a different way.

In the 1950s, I was a big fan of James Dean. I still am. I have a James Dean poster of his movie, *Rebel Without a Cause*. I have a James Dean tee shirt. I never miss any of his three movies when one is shown on television. I can't resist a documentary on his sixteen-month movie career. When I was in high school, I had a James Dean outfit based on his role as Jim Stark in *Rebel Without a Cause.* I wore jeans, a white T-shirt, a red windbreaker, and leather boots. James Dean is the only person I ever knowingly imitated.

I read and reread *East of Eden,* and I saw the movie based on the last third of Steinbeck's novel. The novel was a retelling of the story of Cain and Abel. I remember and frequently recall the lines of Raymond Massey as the father of Cal Trask, James Dean's character in *East of Eden.* "Man has a choice. That's where he's different from an animal." I was deeply moved by James Dean's portrayal of Cal Trask in the movie. I was moved by his plea for a father's approval. I also was aware of James Dean's portrayals of the dark side of life. I wanted to see the dark side, be near the dark side, but I wanted control the danger. When the danger was not under my control, danger scared me. The night of the stabbing unnerved me. Danger had been out of control.

Pascagoula could be a dangerous town at that time. One of many sources of peril was a gang called the "Kitty Kats." Unlike the benignant Gamblers gang, the Kitty Kats were grievous and flagitious, a gang rumored for its violence and cruelty. No one knew exactly who was a member of the gang, but countless bad acts were attributed to the Kitty Kats. One night, I was hanging around Norwood's Drive In on Market Street. A man who we thought was a member of the Kitty Kats also was hanging around and drinking a fair amount of whiskey. Suddenly, he flourished a big silver pistol overhead and used threatening language.

"I'm going to shoot the next son-of-a-bitch comes out the door."

All of us were quiet, really quiet. The night was suddenly black from more than the night. We looked inside Norwood's through the plate glass windows in front. We saw a few people standing around and sitting around. We began to wonder which one would come out the door first. Finally, one did. The blighter we thought was a Kitty Kat fired once, twice, three times. He missed all three times if he actually aimed at the innocent fellow at all.

I knew the trouble was trouble for us all. I ran to my car, a souped-up 1954

Ford with a big flathead V-8 engine, and roared away. I thought everyone else would go to Callahan's Restaurant on Delmas Avenue, which was the main street in downtown Pascagoula. I went instead to the bus station. After ordering a cup of coffee, another kid who had been at Norwood's walked in and sat next to me at the counter.

About thirty minutes later, a policeman walked in, looked around, and came over to talk to us.

"Been some trouble over at Norwood's. You two over at Norwood's tonight?" he asked.

We lied. Mostly, I lied for both of us.

"No, sir. Been here. Both of us. Hung out at the Big Pig and Edd's for a while."

The policeman scowled and said, "I think you two been at Norwood's. There was some trouble. Let's take a look at your cars."

Never minding the lack of a warrant, he probed around mine for a while and found nothing of interest to him. In the other boy's car, he found a knife under the seat, a big knife like a Marine Corps Ka-Bar. For a minute, I thought he was going to run us in, but he let me go. He hauled off the other boy for a concealed weapon, but I knew they wouldn't do anything to him. They just wanted to pressure him into talking. He didn't.

The Scavengers

When I was growing up, I always found ways to make a little money. I picked blackberries and sold them by the quart. I collected cold drink bottles and returned them for the deposit. I sold Cloverine Salve door to door. I sold Mrs. Norman's crochet doilies door to door. I delivered newspapers. I loaded hundred pound sacks of fishmeal onto barges at the local pogy plant. When Shorty Ezell was elected public works commissioner, I was given a job with the city. I repaired gas meters.

When I was seventeen, Dad was still working for the city. He ran public works for the city, working with and for his old buddy, Shorty Ezell. Public works included the garbage dump. A man called "Dutch" operated a bulldozer at the dump. "Scavengers," as they were called, sifted and sorted through the garbage to find occasional things of value and set them aside to be hauled away. These scavengers were down-and-out have-nots, destitute, rough, tough, mean people. Dutch tolerated the scavengers as long as they didn't interfere with his work. Of course, they didn't want Dutch to bulldoze any fresh garbage until they had gone through it for things of value. Dutch accommodated them to the maximum extent possible, which was the overwhelming majority of the time but not always. The scavengers threatened Dutch, and Dutch told my father about it. Dad went to the dump and had a talk with the scavengers. Dad and the scavengers reached an agreement. Dad warned them about any further threats.

One day, Dad came for me at the city warehouse. He asked me to come with him. He was quiet, but he had a firm set to his jaw. The scavengers had threatened Dutch again. Dad was going to do something about it. Dad and I were going to do something about it. I had never seen him this way.

On the way to the dump, Dad pulled over to the shoulder of the road, stepped out of the truck, and went back to the bed of the truck for a moment. When he stepped back into the truck, he handed me a large wrench.

"Put this in your back pocket. You might need it. Use it if you have to."

He briefed me on the background and the situation. He told me where to stand when the trouble started. I understood. I was there to watch his back.

The scavengers were there. Dad pulled up to them and turned off the ignition. I could see through the windshield that they expected him. Their eyes were slits like rats, and their eyes never looked directly at anything, never looked directly at us. They had whiskers from not shaving. They were filthy and smelly.

We stepped down from the truck slowly, and we squared ourselves immediately to confront them. I then turned slowly away from Dad to cover his rear and distanced myself enough that they couldn't rush both of us at one time. *Like Shane and Joe Starrett in the Grafton's barroom fight.*

Dad did not waste an instant. He started calling them names, cussing them, using vulgarity and profanity. He was not yelling, not shouting, but they were scared because they saw he meant what he said in that deep, strong, firm voice. He stood right in their faces one at a time and cussed them, and I could see spit flying out of his mouth and into their faces. He threatened them. He told them what *he* was going to do to them. What he was going to do to them. Not the police, not the sheriff, but what *he* was going to do to them. He told them if they wanted any trouble, he and his boy were ready for them. He dared them to say something, to do something. They said nothing, and they did nothing.

He went back around to each one of them, right in their faces an inch away, cussed them again one at a time and warned them again one at a time and asked each one of them if he understood. Each of them said he understood. They were scared. *We don't know what got into Davis today! We didn't know what he would do next! Man!* It was the only time I ever heard Dad use profanity or vulgarity.

We turned our backs to the scavengers and walked to the truck. Dad started up the engine and drove straight ahead, almost running over them, gunning the truck and never slowing down as he drove through them, watching them dive to either side to avoid being struck. He never looked back.

When we were down the road, he again pulled off the road and stopped. He was shaking. Both hands were gripping the steering wheel so tightly that his hands were bloodless and white. He took a deep breath. After a moment, he loosened his grip and held out his hand, and I gave him the wrench that I had stuck in my back pocket. He took the wrench back to the toolbox in the bed of the truck.

He drove off again and, after a mile or so he reached across me to open the glove compartment. He took a half-pint of Early Times whiskey from the compartment, removed the cap and took a swig, then handed the bottle over to me. I took a drink and handed the bottle back to him. We alternated drinks until we finished the bottle, and then he hooked the bottle over the cab of the truck deep into the woods on my side.

"Dead soldier," he said.

It was the only time I ever had a drink with Dad. Whatever momentary thoughts I ever had about hating this man vanished. I looked at him, looked at his profile, and I loved him. I never had told him I loved him, and he never had told me that he loved me. It would be a few years before he and I would tell each other. On that day, I looked at him, I realized how much I loved him, and

I silently admired him. I saw him. Him. I saw his perfection and his imperfection. I wanted to be like him, as though I had any choice.

What did he do when the spokesman and his hateful group of ignorant followers came to our house and told him to make "niggers" come to the back door and not let them inside? He thanked them for coming, and then he did nothing. His undaunted defiance was silent but nonetheless firm and steadfastly resolute. His black friends kept coming to the front door, and he invited them to come inside. Sitting in our living room, he invited them to have a cup of coffee or a glass of tea, a slice of pie or cake. The spokesman and his group never came back. Maybe they knew what the scavengers knew. This man was nice to a point, but when the wellbeing of others was threatened, he was dangerous. He would put up with almost anything as long as it affected only himself, but he would stand up for others. Come to think about it, that's what Shane did.

Pres and Ed's

One summer, Dad and Mother visited us in Gainesville. Dad loved spicy food, and I suggested that we drive to Pres and Ed's for some barbecue. I had told him all about Pres and Ed's.

Pres and Ed were two black men who owned a barbecue business plunked in the middle of a predominately black neighborhood of Gainesville. Pres and Ed's was a small, fire engine red building that had no inside dining area. If arriving by car, customers joined a queue on a semicircular driveway leading to a window. A black lady would come to the car to take your order. When the customer advanced to the window, the customer paid for and picked up the barbecue. The *menu de repas* listed chicken, beef, pork, ribs, and goat. Customers could choose from four sauces. The four sauces started with mild. The mild sauce was hot and then escalated in hotness to medium, hot, and finally to Mammy Jammy's hot sauce. I think Pres and Ed must have had a military contract to supply Mammy Jammy's hot sauce to the Pentagon. I'm sure Mammy Jammy's hot sauce could have defoliated jungles in Vietnam.

Before I ever went to Pres and Ed's, I had eaten a lot of their barbecue but never had been to their venue. I still remember the first time I went there. When the black lady came to my car to take my order, I asked for ribs in medium sauce. She told me that I wouldn't like medium sauce.

"The mild sauce is hot," she said. "That's what you want. You want mild sauce. You don't want medium sauce."

I told her I had tried the mild sauce and the medium sauce. "I really want the medium sauce," I told her.

She was nice but insistent. "Ed, he don't want us to sell nothing but mild sauce to y'all white folks."

She was nice, very nice, but firm, very firm, black firm. The line of cars behind me was lengthening. Their patience shortened. This whitey was holding up their orders. Suddenly, she said, "I be right back."

In a moment, Ed himself came out of the building in a chef's coat topped by a towering *toque blanche*. Ed came to the open window of my car, bent over, his hands on the side of my car, and appraised me with squinted eyes. He did not speak. After a moment, he stood tall and turned to the black lady at his side. "He looks okay. Let 'im have the medium sauce."

That's how I met Ed. After we were friends, he let me have medium sauce with a little hot sauce on the side. He told me I needed the medium sauce to build up an acclimation to the hot sauce on the side.

Dad looked forward to going to Pres and Ed's. We ordered pork sandwiches and a slab of ribs, both sandwiches and ribs with medium sauce and a little hot sauce on the side. When we neared home with our barbecue, the skies opened up like the deluge of Genesis. It was a typical afternoon Florida deluge. I drove past the house, watching the skies and smelling the barbecue.

"Dad, let's go down the street into the woods. We can eat our sandwiches in the car. We'll save the ribs till later."

In the woods, we sat in the car with the rain deluging in Noachian alluvium. We ate our pork sandwiches with the medium sauce, occasionally dipping into the little plastic cup of hot sauce.

Dad would take a bite of his sandwich, put it down, take off his glasses, and wipe his eyes. "Man, this is good! You can't beat this. My eyes are sweating."

I looked at him and thought, *No, Dad, you can't beat this. It's raining so hard, we can't even see outside the car. It's a two-man world, you and me. You can't beat this.*

After we finished our sandwiches, Dad said, "That hot sauce was something else. I never figured out why people like hot, spicy food. I just know I do."

Dad was looking straight ahead. The rain had let up a little, and the woods were visible again through the windshield. I just looked at him, at his profile. His health was failing. He had a vulnerability that seemed to leave him unprotected. Yet, his profile was still heroic, a time-honored look like that of myth and legend.

"Dad," I said, "tell me again about the little birds that fly south for the winter."

I had heard him tell this little joke many times over the years. I think he made up the joke when he was a boy in Arizona.

He kept looking straight ahead. He had a big grin on his face. His eyes squinted almost shut when he grinned. "You know those little birds that fly down to Mexico for the winter?" he said with a laugh. "They eat those little pepper seeds down there all winter. When they fly back north for the summer, they have to fly backwards."

Anybody who has eaten hot, spicy food caught on to the joke. After eating hot, spicy food one day, anybody wished he or she could fly backwards the next day. Hot, spicy in, and then hot, spicy out.

I laughed once again at his little joke. It was like recalling his childhood, like recalling Arizona. "We'll be flying backwards tomorrow," I finally said.

We both laughed and nodded our heads. I looked at him with moist eyes, and he finally looked at me with that big grin on his face with his eyes squinted almost shut. I could see that his eyes were moist, too. The rain deluged again, even harder. The windows were totally fogged on the inside. It was the last time I ever heard him tell his little joke about the birds flying backwards.

The next day, we took Amanda to Disney World. He and I sat on benches while Amanda enjoyed the rides. He was not strong enough to walk, stand in line, or enjoy the attractions. When we were back in Gainesville, he was sick. He just went to bed. He curled up in his boxer shorts, writhing in pain. It was his gallbladder. I saw his white skin, his scrawny legs. *I see Papaw after he had his stroke. The white skin, the white legs, the white boxer shorts, the white undershirt. I see Papaw before him, and I see myself after him. I see that he is an old man and that I am going to lose him.*

He was white and frail and vulnerable. He said he just wanted to go home, just needed to go home. Later in the week, he recovered enough to be driven home, but I knew and he knew. At that time, I saw his mortality and my own. I knew that the greatest loss imaginable was now also inevitable.

Cancer

When I first became a business school dean, I was living three thousand miles away from Dad in Bellingham, Washington. I was nonetheless true to my determination and commitment to see Dad and Mother at least once every three months. I knew he had cancer, cancer of the lungs from smoking Camel cigarettes. I talked to his doctor and asked him how long. His doctor began the mumbo jumbo about how he couldn't say.

"Dr. Warren, I'm three thousand miles away from Dad. I'm in Bellingham, Washington, and he's there in Jackson, Mississippi. How long does he have? Just tell me the truth."

Six months, maybe two years at most. Dr. Warren was nice, a caring physician who clearly had feeling for my father.

I visited Dad every month. A year later, I decided to interview for the dean's position at the University of South Alabama, located in Mobile, Alabama, only three hours or so by automobile from Jackson, Mississippi. I flew to Jackson with the idea that I would borrow Dad's car to drive to Mobile for my interview. Mother told me that Dad was in the hospital. I visited a few minutes with Mother and then drove Dad's car to the hospital. I immediately saw that Dad was in bad shape. I knew he was dying.

I spent the night with him in the hospital. I sat in an uncomfortable chair alongside his bed, not sleeping at all. I was preparing myself.

Dad couldn't eat anything. The next morning, he tried to eat something for me, tried to choke down some grits for me but couldn't. He wanted to go home.

"You know, I think I could eat some of your mother's chicken 'n dumplings," he said.

I told him I'd get him out of the hospital. I began packing up his things. Dr. Warren came to the room before I finished packing his things. I stood there by my father's side, holding his hand, patting, rubbing, and trying to soothe him.

Dr. Warren held his other hand and said, "Mr. Davis, we've done all we can do for you here. You understand what I'm saying, Mr. Davis? If you want to go home, you can go home. Your boy here can settle up later."

Dad understood, and he didn't flinch or tremble or quiver. Dad looked at him and rasped, "Doctor Warren, I'm not afraid to die. I just hate to put my boy here through all this. You know, my other son and my wife, too. I just hate to put my boys and my wife through all of this. I know it's going to be hard on them. My son here can take me home."

I held up because duty required strength of all kinds. I wheeled him to the car. I wasn't sure he'd make it to the car. Once in the car, I wasn't sure he'd make it home. Once home, I helped him in stages, from the car to the kitchen, from the kitchen to the den, from the den to the bedroom.

He failed steadily throughout the day. He and I talked at times, but briefly. I kept telling him that I loved him, and he in turn kept telling me that he loved me. I never wanted to leave his side. If I could have gone with him and accompanied him to the other side, I would have.

By late afternoon, he couldn't talk. I called Mother to come to his bedside. I told Dad that Mother was there. His eyes were closed. He was motionless, his breathing shallow and infrequent. Mother held his hand. She was strong. She was silent.

"Dad, Mother is here. If you know she's here, squeeze her hand." He squeezed her hand strongly, his eyes closed, and his breath travailed.

Mother told him that she was there and that she loved him. It was time to stand aside and let these two people, husband and wife, father and mother, have their final moments together. Afterwards, Mother retreated to her kitchen.

After I returned to his bedside, Dad died in my arms, sitting up, my arms around him. If he had any hearing left before he died, the last words he heard were mine.

"I'm here with you, Dad. I love you, Dad. I'm here. Like that old refrain of faith, Dad. Here am I. Here am I. Here am I."

Earlier that day, Dad slipped off his wedding band and told me that he wanted me to have it. I returned it to his own finger, whispering, "Not now, Dad." The moment after he died, I slipped the gold wedding band off his finger and slipped it on my own. It is still there inside my own wedding band.

My Father's Son

Dad and I were as close as any father and son ever were. After I was grown and had my own career away from home, I always visited Dad and Mother at least once a quarter, and I always talked to him at least once a week by telephone. A lot of men have trouble saying, "I love you," but he and I didn't have any problem whatsoever. We truly communicated. He understood me. I think he is the only person who ever truly understood me. He took the trouble to know me. I understood him, and I knew him. We enjoyed each other's company.

I am my father's son. I have his mannerisms. Many times, I have startled myself because I realized I had just done something exactly the way that Dad would done it. I think, *My God, that was just what Dad would have done; exactly what he would have done. My God, I am just like him!*

The fourth commandment is "Honor thy father and thy mother…." I think an unwritten commandment is "Be worthy of thy father and mother." Sometimes, I struggle with the issue of worthiness. As a son, I wanted to be worthy of my father who I honored. Dad was a gentle man. In terms of practical wisdom, he was the smartest man I ever knew. People sought him for advice. He was liked and respected by every man and woman who knew him. He was a real man, a good husband, and a great father. To borrow from John Wesley, a perfect man is an imperfect man striving for perfection while realizing he would never reach it. In this sense, Dad was a perfect man. He avoided confrontation because he knew that, if a situation ever reached the confrontation stage, he had failed. He avoided confrontation by averting it through reasoned and measured resolution. To him, the necessity of confrontation was also the evidence of failure.

After my father died, I foolishly told someone, "It'll be a long time before I get over it." No son ever gets over it, only grows accustomed and habituated to the pain of loss. The pain of loss is as great today as it was on June 4, 1982. The pain becomes as familiar as a popular song, but the familiarity binds the pain around me like a shroud. I miss his voice, soft and deep, and his manner, relaxed and gentle.

I attended church with Dad many times in the later years. He couldn't sing a lick, especially after the inflictions of emphysema and lung cancer imposed by Camel cigarettes. He just didn't have the breath for singing. The last time he and I went to church together at Christ United Methodist Church in Jackson, one of the hymns that day was "Faith of our Fathers." I sang the bass part that Auntie taught me, and I looked at his profile out of the corner of my eye. He was looking at me out of the corner of his eye.

Courtesy, Respect, Dignity, and Masculinity

All these years later, I know how much I learned from him. Courtesy, respect, and dignity, an appreciative, deferential regard for all people, regardless of their circumstances, regardless of financial status or means, regardless of gender, race, sexual preference, religion, or any other circumstance. When I grew up in Mississippi, all adults regardless of color or religion or any other accident of birth or choice were Mr. So-and-So or *Miss/Mrs.* So-and-So. To all adults, regardless of color or religion or any other accident of birth or choice, it was yes sir or yes ma'am; no sir or no ma'am. To my family, to my father, that was simple courtesy and politeness arising from respect for all humanity. And "yeah" was never acceptable in our household. The word was "yes," not "yeah."

My father also gifted me with the knowledge and example of genuine, authentic masculinity. To be a man did not mean to be virile with implications of physical strength, vigor, power, or sexual potency. True masculinity meant the best in men and its best expression in a life of brotherhood and fatherhood, characteristics such as loyalty and faithfulness to a person or a cause, accepting responsibilities, making commitments such as providing for the needs of a family. He taught me how to become a man, how to achieve manhood, true manhood, masculine manhood without the foolish ornaments of machismo.

GROUNDS FOR BURIAL

Outside the small town of Wesson, Mississippi, numerous gravel roads once connected communities. In my childhood, people lived along these gravel roads. They were farmers. Driving along these gravel roads, you saw people working in their fields and sitting on their porches. You waved at them, and they waved back. You saw mules rather than tractors. You saw brown and white Guernsey cows as well as fawn-colored Jersey cows, and you knew that these people had rich, sweet milk and butter. You saw hogs and chickens. Dogs, hounds and fice dogs that you knew were good hunting dogs. Along the gravel roads, you would pass an occasional vehicle in support of these people, an ice truck or Gerald Woods's Rolling Grocery Store. It was a simple way of life, and you could see it from the road.

Where two of these many gravel roads intersected, a Methodist Church was founded in the early part of the century. Thompson Chapel has been razed. Thompson Chapel Cemetery is still there. I am related to everyone buried in Thompson Chapel Cemetery.

My grandparents are buried in Thompson Chapel Cemetery. Mamaw and Poppa are buried there, Sally Waldrop Butler and William Edwin Butler. And Mamaw Davis and Papaw are buried there, Ina Warren Davis and Grover Cleveland Davis. I have great grandparents buried there. My great grandfather, Dr. W.J. Butler, is buried beneath a stone that bears the epitaph, "He went about doing good." I have great uncles and aunts buried there. Above his name, Marion Douglas Fuller's stone declares him as "Uncle Marion." Above her name, Lucie Mae Davis Fuller's stone says "Auntie." I have uncles and aunts buried there. I am related to everyone buried in Thompson Chapel Cemetery. It is a family burial ground.

Outside the small town of Calvert, Texas, is the community of Mount Vernon and Mount Vernon Cemetery. In a corner of Mount Vernon Cemetery is another family burial ground. My great-great-great grandfather, Reverend W.W. Nash, is buried there. My great-great grandfather, James Madison Davis, and great-great grandmother, Camilla Jane Nash Davis, are buried there. I am related to everyone buried in the Nash-Davis corner of Mount Vernon Cemetery. It is a family burial ground.

In these two family burial grounds, I have six generations of family buried. I cannot hear the old hymn, "Faith of our Fathers," without imaging these two burial grounds.

In 1993, my daughter, Amanda, attended her first Nash-Davis Reunion, which was celebrating its fifty-fourth year. On the day of the reunion, I drove her to Mount Vernon Cemetery. We stood together fronting the tombstones of James Madison Davis and Camilla Jane Nash Davis, her great-great-great grandparents. She was moved. So was I.

I drove us back to the reunion. After a while, I led her to a book of family photographs. I turned the pages and told her what I knew about these old photographs taken in the nineteenth century. I wanted her to see one photograph in particular and to see her reaction.

Finally, I turned still another page of the family album. On the page, there was the photograph of a man seated and a woman standing. It was a posed studio photograph from the nineteenth century.

I pointed to the woman in the photograph and said, "Amanda, this is Camilla Jane."

It was a photograph of James Madison Davis and Camilla Jane Nash Davis. Camilla Jane when she was a young woman. Amanda's head snapped forward and her eyes widened.

"Dad," she said, "that's me. This is really spooky. It's downright scary! It's like looking at a photograph of me. That's me."

It was the photograph I wanted her to see. After we returned home that night, Amanda was still stunned and moved.

"Dad, I've always wanted children. If I ever have children, I already have names picked for the boys and girls. I've changed my mind about the name of my first girl. I'm going to name her Camilla Jane."

It was her, Amanda, in the photograph. Just like I, Ronnie, am one or all of them in the photographs, one or all of them in the family burial grounds. I am the ones in the family burial grounds. My emotional makeup has come down to me through them. Whatever I am emotionally, I owe to them. *Faith of our fa-thers! liv-ing still. . . . We will be true to thee till death!*

Chapter Five
THE SPIRITUAL JOURNEY

The word "spirit" comes from a Latin root, "spiritus," which is related to a Latin root, "spirare," meaning "to breathe." As a word, therefore, spirit suggests the breath of life. Spirit suggests a kind of vapor that breathes life into flesh and bone, a kind of vapor that animates the body or mediates between the body and soul. Spirit is viewed as breath, a gift of deity, and thus the agent of vital and conscious functions in us. The breath given to us as spirit is the respiratory agent of the soul. Irrespective of religion, soul refers to the essence or substance, the animating principle or actualizing cause of life manifested in thinking, willing, and knowing. The word "spiritual" is simply an adjective that describes something relating to or consisting of the spirit. Spiritual is an adjective dealing with the higher endowments of the mind and with the moral feelings or states of the soul.

CORE VALUES

In business practice and otherwise, core values are the principles, standards, and qualities that a business or organization considers worthwhile, imperative, and so pressingly essential that these core values are the *sine qua non* of the business or organization itself and all of its undertakings. The CEO of a *Fortune 500* subsidiary once told me that core values are the spirit of a business, the vital animating forces that motivate its people from top to bottom. Indeed, core values reflect what is truly important to an organization. They are the underpinnings of company culture, what shores up patterns of behavior, beliefs, and traits that are the expression of the business itself. One company, Whole Foods, declares that its core values "are the soul of our company."

It is so with us. Personal core values give definition to who we are, what we stand for, and what we stand against. Our core values are what we truly believe is important to us. In this sense, our core values are the spirit within us, perhaps the soul at the heart of our individuality. These core values motivate us and shape our priorities. As in the case of many businesses and organizations, many people have given little thought to core values. Consequently, such people tend to follow the core values of others, if they follow any core values at all.

Core values and spiritual growth tend to go together like hand in glove. Special companies with special executives get it right, realizing that core values are the spirit of a business, the soul of a company. They would be the first to tell us that a company culture based on organizational core values thrives on the nutrients of personal core values.

HUMANISM

As an intellectual movement, humanism has its roots in Florence during the latter fourteenth century. As such, it should be designated as Renaissance humanism. By the mid-fifteenth century, humanism was established as a liberal arts curriculum. This curriculum beckoned professors and students alike to the values of reason and evidence in discerning truth. These followers also subscribed to a belief in human worth and individual dignity. The worth and dignity were found in their conviction that everything has a determinate nature, but a birthright of man was the gift to choose his own nature. In this way, choice and core values were at the heart of the intellectual movement.

As humanism unfolded, the movement became a broad ethical philosophy that affirmed the worth and dignity of all people, in turn based on the ability and capacity to determine right and wrong through human means in support of human interests. Ultimately, therefore, humanism rejected the validity of dependence on faith, the supernatural, or divinely revealed writings. Nonetheless, humanism focused on the spiritual aspects of core values, especially ethical considerations of right and wrong. While rejecting deference to beliefs founded on the supernatural, humanism did not reject the beliefs themselves. In other words, humanism rejected the basis for the beliefs, not the beliefs.

Religious Humanism

Religious humanism evolved as a syncretic fusion of humanism and religion. Eventually, the confluence was a rendezvous of humanist beliefs and a form of theism without any necessary alliance with organized religion. Such adherents might consider themselves spiritual but not religious in a functional sense. Indeed, many people might not be traditional theists at all, although they believe in ideals that transcend physical reality or even interpret some experiences as numinous, *i.e.*, uniquely religious. Religious humanists who are participants in organized religion value rituals and ceremonies as periodic means of affirming and celebrating their choice of praxis and often seek profound experiences associated with the presence of God. Christian humanists, for example, have belief in God, traditionally defined.

Scripture, Reason, and Tradition: The Three-Legged Stool

In the sixteenth century during the reign of Elizabeth I, Richard Hooker wrote a multi-volume Anglican apologetic, *Of The Laws of Ecclesiastical Polity*. He claimed that Puritans went too far in their insistence that scripture provided the only source of knowledge, and Roman Catholics were excessive in their claim that the Pope had infallible understanding of faith. Instead, Hooker proposed reliance on holy scripture, human reason, and "voice of the church," eventually interpreted in the twentieth century as scripture, reason, and tradition, the "three-legged stool."

For Hooker, reason was God's greatest gift to humankind. Indeed, reason enabled us to understand God's plan for reality, find a place for ourselves within this reality, and discover proper moral forms of human activity. He believed scripture presupposed reason and required its use. In this way, scripture and reason inform each other. The voice of the church, *i.e.,* church tradition, was a reference to ecumenical council decisions dealing with important matters on which scripture is silent or is offered only in broad hints.

And Experience: The Four-Legged Stool

In the late eighteenth century, still another Anglican, John Wesley, added a fourth leg to the "three-legged stool," *viz.*, experience. In addition to reason, which is rational thinking and sensible interpretation, he added one's personal and communal journey. In this way of thinking, faith was revealed in scripture, necessary for salvation. However, faith was illuminated by tradition, vivified by experience, and confirmed by reason. Even tradition, however, went beyond the voice of the church. Tradition included the influences of beliefs, values, upbringing, and instruction of one's family as well as other encountered influences that have an effect on one's understanding. In a practical sense, reason and experience provided the best *human* evidence of truthfulness.

Secular Humanism

In the twentieth century, the term "secular humanism" originated to disengage from religious humanism. Seen narrowly, secular humanism rejects any theistic religious belief and any supernatural source. Such rejection arises from the basis that religious or supernatural beliefs cannot be supported or validated through rational argument. If not a religion itself, secular humanism is a philosophy that upholds and champions reason, ethics, and justice. At its foundation is a conviction that, whether religious or otherwise, ideologies and traditions should be measured, evaluated, and judged by each individual rather than accepted on faith or on some form of mysticism. This conviction is a commitment to critical reasoning, factual evidence, and scientific method.

Nonetheless, secular humanism is primarily concerned with growth, development, and fulfillment for both individuals and humankind. This concern centers on life and a commitment to making it meaningful through fuller understanding of ourselves and the points of view of those who differ from us in some way. This concern also deals with a search for practicable, workable principles of ethical conduct based on the capacity of these principles to manifest human wellbeing and individual responsibility.

The Point

Personal core values define us and express what we truly believe is important. In this sense, our core values are the spirit within us, perhaps the soul of our individuality. The implied spirituality of these core values is not necessarily religious in their origin. Secular humanists have a strong sense of spirituality, including strong beliefs in right and wrong, ethical conduct, wanting the best for others and themselves, and other values shared by religious humanists as well as those who are steeped in one organized religion or another. That is, whatever the source of these core values, whatever the belief system on which these core values are based, the point is that, once developed, these core values motivate us and shape our priorities. The spirituality of these core values is what makes us human.

Spirituality deals with discerning meaning in life, finding significance in life, deriving purpose in life. Spirituality might focus on personal experience, but spirituality also perceives life as more important, more complex, and more integrated than one's own narrow *weltanschauung*, one's own "look onto the world." In this sense, spirituality has an appreciation for a transcendental dimension of life beyond self. Spirituality also deals with values, *i.e.,* the beliefs, ethics, and standards that one cherishes as well as connections of self to others, nature, and perhaps to a divine being. The framework of cherished beliefs, ethics, and standards imply proper connections.

Some of us are brought up in a Christian, Jewish, or Muslim family and culture. We follow the spiritual path impressed on us in our upbringing. Others are brought up in a secular family and culture, and follow a different spiritual path through life. Whatever upbringing in which we are situated, we must find a way to mature spiritually, developing and maintaining core values that serve as a guide to right and wrong behavior and proper connections to others.

In my personal case, my upbringing was Christian in religion, humanist in philosophy. Upbringing, however, only points me or anyone else in a certain direction and leads us only so far. After upbringing, the rest of the journey is up to us. Whatever the upbringing, the subsequent journey is a lifelong confrontation with one fork in the road after another, each requiring choice.

FIRST METHODIST CHURCH

When I was a boy, my parents were members of the First Methodist Church in Pascagoula, Mississippi. First Methodist Church was located on the northeast corner of South Pascagoula Street and DuPont Avenue. It was air-conditioned. Indeed, a sign out front at one time declared itself, "The Air-Cooled Church With A Warm Heart." At another time, the sign proclaimed, "Everything Air-Conditioned But The Pulpit." In the 1950s, air conditioning evidently was more important than theology in matters of church life.

Located across DuPont Avenue on the southeast corner was Central Elementary School, which I attended through the fifth grade. Central Elementary School was not air-conditioned. Across South Pascagoula on the northwest corner was Pascagoula High School, from which I was graduated in 1959. Pascagoula High School was not air- conditioned. Cater-cornered on the southwest corner was the residence of Mr. Frank S. Canty. Mr. Frank S. Canty was the mayor of Pascagoula when I was a boy and again when I was in high school. He also was an inebriate, both when I was a boy and again when I was in high school.

Frank S. Canty vs. Brother Hilbun

The minister of First Methodist Church was known as Brother Hilbun. Brother Hilbun thought it would be a swell idea to install a sound system in the sanctuary along with prodigious speakers in the steeple to broadcast carillon recordings each evening at 5:00 p.m. for about fifteen minutes. These carillon recordings could be heard several miles away. At 5:00 in the afternoon, Mr. Frank S. Canty, Mayor Frank S. Canty, would generally be in his home, often sleeping off a drunk or nursing a skull-splitting hangover after a night of hard drinking in seedy bars from Biloxi to Mobile, driven from one joint to another in a police cruiser, sometimes causing a disturbance with his obnoxious behavior, sometimes resulting in a skinned place on his nose where a strategically placed punch had landed.

Mayor Frank S. Canty first asked politely, and when politeness didn't work, then demanded impertinently that Brother Hilbun either turn off or at least turn down the carillon recordings. When polite requests and impertinent demands didn't work, Mayor Frank S. Canty threatened Brother Hilbun. If Brother Hilbun didn't turn down or turn off the carillon recordings, Mayor Frank S. Canty threatened to come across the street and bust Brother Hilbun's skull open with a baseball bat. Probably to give Brother Hilbun an idea of what Mayor Frank S. Canty's own skull felt like at 5:00 PM when the carillon recordings were detonated.

One day at 5:05 PM, Mayor Frank S. Canty showed up at First Methodist Church with a Louisville Slugger in his hands, brandishing the baseball bat menacingly like a halberd. Brother Hilbun espied him first, however, and did what any sensible man would do. He ran. Brother Hilbun bolted down the corridors, Mayor Frank S. Canty a scant step or two behind him with bat held high, through the Sunday school rooms, through the music rooms, by the pulpit that presumably was not air-conditioned even during the week, down the aisles of the sanctuary. The two of them soon burst from the church building and ran around the churchyard, through the gardens. Brother Hilbun was outlasting Mayor Frank S. Canty.

At this time of day, a lot of people were driving through the busy intersection. They pulled their automobiles to the side of the street to watch with amusement Mayor Frank S. Canty chasing the clergyman with a Louisville Slugger, a momentary mockery of America's pastime. Sooner or later, one of these motorists was certain to have no sense of humor. Some humorless killjoy called the police but was told the police couldn't do anything because Mayor Frank S. Canty would order them not to arrest him, if not order them to hold down Brother Hilbun while he took his requisite cuts. This worrywart then called the Jackson County Sheriff's Office, and deputies showed up to arrest Mayor Frank S. Canty.

Mayor Frank S. Canty was booked and locked into a cell at Jackson County Jail. He was talked into resigning by one of his drinking buddies, Mr. Robert Gulley, and a delegation from the Chamber of Commerce. In exchange for resignation, an agreement was reached. Mayor Frank S. Canty would be released immediately, and Brother Hilbun would not press charges. The former part of the agreement was paramount. Mayor Frank S. Canty said he wanted out of jail and wanted out of jail now because he needed a drink. Brother Hilbun had run and not grown weary, and Mayor Frank S. Canty, for all the swishing of his baseball bat, like mighty Casey, had struck out. He had another appearance at the plate, however. Mr. Frank S. Canty was elected mayor again in 1956.

My father, Marion Fuller Davis, was hired by First Methodist Church, hired by Brother Hilbun himself to do all the rough and finish carpentry to install the sound system in the sanctuary and the speakers in the steeple to broadcast the carillon recordings. You might say that Dad's craftsmanship started all the trouble. He set the table for a moveable feast, although the feast day of Canty v. Hilbun was not in response to Easter.

Confirmation of What?

At First Methodist Church, I sang in the children's choir. At this time, the minister was Dr. Sutherland, a stiff, imposing, pompous, ostentatiously self-important man with a pate as bald and denuded as a baby's behind. His wife, Mrs. Sutherland, was a stiff, imposing, pompous, ostentatiously self-important woman with an intricate hairdo, certainly more complexly arranged than absolutely necessary. Children in the choir wore homemade robes made by mothers from white percale sheets according to a common pattern chosen by Mrs. McRae.

Mrs. McRae was in charge of the children's choir sort of like the Commandant of the Marine Corps is in charge of the Marines. In fact, she had the eye of a Parris Island Drill Instructor on us when we sat as a choir in the sanctuary. She gave demerits for reproachful behavior and made these demerits a matter of public record by posting them on a bulletin board for all to see. I led the choir every year in demerits. I figured, what are they going to do to me?

When I reached the age for Confirmation Class, I listened and responded to questions with answers I knew would please our earnest Confirmation Class teacher, Mrs. Dawson. I easily memorized what we were asked to memorize. On Confirmation Sunday, we were confirmed as believers, and we took communion. No one of us understood what he or she was doing. I certainly didn't.

Catholic Girls

I continued to go to First Methodist Church until I was old enough that Mother no longer made me go to church every Sunday. When I was in high school, the only person who could lure me to church was a girl, any girl as long as I was dating her.

For a short time, I dated a girl named Sissy, who recently had broken up with her boyfriend. Sissy was Catholic. Our next-door neighbor was an older woman who was a bigoted Southern Baptist. She was a troublemaker, telling my mother that I was dating a Catholic girl and thus popery implications of sin and iniquity. In this singular act of mean-spirited gossipy cruelty, she planted wicked seeds of deep maternal worry and concern in my mother's mind, the mind of one who had grown up in the insular piney woods of Mississippi on the banks of Beaver Dam Creek where there were no Catholics save those putative Catholics of rumor.

Mother was rarely direct about anything. She was a subscriber to and a practitioner of circumvention and convolution. One morning after I had taken Sissy out for the fourth or fifth time, Mother initiated a discussion with me at breakfast when the two of us were alone in the kitchen.

"I don't know who you're dating, but I'm sure it's a nice girl. I'm sure it's not a Catholic girl. They tell me Catholic girls can do anything they want, then all they have to do is tell a priest about it, and it's okay."

Of course, this declarative was word for word with exacting fidelity from the malicious Southern Baptist gossipmonger. Nevertheless, a mother should never tell a teenaged son this kind of thing. My *tabula rasa* took off like a skyrocket and bloomed in pyrotechnic brilliance! My hormones were aroused, inciting an erotic insurrection. *If that's true,* I thought, *I'll date only Catholic girls!* I never had thought about it. My libido was ablaze. A lot of good it did me. Sissy went back to her old boyfriend, who was Catholic.

DR. SKELTON

In high school, I socialized with kids in the class ahead of me. All of my good friends were sophomores when I was a freshman, juniors when I was a sophomore, seniors when I was a junior. The girls I dated were in the class ahead of me. When I was a junior, I started dating a senior girl who was Southern Baptist and who sang occasionally in a girl's quartet at First Baptist Church. I began to go to church with her, particularly to hear her sing.

The minister was Dr. Skelton, who was a truly exceptional man and a gifted speaker. Dr. Skelton once delivered a series of Sunday evening lectures dealing factually rather than judgmentally with other denominations of Christian faith. He wanted to speak educationally about whom these other denominations were and what they believe. He actually supported the fact of different denominations on grounds that people are different, and their personalities are different. Some respond more and better to one approach than to another, and different denominations meet this need arising from differences in people. This departure was highly irregular in those days because Southern Baptists were highly creedal, every bit as creedal as Catholics.

One of Dr. Skelton's Sunday evening lectures was, "Who are the Catholics?" Dr. Skelton invited all local Catholic priests and nuns to attend the evening service. Most of them were there, and all of the priests and nuns were surprised and very pleased with what they heard. The lecture was in keeping with 1 Corinthians 12:5, in which Paul writes to his followers in Corinth, "And there are differences of administrations, but the same Lord." Dr. Skelton's message was different denominations and different religions but one God.

When I was a senior, I joined First Baptist Church and was baptized, immersed in the baptismal pool by Dr. Skelton. Just in case. Methodists could take their chances. I was covered if baptism by sprinkling didn't take. Baptists are creedal. Unless immersed, baptism doesn't count and doesn't take.

It was the singer, not the song. I do not mean the senior girl who sang in the girl's quartet. I mean Dr. Skelton. I kept going to First Baptist Church, captivated by Dr. Skelton, moved by the man, unmoved by the message. After I finished high school, Dr. Skelton left First Baptist Church and Pascagoula. I think he left to work with American Indians in Arizona. His son, Henry, was in my graduating class.

Too Late

One of my first cousins, Richard, is my age. He and I grew up together. Richard's father, my uncle, was a Southern Baptist minister, Dr. R.P. Butler. All of his life, Richard rebelled against his father. At the time of his father's death, Richard and his father were as estranged as ever. Most of us wondered whether Richard would attend the funeral. He did. Before his father's funeral service, at which I was a pallbearer, Richard pulled me aside with tears in his eyes.

"I've been thinking a lot about my father since I learned he passed away. Until the last two days, I never realized what a great man he was. I'd give anything in the world to see him one more time. Some things I'd want to tell him. I know what I'd say to him."

Then, he added two of the saddest words in the English language. "Now, it's too late," he said.

Too late, two of the saddest words in the English language. *It's too late to ask forgiveness. It's too late to seek reconciliation. It's too late to experience repentance and redemption.*

Reconciliation is a great theme, perhaps the theme of both the Old Testament and the New Testament. Old Testament is an insult to Jews. The Hebrew Bible or the Jewish Bible is a little better, but to Jews it is the Bible. Nevertheless, reconciliation still is a great need for us today. Sometimes, it is too late for reconciliation in this world.

I told Richard to write down what he wanted to say to his father in the form of a letter and take the letter to his father's gravesite. "He'll get it," I said.

I didn't know whether his father would get it or not, but I thought writing the letter would be healing for Richard, a soothing balm for his pain of guilt. I don't know if he ever wrote a word or if he ever took anything at any time to his father's grave, then or later.

THE ALIBI

In 1971, I resigned from the faculty at Iowa State University to join the faculty of the University of Florida. We moved to Gainesville. On my way home every day, I passed through the intersection of Newberry Road and 34th Street. On the left was a Publix grocery store. Publix was and is the touchstone among grocery store chains in Florida. Each one had a large neon sign with the Publix name written in a sort of emerald green. At the time, the neon sign at each store was emblazoned with the words, "Where Shopping is a Pleasure."

When my daughter, Amanda, was about age eleven, she and I were riding past this particular Publix store at night. The first three letters of "Shopping" had gone dark in the neon sign.

"Dad, look at what the Publix sign says." She read aloud, "Publix. Where pping is a Pleasure."

We laughed hysterically. Even now, years later, when anyone ever mentions Publix around the two of us, we turn to each other and say simultaneously, "Where pee-peeing is a pleasure." Then, we die laughing.

The Gang of Five

At the same intersection across from Publix was a blue-collar, neighborhood tavern called the Alibi Lounge. When I first moved to Gainesville, several of my new colleagues in the economics department became good friends. I had known two of them, Blaine Roberts and Dave Schulze, when they were students in the doctoral program at Iowa State University, where I served on the faculty immediately prior to joining the faculty of the University of Florida. On Friday afternoons, Harold Black, John Morrall, Dave Schulze, Blaine Roberts, and I would meet at the Alibi and drink cocktails while our wives collected at one house or another to drink wine and cook a fabulous dinner. When dinner was ready and the wives were ready for us to join them, they would call us. We would join the ladies, join the wine drinking, and eat a splendid dinner that the five wives had prepared together in the kitchen.

After dinner, the men played chess, and played it well. All of us were students of this curious game that is a kind of war of egos. I know chess is only a game, but when I lose a game, I feel crushed. My personality, who I am, feels like it is disintegrating. Bobby Fischer, the American who won the world championship of chess in 1972 when he defeated the Russian defending world champion, Boris Spassky, once said that the greatest moment in a game of chess comes when his opponent drifts in a lost position "and I feel I can crush his ego."

Charlie

After a year or so, the gang of five began to break up. Blaine Roberts and John Morrall accepted appointments with the Nixon Administration, and they moved with their wives, Martha and Annie, respectively, to Washington, D.C. John and Annie asked us to keep their Boston terrier, Charlie, until they returned to Gainesville. My daughter, Amanda, answered for us, "Yes."

We already had a seven-pound toy poodle named Mimi, who was a mindless, brainless little nitwit of a dog who was totally sweet but who also was dumb as a football huddle. Mimi never caught on that she was supposed to be our daughter's dog rather than mine. Charlie caught on. Charlie and Amanda were close.

Charlie was badly deformed at birth but was spared by Annie, who refused to let him be destroyed. He had serious respiratory problems that made him sound like he was gasping for breath, and he always snored when he slept. Charlie was the only dog I ever knew that made a noise when he broke wind. He was the smartest dog I ever have been around. Ever. Charlie was a dog genius with a canine IQ as high as if not higher than the human IQ of Marilyn vos Savant.

In Washington, Blaine and Annie had an extramarital affair and suddenly announced to their respective spouses that they wanted divorces so that they could marry. Martha ended up with their little girl. John ended up with their two little boys. We ended up with Charlie.

In the 1970s, Amanda wanted to go to summer camp with her friends, who were Jewish. During each of three or four summers, Amanda went to Mountain Lake, a Jewish camp in North Carolina. Mountain Lake was an eight-week experience. The food was fantastic. After all, Mountain Lake was a Jewish summer camp. Being a Jewish summer camp, they thought Amanda Davis's name was Amy Davidson.

The second year that Amanda was at Mountain Lake, Charlie dropped dead on the patio only a few days before she returned home. I thought I should break the bad news to her face to face rather than by telephone, break the bad news at home where I could show her where I had buried Charlie and placed my best and biggest Fontana rock over his grave. We picked up Amanda at the airport, and just before we made the last turn to our subdivision, she said she just couldn't wait to see Charlie. It was the second toughest thing I ever had to tell her. The toughest was when I had to tell her that her mother and I were getting a divorce.

The Regulars

When Blaine and John took positions in Washington, Dave and Harold stopped going to the Alibi on Fridays, and the remaining wives stopped getting together to drink wine and cook. I kept going on Fridays. I met some of the regulars, who were good and decent people and mainly blue-collar workers. Paul, called "Cajun" because he was one, was a telephone repairman. Tommy managed the local livestock market. Jimmy, called "Redneck" because he was one, was a rental property owner. Henry was a pharmaceutical salesman. Jan was studying to be a physical therapist. Walter was so big that, as a joke, we once brought out two bathroom scales to weigh him. Windy was a barber who once ran a close race for the county commission. Billy was the boyfriend of Pam, the bartender who was studying for a degree in special education. Of course, there were also various, sundry, and miscellaneous others on a given night. All the regulars knew me because I had become a regular.

There was both pain and fun among the regulars. The fun masked the pain. There was a lot of pain. We divided the pain so that it was bearable.

Paul's wife left him for the dentist she worked for, and she took the children. Paul was hurting every minute of every hour of every day.

Henry had a wonderful wife and children, but he was in love with Jan, who thought of Henry as a good friend but had no romantic interest whatsoever in him. Henry showed one of his physician customers a dark spot on his arm and was told it was a melanoma. He and I were the same age, and he had cancer, a very dangerous cancer.

Jan was romantically interested in a buttoned-down lawyer, Jack, but he was married. Jack had enough romantic interest in Jan to get her pregnant, but not enough decency to admit paternity even when it went to court. He should be thankful that DNA testing was not commonplace in the early 1970s.

Walter loved Secretariat, the magnificent horse that won the Triple Crown in 1973. The regulars, including Walter, collected to watch each of the three races won by the wonderful, giant horse. After Secretariat won the Triple Crown, Walter dropped dead one day. His heart exploded at home one day while he was in his favorite room, the kitchen.

Windy passed away and had one of the biggest and most moving funerals in Gainesville history.

With each one of the regulars ministering to the other one regarding his or her hurt and pain, there was a lot of co-dependency among us. Nonetheless, we had fun, often romps and larks of lifelong memory.

One night, a well-dressed man who no one knew came into the Alibi and drank heavily. He probably had not been sober when he arrived. Before anyone really paid attention to him, he passed out at a table by the front door. He slumped at the table with his arms folded on the table, his head resting on his arms.

The bartender, Pam, felt bad about the unfortunate fellow who probably was an out-of-towner. Concerned about the man, Pam asked Jack, the lawyer, what she should do.

Jack turned slowly on his barstool to look over his shoulder at the unfortunate but well-dressed fellow, probably seeing dollar bills.

"Why don't you call the police, and I'll put one of my business cards in his shirt pocket."

Nice guy, huh? Well, nice for a lawyer. Lamar Hunt once said, "My definition of utter waste is a coachload of lawyers going over a cliff, with three empty seats."

Roger Maris

In 1961, Roger Maris hit sixty-one home runs for the New York Yankees, breaking the major league record of sixty hit by Babe Ruth while playing for the same club, although Maris played a 162-game schedule but Ruth only a 154-game schedule. Hence, "the asterisk." Maris finished his career in St. Louis as a Cardinal. The Cardinals team was owned by the Busch family, which also owned the Budweiser beer empire. Upon retirement, Roger Maris was awarded a Budweiser distributorship in Gainesville. On occasion, he came into the Alibi, but not for a beer. He was a whiskey drinker. He was not easy to like. His rude, surly arrogance and condescendence were wide and deep.

Late one Friday afternoon, Roger Maris came into the Alibi. He stood at the bar next to Jimmy, the Redneck. Maris ordered a drink and placed a crisp, new twenty-dollar bill on the bar.

Jimmy slurred to him, "Maris, why don't you buy us all a drink?"

Maris turned to Jimmy with his signature snarl and said with contempt and invective, "Go to hell, Redneck. I'm not buying anybody a drink."

Jimmy retorted caustically, "I know why, Maris. You're too cheap. Money means too much to you."

Maris then turned his considerable body and stood looming over little Jimmy sitting red-faced as always on the barstool. Maris snapped at him loudly for all to hear, "Money means nothing to me, Redneck!"

The filled barroom quieted. Eyes turned to watch, ears to listen. We were congealed in wonderment, hyped in anticipation of what would happen next.

Jimmy reached slowly for the twenty-dollar bill on the bar, picked it up, tore it in half, then tore the halves in half, and eventually tore the twenty-dollar bill into countless tiny pieces and dropped the pieces to the floor of the bar.

It happened so unexpectedly, Maris simply watched wide-eyed with disbelief.

"What the hell you doing, Redneck? Just what you think you doing? That's my twenty-dollar bill you just tore up!"

Maris had the attention of the entire barroom, which suddenly was totally hushed. All faces turned to Maris and Redneck.

Jimmy grinned boozily and said, "What do you care, Maris? You said money don't mean nothing to you."

The whole bar erupted in loud laughter. The unlikable Maris had been ridiculed, and we were blissed out with delight seeing this cock-a-hoop swellhead brought down. Looking around the bar, his face hard, deep-set eyes black in the low light, infuriated and humiliated, Maris turned and stalked out the Alibi door amidst the uproar of laughter. Jimmy drank free the rest of that night. Everyone bought him a drink. No one ever saw Maris again in the Alibi.

Meaningless but Harmless

The days and weeks and months at the Alibi continued. My wife joined me at times. On her way home, she would swing by to see if my car was at the Alibi and join me when it was. She became close friends with Jan. On her way home, she would swing by to see if Jan's car was at the Alibi and join her if it was. The whole experience was shallow, meaningless, and purposeless, but it was harmless. My teaching, research, administration, and consulting were going well, and I enjoyed the break from pointy-headed intellectuals I saw all the time on campus. I was governed by rationality and reason so fully in my work that I enjoyed the interregnum of irrationality and insanity in my play. That was a rationale, of course. It was my excuse. It was my alibi, and I was sticking to it.

O, DEATH, WON'T YOU SPARE ME OVER TIL ANOTHER YEAR

One Saturday night, I was not at the Alibi. I was home. My wife and I were sitting on our sofa watching a college football game on television. The next day, Sunday, we were supposed to take a covered dish to the Alibi. The regulars planned to set up covered dishes in the booths and watch NFL games on television. Suddenly, in an immediate, instant burst, my mind opened to indescribable horror and then closed again. In that infinitesimal flash, I saw total abhorrence. I cannot say what I saw. I can say only that I saw abject horror and abhorrence. I cannot say what was horrible or abhorrent. In that instant, I bolted to my feet in alarming fear and dread, and I walked hurriedly but silently to the master bedroom bath, where I stood and looked at myself in the mirror. I thought, *"What's the matter with me? Am I losing my mind?"*

I knew what I had seen. I had seen death. Darkness, doom, ruin, and fear.

I didn't tell my wife about this horrifying experience. I didn't tell anyone. The next day, I went to the covered dish luncheon at the Alibi, and I watched the NFL games. I did not drink a beer, a cocktail, or anything. I was a man who had seen death. I never went back to the Alibi. It would be more than five years before I would drink even a glass of wine.

Now and then, I ran into the old regulars, perhaps at the grocery store or wherever, and they would say they never saw me anymore. They said everyone missed me.

"What's the matter? You too good for us now?"

"No. It's not that," I would say.

"Then what is it?"

"I don't know what it is," I would say.

My wife reprehended me for abandoning my friends, her friends. My friends at the Alibi denounced me for abandoning them. I had not abandoned anyone. After seeing death, I simply had no sense of belonging to the situation and environment of the Alibi. To paraphrase the first law of wing walking, "Don't turn loose of one thing till you get hold of something else." I had turned loose of one thing without at that time having hold of anything else.

I don't watch television much for entertainment. I mostly watch television to be informed. I haven't seen many episodes of a network television series since color television was invented. I never, ever watch celebrity interviews. Airheaded celebrities are overexposed on television if they are interviewed at all.

I'm a sports fanatic. I played baseball. Curveball pitcher, no fastball, couldn't hit a baseball. I played football. Center and linebacker on a championship peewee football team representing an elementary school I never entered and later a state championship junior high school team. I ran track.

In winter, I boxed. It started when I learned that during local wrestling matches, they let boys in the back door, strapped sixteen-ounce boxing gloves on them, and put them in the ring between matches. Put them in the ring *blindfolded*. The spectacle was a ring full of blindfolded boys flailing away blindly at each other. The wrestling crowd had a lot of laughs watching all of the blindfolded haymakers being thrown and the few that connected. I'm sure it was almost as funny and every bit as dignified as midget wrestling. Afterwards, the crowd threw money in the ring. If a kid put on a good show and exhibited some spunk, a guy sitting on the aisle might slip him a dollar on the kid's way out. I was one of those boys.

I ended up entering a lot of Golden Gloves fights, usually under the name of Jimmie Davis so that my father would not find out about it. He found out. He never said a word to me about it at the time. He never told my mother. Never.

I'm still a boxing fan. Everyone is entitled to at least one intellectual weakness. Mine is watching a couple of guys beat each other's brains out. After Muhammad Ali knocked out George Foreman in the eighth round of their championship fight in 1974, the fight in Zaire when Ali used his famous "rope-a-dope" strategy to wear down the behemoth and seemingly invincible Foreman, I turned on television one evening and chanced across George Foreman as a guest on some program. As a boxing fan, I had to watch and listen to the unpopular prizefighter at the time.

George Foreman said that after knocked out by Ali, he was placed on a stretcher in his dressing room. George Foreman said he actually died. I sat transfixed as I heard him say that he actually died and he actually saw death. Death, George Foreman said, was horrible. He could not describe it, George Foreman said, but he saw it.

I saw it, too. George Foreman said he actually died, and God let him come back from death for a purpose. As a direct consequence of this vision of death, George Foreman retired from boxing to take up preaching for a while. Now, George Foreman is an immensely popular figure. Of course, he is *immensely popular.* Anything George Foreman does is immense.

FONTANA

In 1971, I was appointed as a tenured associate professor on the economics faculty in the College of Business Administration at the University of Florida.

I was promoted to professor in 1974. Living in a university town like Gaines-ville, Florida, was an enriching experience. Home of the University of Florida, Gainesville was a good town in which to live and work. Football weekends were magical and enchanting even when the highlight film for the year was a tie with Georgia Tech, long before the Gators won the national championship in 1996 and back-to-back in 2005 and 2006. Now, even home basketball games are exciting.

Most of the year in Gainesville, we had better weather than other people in the country. July and August, however, were brutal. We had day after day of hot, humid weather that was enervating and oppressive, highs in the upper 90s if not over 100. Overnight lows in the lower to middle 80s and thunderstorms that ran up the humidity to equal the temperature.

Beginning in 1972, I took up jogging after reading Dr. Kenneth H. Cooper's book, *Aerobics*. In 1977, I ran my first of more than one hundred marathons, the Marine Corps Marathon in Washington, D.C. I regularly competed in com-petitive long distance races representing the Florida Track Club. At that time, the Florida Track Club was no average, ordinary, run-of-the-mill track club. It was not a club for joggers at all. It was a club for highly competitive track and field athletes. When Frank Shorter won the gold medal in the marathon in the 1972 Olympics, he was a member of the Florida Track Club. When Dave Rob-erts set the world record in the pole vault, he was a member of the Florida Track Club. We also had Marty Liquori, Barry Brown, Jack Bacheler, Jeff Galloway, and other world-class athletes as members.

As part of my routine long-distance training schedule, I can remember ris-ing at 5:00 during July or August to run before the sun was up. One day, I saw a bank thermometer reading 87 degrees in the pitch black of pre-dawn morn-ing. It was the overnight low, I suppose. As a college professor, I could take advantage of a slow academic calendar in the summer to escape the heat and humidity. My wife was an administrator, Associate Dean of the nursing school. I began to think about a place where we could go for a week or two in July or August to find cooler temperatures and dryer air.

At the time, I was a student of restaurants around the country. In advance of any professional meeting, conference, or convention, I always made reservations for eight or twelve people at what I regarded as the best restaurant in the site city. My academic friends around the country knew they could count on me, and they would find me at the front end of such gatherings and ask, "Well, where have you made reservations for us to go to dinner?"

I found the *Mobil Travel Guide* to be reliable as a source of information about restaurants and accommodations. I looked in the *Mobil Travel Guide* for the Middle Atlantic States for some ideas about where we might go to escape the heat and humidity. Listed in North Carolina, I found a place that intrigued me. Fontana Village was referenced under the sub-heading, "Resort." I read that Fontana Village was located at the southwest edge of the Great Smoky Mountains National Park. The Village itself was comprised mainly of work cabins originally built for the construction crews that built Fontana Dam, which still is the tallest dam in the Tennessee Valley Authority (TVA) system. I discovered that Fontana Dam was birthed in the early 1940s when America was at war and needed additional hydroelectric power. Fontana Dam actually crossed or was crossed by the Appalachian Trail.

To me, Fontana sounded idyllic. Fontana had to be cool in the mountains, Fontana had to be wooded, and, as far as I could tell from the description in the *Mobil Travel Guide,* Fontana had to offer absolutely nothing whatsoever to do there. Cool nights, mild days, endless woods, and absolutely nothing to do. Perfect. Brilliant! Fontana was my kind of resort. I was sold. I made reservations. I was not disappointed.

We drove from Gainesville to Atlanta, where we dined at the Midnight Sun, stayed the night, and then drove to Fontana the following day. We arrived in mid-afternoon. I first noticed that the entire front porch of the main lodge was filled with side-by-side rocking chairs. I bounded up the steps to register. I was in love at first sight. We were given a cabin on Licklog, a kind of country cul-de-sac with rustic cabins totally shaded by hardwoods and other deciduous trees, laurel, dogwood, hemlock, sourwood, and tulip poplar. The cabin itself was comprised merely of a sitting area, a tiny kitchen, bedroom, and bath. It was one of the original cabins provided for the men who built Fontana Dam in the 1940s. Some of these men lost their lives during construction. No air-conditioning, no television sets, no telephones.

My wife and daughter went for a walk. I took a nap. I fell asleep thinking, *I wonder if this is the cabin of one of the men who died during construction.* While I slept, it rained for a time. I could not wake up fully. The rain fell straight in the stillness of the mountain. No lightning, no thunder, no wind to drive the rain at angles. The rain fell straight and gentle, and the sound that the rain made as it fell on the leaves of the trees was a sound like no other. That sound was like a narcotic, and I was its narcoleptic victim. Let others go to beaches to relax. Let me go to the mountains where the rain falls straight down on hardwood leaves. *It's raining,* I thought. I heard the rain, and yet I slept. I slept, thinking, *I wonder what "it" refers to when we say, "It's raining."*

That evening, we went to the cafeteria for our first dinner. The food was just good country cooking. I loaded up on the kind of cooking I was raised on: greens, rutabagas, and sweet potatoes. Now, I was in love at first bite. Every day of my life until I left home to go to college, my mother made biscuits in the morning and cornbread at night. Fontana had biscuits in the morning, drop biscuits, and they had cornbread, good cornbread, real cornbread made from real cornmeal and cooked in an oven in a real iron skillet.

My wife and daughter left room after dinner for ice cream. I didn't, but I had some anyway. We licked our cones as we sauntered and strolled and shuffled along, heading like moths for some lights in the early evening darkness. A soft-ball game was underway. We sat in the grass beyond third base and watched, dodging the occasional foul ball when hit our way.

I overheard a lady with a whiney northern accent talking to a weathered and wizened old man who seemed to be a local resident, who probably was one of the workers at Fontana. She asked him which one of the two roads up the mountain to Fontana was the better one to take.

Without a moment to think about it, the grizzled old timer said, "Neither one of 'em. You take one, you wish you'd 'a' took th' other 'n.'"

Perfect. Brilliant!

Lewellyn Cove and Cascade Falls

The next day morning, I discovered Lewellyn Cove, a tree-sheltered creek that cascades down the mountain on a bed of smooth, worn, flat rocks and large, irregular stones wedged by nature at the edges like masonry walls. Fallen tree limbs and moss-slicked logs clutter the way in chaotic patterns. I saw rocks I wanted, and I toted them to the trunk of the car, thus beginning my practice of always going home with "a little piece of the rock." In the afternoon, I discovered Cascade Falls, a wide, shallow flow that actually falls three or four feet. Below the fall itself, Cascade Falls is bedded with more rocks than I could take home in a lifetime. I know. I tried.

The Appalachian Trail

The following day, I decided to walk up the mountain to the Appalachian Trail. I found a weathered wooden sign that said simply, "Appalachian Trail," with an arrow. I followed the arrow. At first, I walked along broad, rocky paths through totally shaded woods and barely running water over moss-covered rocks, and then I walked up, and up some more, and then along switchbacks that suggested ancient trial-and-error stabs at finding access, and then up again. I thought I had lost my way more often than I thought that I was on my way. After an hour of walking and climbing, I suddenly stepped onto a well-worn clearing with a broad path running in both directions, east and west at this point. I was thrilled. I knew it was the Appalachian Trail.

I thought about my family who had come to this country from Scotland after fighting on the losing side in April 1746 for Bonnie Prince Charlie on Drummossie Moor, near Culloden House, and I thought about the first of my family born in this country in Albemarle County, Virginia. I thought about the migration to Kentucky, and then the inevitable movement down the Shenandoah Valley, down the Appalachian Trail to Alabama, then to Mississippi, then Texas, and then Arizona. They skipped right over Louisiana.

They were highlanders, I thought, and they defended Mary, Queen of Scots, and James Edward and Charles Edward. Highlanders must have been Roman

Catholics. When did highlanders become protestant? Was it somewhere in the Shenandoah Valley? Was it somewhere on the Appalachian Trail? Why? Why did the highlanders, who had their names proscribed and suffered grave privations after 1746, who joined one of the great migrations to America, and who were Catholic and defenders of the Catholic Mary and Charles Edward, why did they reverse their fervor and profess their faith through protestant churches? When? Where? Why?

Lookout Rock

Standing on the ridge, I noticed another simple sign, the first I had seen since leaving Fontana. It was another wooden sign, whitened by the weather, "Lookout Rock," and again an arrow. I followed the arrow along the Trail. Lookout Rock was a short walk from the sign. A little off the Trail, I found it, a vast, massive rock that projected out the side of the mountain with an uncluttered view over the treetops. The circle of rolling mountains and valley suggested an immense, natural amphitheater of heroic, god-like proportions, a kind of Valhalla where Odin received the souls of slain heroes. The top of the rock itself was practically flat. At first, I stood there and then sat there introspectively and self examined my thoughts and feelings.

Lookout Rock was a special place, perhaps because I appropriated it by my own vow and thus consecrated the rock as hallowed. Perhaps it was ascribed with intrinsic holiness especially for me and thus was hallowed for me on my behalf. For whatever reason, this place was my place, this rock my rock. I had no awareness of faith, no sense of faith except a conviction of science as the means of understanding and explaining nature.

Plutarch

Eventually, I came down from Lookout Rock and down from the Appalachian Trail. After dinner, all three of us sat in our little living room. We played Scrabble. I listened to a baseball game on the Armed Forces Radio Network, which I received on my portable shortwave radio. In packing for the trip to

Fontana, I brought a book I would never read if I had any other books to read. Late that evening, I began reading Plutarch's *Makers of Rome,* which I once had bought when I was feeling noble or intellectual. I knew I never would read Plutarch as long as I had any other book around even if the other book was Beatrice Potter's *Adventures of Peter Rabbit.*

I read Plutarch with deep interest. My favorite Roman was Coriolanus, the first of the nine lives chronicled by Plutarch in the Penguin Classics publication I had brought with me. I knew I was reading a tragedy. I was deeply moved as I read about his death. "They rushed upon him in a body and cut him down, and not a man stepped forward to defend him. . . . When the Romans heard of his death, they took no action either to honor his memory or to condemn it." I wondered if I would die in the same way, no one to honor my memory but no one to condemn it.

HEARING VOICES

The next year, we returned to Fontana. After a week, we were nearing the end of our mountain retreat. On our last morning, I woke to the velvet, melodious, honeyed sounds of dawn in the Appalachians. After a quick morning routine, I held the screen door open, stepped soundlessly onto the wet wood of the raised porch, then eased the door shut without sound.

Standing apart from the light, swaddled in the deep shade of ancient trees, both hands grasping the porch railing, I cocked my head and listened to the early morning sounds of the mountain. I heard the small birds nearby, chirping and quarrelling with their tinny voices and flitting nervously from branch to ground and branch again. In the distance, great birds soared and screamed as though horrified at what they saw on the wooded land below. I breathed the cool, dank air of dawn, and I looked through the dim, obscure leaves of the trees to the blue ridge of the mountain where the black horizon was suddenly blood red from the rising sun. I stood solitary on the cabin porch, and I felt alone among the other cabins, alone in the forest, alone in the world, desolate and forlorn. As Kafka wrote, ". . . as forlorn as children lost in the woods." I was a child lost in the woods.

I was an average-looking man, almost but not quite six feet tall, athletic in build, although I had the slightness and gauntness of a long-distance runner. The tortoiseshell frame of my glasses was more or less the color of my brown hair and hazel eyes. I had the look of a college professor, which I was. I also had the look of a downtrodden man who wanted more from the morning, more from the day, more from life.

I stood laser straight, erect as a totem. When I looked to one side, my eyes moved behind the glasses, but my head remained unmoved. I finally looked down and stared emptily at the bare ground beneath the porch. My mind was both filled and empty, and I vaguely heard soft babbling from a spring-fed brook of mountain water that snaked its way sinuously between cabins, and then heard a screen door slam shut in the remote distance. Although muffled and muted, the slam stirred movement as my head turned slowly in the direction of the dull sound, and it reminded me that distant people were here.

I wore the green signature shorts of a competitive runner and a white singlet with MISSISSIPPI emblazoned on a magnolia blossom printed across the chest, the competitive singlet of the Mississippi Track Club. My long, tapered legs were well defined with muscles and bare to my lightweight racing flats.

I walked slowly and deliberately down the slippery steps to the forest floor, wet and soaked from overnight summer rain. I almost tiptoed across the moist, soggy ground to the macadam pavement and then almost reluctantly walked the short distance down the pavement to the main road. As soon as I stepped onto the main road, I began to run down the sharp incline of the hill, and, when I reached the bottom, I bore to the left and to the left again, and began to run up the steepness of the hill, and, when I reached the top, I bore to the left and to the left again, and ran down the hill and then up the hill, turning left and left again, repeating and repeating the up and down intervals for one hour, two hours, and then it was over, my legs dead, my mind exhausted, and yet I felt the goodness of tiredness all over my body.

Now, the sun was up but not over the mountain, and the trees and cabins were congealed in the stillness, shaded in the diffused yellow light of summer. I walked the pavement, head down, eyes fixed, and my mind blank. Where the macadam ended, I walked the bare dirt road cut into the woods, beyond the bridle path rutted by old, worn-out walking horses ridden each day by children and their watchful parents, beyond the ageless rocks and stones cleaved and left as lapidary detritus of glaciers of another age. Then, I walked on the russet path up the side of the mountain, at times flat with switchbacks and at times steeply vertical with rock-lined steps made treacherous with worn and wet slickness. In my mind, I knew only my destination, the Appalachian Trail and then Lookout Rock where I knew I could see the green of the land, the gold of the sun, the blue of the sky, though all seen darkly through the smoky mountain air.

I took the last remaining step to the Trail with a sense of familiarity. At once, my muscles had memories that recalled each time I had climbed and walked here. My mind held memories that recalled the meaning of place, this place. I sensed another familiarity, knowing that people, my people, had walked here before me. I felt small in their sudden company through remembrance. I plod-ded privately along the Trail, each flat-footed step one that I had taken every day, taken last year. I knew somehow that this place was mine, where I ought to be, and I knew somehow that I belonged here. Finally, I reached the place where I left the Trail and walked the few grassy steps down to and then onto the bare, smooth stone of a great rock that was a kind of monolithic sentinel unto a good land.

I stood at first akimbo, then sat cross-legged on the hard rock. I had an un-obstructed view from this special place. I thought about both lookout and out-look on this rock. What I saw from the rock was a most beautiful place, verdant and unsullied, rising and falling and rolling with the mountain itself, remind-ing me of a heavy crystal snow scene that as a boy I held in my hands each time I visited Auntie and Uncle Marion. What I saw from the rock was myself, my life, viewed at once in snapshot glimpses and flashes.

I lost any sense of time and occupied only this place in timeless thought. In my thought was the image of a photograph of my father as a boy sitting on a monumental rock in the Dos Cabezas Mountain of Arizona, seeing in my thought how I looked exactly like my father and how I too now sat on a great rock. I imaged a story my father told me of sitting on that rock and seeing movement down below on the desert floor in the distance, discovering through the hot, wavering, desert air that the movement was a small Indian boy running among the spiny mesquites, chasing a lone jackrabbit at an even pace though the jackrabbit darted in fits and starts first one way and then another, and then noticing in the big sky overhead a soaring eagle following the boy and keeping an eye on the jackrabbit, all three somehow connected, all three somehow linked unknowingly through meaning and purpose.

Time passed or time stood still. I did not know. I knew only that all was still and calm. The world as I saw it did not move. *The passage of time is what allows us to observe motion, I thought. No motion, no passage of time? No sound? Of course, there was sound.* There was the constant, unchanging sound of cicadas and tiny, green tree frogs taken together, a continuous one-pitch noise that whirred and vibrated everywhere and yet was unheard consciously, and the occasional bird that blurted out discrete, raucous cries, rhapsodic disturbances that seemed to leave jagged wounds in the quietness, wounds that healed slowly in the stillness. I knew I was alone. I felt alone. For all I knew, I was in bardo, intermediate between two lives on Earth, after death but before the next birth.

Shattering the brooding introspection, I thought I heard a sound. Not the cicadas and frogs, some other sound. Then, when I listened intently, it was not there. A moment later, I thought I heard the sound again. Then, it was not there, only the cicadas and the frogs. Now, I was aware of time, seconds when I heard something. *What? Followed by seconds when I heard nothing. Had I heard anything in the first place? No, I thought, it was not real, not palpable.*

Next, I heard voices. It was voices I heard. I rose quickly and jerkily to my feet and stood on the rock, alert with heightened senses, looking around me with eyes that suddenly seemed to exceed their vision and listening with ears that went beyond their hearing. It was voices I heard, and the voices were drifting eerily up the mountain from the valley below, fading in and fading out, but I heard the voices.

As I stood there aroused and alert, head back and eyes lifted, I heard the voices and realized the voices were singing. It was voices singing that I heard, and I heard their song when it reached me after climbing the mountain as surely as I had ascended each path and each step. It was voices I heard, and the voices were singing, and I heard their song:

> . . . And grace my fears re-lieved;
> How pre-cious did that grace ap-pear
> The hour I first be-lieved!
> Thro' man-y dan-gers, toils, and snares,
> I have al-read-y come;
> 'Tis grace hath bro't me safe thus far,
> And grace will lead me home.

I stood mute but I heard their song, and in my mind I sang with them, sang the bass part I learned as a boy, sang the words I learned when I stood behind Auntie playing the piano. It was Sunday. I had forgotten. It was a church. I was unmindful of churches. It was Sunday, it was a church, it was people, it was their voices, and it was their song. They lifted up their voices to me, I received their song, and then it was gone.

I felt inadequate and unworthy, feeling that I was not the man the boy was meant to be. I was overcome with the sudden sensibility of total love for my father and mother, my daughter, and for all of my family, even those who had gone before me, some I had never known. All of these emotions were felt in an instant portion of time. My hazel eyes moistened and tears ran down my cheeks in silent streamlets, and a salty taste arose in my mouth. I heard only the insects and frogs and their one-pitch song vibrating and whirring in my ears. The voices were gone, and the song gone with the voices.

Then, I heard the voices again, fading in and fading out, their song rising and climbing up to me, and I heard the bits and pieces:

> . . . O how our hearts beat high with joy
> Whene'er we hear that glo-rious word!
> Faith of our fa-thers! ho-ly faith!
> We will be true to thee till death.
> . . . And preach thee, too, as love knows how,

By kind-ly words and vir-tuous life:
Faith of our fa-thers! ho-ly faith!
We will be true to thee till death.

Again, in my mind, I sang the bass part, and in my mind, I saw myself as a boy standing behind Auntie, learning the parts she taught me, reading the words from *The Cokesbury Worship Hymnal*. My throat was constricting and my eyes were blurring my vision, but this time I sang aloud in a choked, cracked voice: "Faith of our fa-thers! ho-ly faith! We will be true to thee till death."

Then, it too was gone. The song, the voices, the people, the church, they were bygone and bypast, imploded inward to a silence that drifted down like flakes of snow. Yet, I was there in a special place, and I knew I belonged. The cicadas and frogs were there, too, and their rhythmic, whirring, one-pitch song was stilled for a moment, and then went on. My legs failed me, and I fell painfully to my knees on the insusceptible stone of the great rock. I bowed my whole body over and down until my arms were fully extended as though hugging the ageless rock and my forehead was flush with it.

I was mindful of Deming, who months earlier had given me the urge of transformation from the man I was to the man I could be and ought to be. I also realized that I had left spiritual growth behind, as Dr. Knapp said years earlier. Not religion but rather spirit, the breath of life that makes us human.

TRINITY: THE FIRST SUNDAY

After returning to Gainesville from Fontana, I wanted to take my family to church. My usual Sunday was going for a long, relaxed run on back roads, taking a "senility snooze" to recover from the run, and then reading a book while keeping one eye on the Chicago Cubs game televised on WGN. Even at that time, however, I knew the difference between adequacy and availability. I didn't feel up to or sufficient for the purpose. I nevertheless made myself available, placing myself at the disposal of my teenaged daughter who said she wanted to go to church as a venue for meeting other teenagers.

I said, "You pick the church, and we'll go."

The conversation had occurred mid-week when Sunday seemed a day in the remote future. Now, Sunday was the immediate present. Somehow, the remote future doesn't involve giving up one thing to do another, but the immediate present heightens in a confining and stifling way the sense that you must give up this to do that. As an economist, I understood the essential nature of choice and the inevitability of cost. When choice is made, the cost of doing something is the value of lost opportunity to do something else. Like a cynic who knows the price of everything and the value of nothing, I was thinking in terms of "opportunity cost," *viz.,* the cost of going to church was the high value I placed on running, napping, reading, and watching the Cubs, all of which I was forgoing.

I was dressed and ready. My wife and daughter were not. I supposed Amanda was in training with her mother to be late so that one day she would be practiced in driving her husband nuts. If we were to be seated in church for the beginning of the worship service, we needed to leave. We were not leaving. I sat and waited for five minutes, then six minutes, seven minutes, eight minutes, and then nine minutes. We left ten minutes late.

In the car, I asked, "Tell me again. Where we going?"

My wife said, "Amanda wants to go to Trinity United Methodist Church on Eighth Avenue. They have a good program for young people."

As I drove us to church that Sunday morning, I saw it was a beautiful morning. If Montana was big sky country, Florida was big sun country. The sun was big that morning, the grass was green and perky, and the air was light and still and almost cool on that early fall morning. On my side of the car, I drove with the window down.

We looked beautiful. Both my wife and daughter looked pretty in their dresses, and I had told them how pretty they looked. My wife was dressed professionally like the Associate Dean that she was. My daughter was dressed like the daddy's little girl I wanted her to be the rest of her life. As I glanced over my shoulder at Amanda in the back seat, I wondered, *Why did she stop giving me a kiss before she goes to bed for the night? When was the last time?* I was just dressed. Brooks Brothers would have been proud of me: blue suit, red silk tie, and accessorized with shoes, belt, and watchband of matching leather.

We arrived late. I was sure the service already had started. We left the car parked on a grassy, unimproved area as directed by a rather peculiar parking attendant inexplicably wearing a pair of pink bunny ears. I supposed he had been called to the parking ministry, for which the vestment is highly irregular and stylized as in the choice of one's own miter. Actually, the bunny ears looked no wittier on him than, say, the miter looked on the Pope.

We walked rather quietly towards the front door of the church building, a rather unimposing, unimpressive structure situated next to new construction that I took for the future home of Trinity United Methodist Church, which in turn I took to mean that Trinity United Methodist Church had prospects. *When I was a kid in Pascagoula,* I thought, *we just went to the Methodist Church. I guess we weren't united. Maybe we didn't have the need for it.* The old church building looked like it had been built by the low bidder, and the low bidder had come in under budget.

As we opened the doors, we entered a vestibule. In the instant that I stepped over the threshold and into the sanctuary, I saw that the nave was packed with people in pews from the narthex to the chancel, and I saw the people, and I heard their voices, and I heard their voices singing,

> Thro' man-y dan-gers, toils and snares,
> I have al-read-y come;
> 'Tis grace hath bro't me safe thus far,
> And grace will lead me home.
> When we've been there ten thousand years,
> Bright shin-ing as the sun,
> We've no less days to sing God's praise
> Than when we first be-gun.

I knew that this place was where I belonged. I belonged in church, in this sanctuary, which I knew was not the modest building that sheltered these people, but the people themselves. It was where I belonged. Others might have the equivalent sense of belonging in a synagogue or mosque or even the same sense of belonging in the company of humanists. I just had the sense that I was meant to be here.

The three of us sat together in a back pew. The worship service continued, and I watched with my eyes, heard with my ears, and felt with my heart. Without knowing these people, I knew their presence and knew their positive fervor, their aliveness, and their genuine relationships to each other.

I did not care for the religiosity of the church. I was a nonbeliever in a place of belief. I knew the religion but didn't believe the details. Yet, I sat in that back pew on that Sunday and had a deep, profound spiritual experience that also was physical, intellectual, and emotional at once. It was not religious, but it was spiritual. It must have been like John Wesley sitting in Aldersgate where he said his heart was "strangely warmed." John Wesley, that famed Anglican who if he were to reincarnate suddenly in America would ask, "Where is the nearest Episcopal Church?" He never changed his religion from the Church of England. Jesus never changed his religion, either. He would ask, "Where is the nearest synagogue?" Every year, I observe the eight days of Hanukkah by lighting candles in a menorah. After all, Christmas celebrates the birth of a Jewish child.

In that one hour, I felt the breath of life in my nostrils, making me human. The mature spiritual relationship was not based on restraint and certainly was not the work product of some self-promoting preacher who trucks in shameless emotional manipulation. Indeed, the spiritual relationship was not religious. In that one hour, I began to make a little sense of my life, and I could see the meaning if not the purpose of personal experiences that had been perplexing to me. I thought about Fontana and Lookout Rock, where I had heard the eerie sounds of "Amazing Grace" wafting up the mountain to me, driven mysteriously by some unknown impulsion. I thought about my experience of seeing death. I knew why I did not have the sense of wholeness. I knew I could endure and prevail, achieve the wholeness and completeness I sought and overcome any destructive forces in my life.

FONTANA: SPIRITUAL BENCHMARK

Each year, we returned to Fontana for a week or two on Licklog. At times, my wife and I returned without Amanda when she was Camp Mountain Lake, the Jewish summer camp. At times, it was all three of us. One year, it was the three of us, my brother and his family, and my father and mother. We stayed in a "mountain mansion" that year. Dad told me it was the first vacation on which he had ever been.

Each year at Fontana was a benchmark to measure growth, accomplishment, attainment, fulfillment, or failure against the standard of the previous year. My marriage was failing. Two people, two careers. Two high school sweethearts who married too young and who married for the wrong reason. Two adolescents who had a little in common, now two adults who had grown in different directions, had developed different values, and who got along by going along. With Fontana as the yearly benchmark, I knew that life was ebbing slowly and measurably from the marriage. Big talk was becoming small talk, small talk becoming no talk. Communication of any kind, physical, emotional, intellectual, or spiritual, was dwindling, subsiding to nothingness.

Dad said about politics, "You can't beat somebody with nobody." In a marriage, you can't beat something with nothing. Each year at Fontana, I saw more and more clearly the hopeless situation that I could not beat or overcome in any way on my own. You can beat back the waves, but you can't beat back the ocean. I was beating back waves. Yet, I did not believe in divorce. When all options were placed on the table, I had but one to choose. Endure. I endured until 1979 when even that option was taken from me, when I was told that the marriage was over and that I should do the noble thing. Move out. Ultimately, I returned to Fontana alone.

Fontana was special, singular. My increasing sense of despair was bearable there. From hopelessness, I would snatch solace through introspection in the natural peace I observed from the lofty Lookout Rock. From that high place, I had a macroscopic view of the world where no opposing forces could be seen, only the world in orderly harmony. I was above my own fray and perhaps my own petard, removed from my own conflicts.

As I sat in the back pew of Trinity on that Sunday, I began to make sense of my experience on Lookout Rock when I heard the voices singing. Something divine or otherwise had drawn me there like a magnet pulling on iron. The metaphor of the rock did not escape me. I heard the voices, and the voices unknowingly sang their message to me and for me. Somehow, the voices had found a way, a means of reaching me and speaking to me. Sitting there on the back pew, I made a commitment. *Next summer, I will find that church. I will add my voice to theirs, and I will sing my bass part so that "Amazing Grace" will drift eerily, uncanny and unearthly up the mountain, fading in and fading out but finding ears to hear.*

ACT YOURSELF TO A NEW WAY OF THINKING

As I sat on the back pew of Trinity United Methodist Church that Sunday, I knew I had left my spiritual side, left the spiritual characteristic of my individuality behind, and I knew that my growth and development had been unbalanced. I didn't experience personal integrity because the dependent and interrelated parts of my individuality did not complete the whole.

As Dr. Knapp had pointed out years before, I had to think about and work on my spiritual growth. I sat there and made my commitment, the commitment that I needed to make. I was determined to grow spiritually, to mature spiritually beyond childhood, beyond adolescence, and to develop spiritually commensurate with my physical, intellectual, and emotional development, and thus to make my spiritual resources more available and usable and to make latent values active in providing direction and purpose and fulfillment.

As I sat on the back pew thinking and willing and knowing, I heard the minister, O. Dean Martin, speaking. He was a rather quiet man, a handsome man, athletic in build, chaplain for the Florida Gators. He was a pastor who was articulate and positive, talking about what could be done for you and what had already been done for each of us. He was a man who had struggles himself and knew firsthand what struggles were like.

As I sat there, I heard Dean Martin speaking at the moment I was making the commitment I needed to make.

"It is easier to act yourself into a new way of thinking than it is to think yourself into a new way of acting."

I needed to hear that message at that moment. I accepted it then, and I accept it now. He didn't say that either way is easy. Neither way is easy. One is just easier than the other. I was both beginning and continuing a lifelong struggle. I was thinking too much, taking action not enough.

After that Sunday, my wife and daughter and I continued to go to Trinity. Eventually, we joined the church and joined Sunday school classes. My wife and I joined the Fisherman Class, comprised of a large group of outrageously extroverted people of all ages. They liked to sing old songs from the Methodist Hymnal, and they were dedicated to *Bible* study. Each Sunday, a member of the class taught the lesson from Methodist literature for adult classes. I began to grow spiritually, and the growth was real, having essence and substance. Unlike the charlatan television preachers, no one was manipulating me.

Every Sunday, we went to the worship service and then to Sunday school. On occasion, I taught the lesson. Not being particularly religious, I probably was more humanist than the class wanted me to be. I took a turn now and then as usher for the worship service. A church friend and I started a Methodist Men's Club, and about seventy-five men joined us once a month for a speaker program and a supper. I was called to the cooking ministry. I always cooked the supper.

One Sunday, an engineer in the Fisherman Class invited a friend of his to speak about an experience he could not explain. It involved a dispute between foreign students when he was a graduate student. He resolved the dispute by speaking a language he had not learned. He spoke to the leader of one group of these foreign students in the leader's own language and uttered a message he did not understand himself. He had to ask the student leader what he had said. He had spoken in a foreign language he had not learned. This understanding is the true meaning of speaking in tongues, not the ecstatic mumbo jumbo gibberish of Pentecostals.

This man held a doctorate in engineering. He obviously was moved by the isolated experience, and all of us could tell that he had genuine difficulty in telling this highly personal story. Not a religious man himself, he was apologetic, hoping the story had not offended anyone.

Afterwards, on the way home, my wife declared that she was not going back to the Fisherman Class or to Trinity. Period. Why? That man was obviously crazy, she said, and she was so put off that she was not going back. I kept going to Trinity and to the Fisherman Class each Sunday. Alone.

PLACE: THE TRIANGULATION OF SPACE, TIME, AND MEMORY

At one time or another, all of us tell others where we learned of something historical or of something otherwise significant to our interests and where we experienced something of note. My memory is linked and geared to emotion. I remember feelings, and I remember place. The physical environment and physical surroundings give fixity to the feelings so that I know where to find the feelings in my memory. Without emotion, my memory is less reliable. I don't remember the plots of books unless an emotional dimension triangulates on my feelings. I don't remember movies unless emotions are aroused. I have detailed memory of books and movies that aroused and evoked feelings.

As I sat in the pew in Trinity United Methodist Church on that first Sunday morning, I remembered. I remembered time and place and feelings. As I sat in that pew on that first Sunday morning, I understood. I remembered experiences, and I began to understand their meaning. Now, years later, I remember every detail of that pew on that first Sunday morning. I remember the place. I remember every detail of what went through my mind in that one hour. As I sat in that back pew on that first Sunday morning, I knew I had seen death and separation. I felt like a privileged vessel. It was horrifying and terrifying, but it was a privileged sight to be chosen to see death and separation. I had turned loose of one thing, but I now had hold of something else. I had found a place. I had found a safe place. I had found a home. Grace had led me home. It was not the religion. It was a place where I felt I belonged. As Robert Frost said, "Home is the place where when you have to go there, they have to let you in." I had the feeling of home.

D-I-V-O-R-C-E

Sometime in 1978, my wife and I were sitting under the large oaks behind our house, looking quietly over the cornfield where the owner ran some cattle and the red-tailed hawks soared and swooped to seize field mice. By that time, she had her own doctorate and held the position of Associate Dean of the School of Nursing. The setting was quiet and peaceful. We were quiet. Suddenly, she broke the silence.

"We've grown in different directions. I'm not going to follow you and the direction you've chosen. There's too much distance between us. I think I want to go my own way."

I didn't believe in divorce. I didn't want to hurt others. I didn't want to hurt my daughter, my father, or my mother. Nevertheless, I told my wife if she ever decided to go her own way, I would move out and find my own way.

"It's very noble of you," she said.

A year passed without another word on the matter. The distance between us grew exponentially, but she didn't speak further about going her own way. One Friday night in the spring of 1979, I again sat with my wife under the same oaks, watching the lightning bugs glow around us, listening to cicadas and green tree frogs whirr and peep above us. Suddenly, she broke the silence.

"You once offered to move out if I ever decided to go my own way. It was very noble of you. I think I've decided to be on my own. Could you give me a couple of hours to think about it some more? I need some time alone to think about it."

I walked to my car, a silver 1976 Oldsmobile Cutlass, and I drove down Newberry Road under I-75, turned left on Eighth Avenue, drove by Trinity where I slowed to look at the new sanctuary and kept going, just staring into the oncoming headlights, driving without any sense of destination. Then, in the distance I noticed some lights, lights installed high on standards, lights illuminating a baseball field. I parked the car and walked out of the darkness and into the light. It was a Little League baseball game. I sat on an embankment midway between home and the left field fence. I watched the game, the little boys playing the game, the little girls screaming in the stands, the mothers and fathers cheering their little boys on the field. When the game was over, I walked out of the light and back into the darkness. I knew that my marriage also was over.

AVAILABILITY, NOT ADEQUACY

In 1979, I was a stronger person than I had been. I had the strength of integrity, the wholeness and entirety and fullness and soundness of integrity that came from spiritual growth and development to match physical, intellectual, and emotional growth and development. I knew I would need the availability of all of these resources. Yet, I felt unworthy. I felt I had disappointed my family and my minister, Dean Martin. I felt I was not adequate to do what he had asked me to do.

Dean had asked me to teach an evening Discovery Class, which targeted new and renewed Christians with the intent of giving them the basics of Christian faith so that they could enter a regular Sunday school class without feeling out of place. I had knowledge of these Christian basics even if I did not believe them. As other religions have been, it was man who excogitated Christianity. I didn't feel I could do it. I also felt that if Dean knew I was going through a divorce, he wouldn't want me to teach the Discovery Class.

I made an appointment with Dean Martin. I was embarrassed as I sat before him. I started at the beginning and told him the entire story leading to the divorce. I didn't know what he would say. When I finished my story, Dean had two comments.

"First," he said, "I knew you were coming to church alone. You should have got out a long time ago. You did everything anyone could expect you to do to save your marriage, and you even did some things you shouldn't have done. Second, I know you don't feel adequate right now. God doesn't want your adequacy. He wants your availability. God can use any experience."

I taught the Discovery Class. I didn't feel adequate, but if Dean wanted my availability, he had it.

A woman in her early thirties was in the class. She had dark hair, she wore glasses, she was tall, and she was well proportioned. She was an ordinary looking woman. She was quiet during the first class. She introduced herself as a nurse. Before the second class the following week, she said she wanted to talk to me after the class if I had the time to listen. Afterwards, she and I stayed in the classroom. She said she had a dream after the first class. Maybe it wasn't a dream, she said. Dream or not, something told her to talk to me.

She began to cry quietly. She told me her husband was seeing another woman, and he couldn't make up his mind whether to stay with her or to leave her for this other woman he was seeing. She had done everything she could, but she just couldn't take it any longer. She had driven her automobile at a high rate of speed along a highway north of Gainesville, a road I knew well because I had run an out-and-back marathon along the highway. It was lined with huge oak trees on both sides, and the road was designated as a scenic highway. She told me she kept hoping she would lose control of her automobile and hit one of the oaks.

She looked at me and said, "I know what I'm doing. I'm trying to kill myself."

She kept saying she didn't know why she was telling me this story. Something just told her to talk to me. I told her what I thought about her situation, and I also told her my own story. Because of my situation, I didn't feel adequate to give advice, and I told her that she might want to discount any advice I gave her. She listened.

She finally said, "This has really helped me. What helped the most was hearing your own experience. I don't think what you said and what you advised would have meant as much to me if you hadn't experienced the same kind of thing I'm going through. You know what it's like to be betrayed and rejected."

Yes, I thought, *I know what it's like to be rejected. Rejection is what we fear the most. You probe beneath the surface of almost any fear and you'll find the fear of rejection.*

She kept saying that something told her to talk to me.

"You saved my life," she said, "and my soul."

I thought, *Dean, you were right. You or God can use any kind of experience. You were right, Dean. You wanted my availability, not my adequacy.*

THE HARDEST PART

My marriage failed. My mother and father came to Gainesville for our daughter's high school graduation in 1979. My wife asked me to tell them about the divorce while they were there. She also asked me to tell our daughter. She left me alone with my parents.

Mother, Dad, and I sat on the screened back porch. As I told them, I looked beyond the oaks to the cornfield where the cornstalks stood tall and straight, verdant and gold, waving at us, moving, growing, and maturing. My mother became tense and jumpy and quiet and resentful. My father did all the talking for them. He made it as easy as he could for me. I knew I could count on his support.

After her graduation, I told my daughter. Emotionally, I held up and held myself together. Amanda kept saying, "I don't know what to say." She cried. When I said all that I could say and she had cried herself empty and dry, she said she just needed to go out for a while and have some time for herself, some time to think. She left the room and left the house for the rest of the day.

I walked back to the master bedroom, looked out the sliding glass door, looked beyond the oaks to the cornstalks, but I couldn't see them. I couldn't see anything. I sobbed noisily, and I hoped the tears would wash away the hurt and pain. I sobbed uncontrollably. The pain and the hurt were still there. I loved my daughter so much, and the last thing I wanted to do was hurt her. The pain and hurt were more than I could bear alone. I knew that Amanda thought divorce was my decision.

RECONCILIATIONS

Over the years, I have been active in public speaking and lay speaking. One year in the 1980s, I gave an even hundred different speeches. That year, I was asked to speak at a Methodist church. I spoke on "Living in the Wake of Three Deaths," a personal message dealing with conflict and the need for conflict resolution. The three deaths were three kinds of death, *viz.*, death of a loved one, death of a marriage, and death of a dream. It was a message that dealt with the need to make us whole again, the need to restore us to soundness. It was a message that dealt with reconciliation.

Reconciliation is a need that arises from brokenness. The three different kinds of death were three different kinds of brokenness. All three kinds of brokenness represented separation, a violent separation into parts. When we are broken by life's setbacks, our wholeness is separated back into its parts. From this separation into parts, from this brokenness, a need arises to be made whole again. We need and yearn to be restored to our original soundness. In some cases, reconciliation is the process of making whole again or restoring to soundness. In other cases, reconciliation is the process of resolving dispute and returning to harmony.

When I spoke on the death of a dream, I made a reference to my daughter, Amanda. At the time, a distance separated us. She was twenty-five years old. She lived on her own. She had finished her degree in business at the University of South Alabama. I was her dean while she was a student there. I called her name at graduation. Yet, we were distanced. We were separated. We were broken.

I moved to New Orleans in 1989. Amanda continued to live in Mobile. She took a job with FDIC as a bank examiner. We rarely talked by telephone. We rarely saw each other. In 1990, Amanda called and said she wanted to visit me in New Orleans. I was thrilled.

When Amanda visited me in New Orleans, we went to Feelings Café in the Marigny Foubourg north of the French Quarter. It's an old slave quarters. We sat in the dining room and had a magnificent dinner. The talk at dinner was light and breezy. Amanda and I told some old stories about her childhood and adolescence. After dinner, we sat in the courtyard for an after dinner drink of Courvoisier.

Finally, after a long moment of reflection, Amanda reached for my hand. We sat together at the cast iron table and totally reconciled and restored our father-daughter relationship to wholeness.

Amanda simply said, "Dad, I love you. I want you to know that I...love...you." Tears were running down her cheeks. She continued. "Dad, I am so sick of the distance between us. I am tired of rebelling or whatever I've been doing. I want to love you, and I want to let you love me. I know you love me."

Love and be loved. All that matters. All we want. All we need. All we expect. After years of blaming me for divorce and more, all that mattered, all Amanda wanted, needed, and expected was to love and to be loved.

We sat in the courtyard a long time that night. We sat in the courtyard of Feelings Café and talked. We said the things we needed to say to each other. It was as though neither of us ever wanted to leave the preciousness of the time and place. It was as though we wanted to catch up all at once. Amanda and her Dad were reconciled. Amanda and her Dad were made whole again. Amanda and her Dad were restored to soundness. Amanda and her Dad were returned to harmony.

Amanda is doing well in her career. Amanda is doing well in her life, married to a college sweetheart, three stepchildren who she adores as her own. I am very proud of her. I love her. She loves me. Love and be loved.

I also spoke on the death of a marriage. The divorce I experienced was friendly. Our marriage came to an end. Amanda's mother and I recognized we would be our daughter's parents for the rest of our lives. She was no longer my wife, and I was no longer her husband. However, she would always be the mother of our daughter, and I would always be the father of our daughter. We would always be the mother and father of our daughter.

In 1992, Amanda wanted to have a birthday party. She was turning thirty-one. As a bank examiner, she was where the banks are during weekdays. As a rule, she was home only on weekends. Her birthday was on a Saturday, and she wanted to invite all her friends to a party. She wanted to have a band. She wanted to have her party in Mobile on the Dog River at a little place called The Dock, which sold fuel, beer, bait, and gear.

I paid for the band. I drove from New Orleans to Mobile for the party. Amanda's mother was there. She had remarried, and I met her husband. Her mother's sister and her husband were there. Amanda's mother and I took the dance floor, which was the dock itself, and danced a wicked jitterbug the way we did in the old days.

It was a great party. During a break, Amanda's family was gathered around her. Amanda suddenly said, "This is great! I want to thank everybody for being here together."

She looked at her mother and then at her father. Then, she said, "It's so. . . ." She paused, trying to find the right word. "It's so . . . *civilized.*"

I was proud of her. I was proud of all of us, all of us together. We were reconciled. It was so civilized.

ARTHURINE

Over the holidays of 1999, I stayed with John and Wanda Filer in Mobile, my best friends, and their teenage son, Jason, my godchild. Jason's former elementary teacher dropped by one evening, and I invited her to visit New Orleans sometime in January. I looked forward to her weekend visit.

On January 7, 2000, I began teaching my managerial economics course for Class 4 of the Executive MBA program. Executive students meet for classes every other weekend. On this first day of class, I asked one of the executive students on the front row if she knew how to make reservations for one of the romantic dinner cruises on the Mississippi River. I was directed to another student in the class, who was described as the all-knowing maven about social life in the city. After talking to her, she offered to email me a list of romantic venues. She even offered to make reservations for me.

The romantic weekend cratered. My invited weekend guest was unable to visit the Big Easy because of illness. Oh, well. As we say, easy come and easy go. Maybe the whole thing was fate. Thomas Hardy would have understood.

Still another student in Class 4 was a personal trainer, Leilani Heno. She talked her fellow students into gathering at City Park on the off Saturdays to run, walk, bike, or just hang. Knowing I am a runner, I was invited to join them. The following Saturday, January 15, I rose early, went for my usual sixteen mile run to Fontainebleau State Park and back, went to Morning Star Church for the prayer service at 9:00, and then left Mandeville at 10:00 for City Park.

I arrived just in time to run with the executive students. One of the executive students and his uncle were excellent runners. The three of us headed the pack, running at a five-minute pace or so, thus finishing a five-mile course under thirty minutes. Not bad, considering I had already run sixteen miles earlier that morning.

Afterwards, we waited until all others completed their run, walk, or whatever. Someone suggested we should go to Nick's for lunch. Sounded good to me, considering that I had run more than twenty miles without eating anything. Rather than take all cars, we decided to take four or five cars. My car was parked in front of the New Orleans Museum of Art where we were standing. The executive student who was reputed to be the all-knowing maven about social life in New Orleans went with me along with three others in the back seat. She was wearing a slinky running outfit. I noticed. I noticed a lot. She sat in front.

Minutes after we left, we were halfway to Nick's. Suddenly, I heard this voice from the passenger seat.

"I left my purse and wallet locked in my car. I don't have any money. I am so embarrassed. I'm sorry."

Being a gentleman, I offered to treat her to lunch, meaning she had to sit next to me at Nick's. Maybe the whole thing was fate. Thomas Hardy would have understood.

Her name is Arthurine Payton. At lunch, I decided I liked her. A lot. She was very pretty, very smart, and she wore the slinky running outfit that caught my attention. Afterwards when I dropped everyone back at City Park, I asked her if she would like to go to the Lake and talk for a while. She would.

We sat on a bench looking over Lake Pontchartrain. We talked for an hour or so. I asked her if she would like to meet somewhere for a casual dinner that night. She would.

We agreed to meet at Vasquez at 7:00. That night on the way to arrive early, I was caught in a delay on the twenty-four mile Causeway from Mandeville to New Orleans and arrived at 8:00, wondering if she was still there. She was. We had a nice dinner and talked still further. In one of the cheesiest pickup lines ever, I asked if she would like to hold hands so that people would know we weren't there on business. She wouldn't.

By now, I knew she had three sisters, the four of them known as the Payton girls, and that her father died just before she was born. Her father's name was Arthur, and her mother named her Arthurine in honor of her late father. She made a feminine name of Arthur like others made a feminine name of Gerald or Joseph, thus Geraldine or Josephine. Arthurine is not a unique name. There are at least two other ladies named Arthurine in New Orleans alone.

After dinner, I walked Arthurine to her car and being a gentleman, I opened the door for her. As she stood at the door, she kissed me. Not a grandmotherly peck on the cheek. She kissed me on the lips. My heart thumped all the way back across the twenty-four mile Causeway to Mandeville. In this way, Arthurine and I began our romance, which we kept separate from the classroom. She genuinely earned an A for the course as she did in her other courses.

Before meeting Arthurine, I had never been to a Mardi Gras parade, never been to Jazz Fest, never been to the French Quarter Festival. Sometime in late January, Arthurine told me I needed to know she went to every Mardi Gras parade, every day of Jazz Fest, and she was on the Board of the French Quarter Festival, meaning she certainly went every day of FQF.

She asked, "How about you?" I said, "Me, too." You'll say anything when you're courting a beautiful woman. So, I went to all of the Mardi Gras parades that year.

Arthurine also wanted to go to the Zulu Ball. New Orleans has a number of social aid and pleasure clubs. Founded in 1916, Zulu is the best known. It is a predominantly black carnival organization, and its parade rolls at 8:00 AM on Mardi Gras right before the famed Rex parade. Indeed, the first Zulu parades were parodies of Rex, King of Carnival. All Zulu riders in the parade wear outrageous black face and grass skirts.

On Saturday night before Mardi Gras, we went to the Convention Center for the Zulu Ball. I was one of few white men there. We were guests of Herbert McCarver, Leader of the Pin Stripe Brass Band, the official brass band of Zulu. Arthurine is beautiful. She is petite, weighing only ninety-six pounds, wearing size zero. At the Zulu Ball, she had on a sleek, colorful floor length gown. She certainly stood out in the vast hoard of revelers. I was proud to be in her company.

So it went that year, every parade for Carnival, every day of Jazz Fest, every day of French Quarter Festival. So it went every year after that first year.

In the fall of 2000, Arthurine went to Paris, France, with her classmates for their international experience. When she returned to New Orleans, I was at the airport to welcome her back home. I suggested dropping by the Bombay club, famed for its martinis. We sat at the bar while Gina made our martinis. When she served our martinis, I lifted my glass. Arthurine probably thought I would propose a toast to welcome her home. Instead, I said, "Will you...." She said, "Yes." I never finished the sentence with "...marry me?" Arthurine accepted my proposal before I finished it.

On May 26, 2001, Arthurine and I were married at St. Michael's Episcopal Church. Father Roy Pollina presided. My daughter, Amanda, was my best man. Yes, my daughter was my best man. The church was filled to overflowing. It looked like the U.N. Many of my students at one time or another attended, many of them international students. In addition to people of many different countries, people of different religions attended. Christians, Jews, and Muslims were our guests. Indeed, many of my Muslim students and friends had never been inside a church, never seen a mass, never seen a Christian wedding until that day.

Differences. Different countries. Different cultures. Different religions. I am a difference seeker, and I was very pleased that day with the consecration of our marriage midst such differences that brought us all together.

Oh, I forgot to mention that Arthurine Payton is black. Let me add, however, that black plus white does not equal gray. We lead very colorful lives.

BANGLADESH

In 2003, a fellow faculty member in the Department of Economics and Finance, Kabir Hassan, walked into my office. I knew he was from Bangladesh. Kabir surprised me. He said he was representing the President of his country, who also was the Chancellor of North South University, the first private university in the country. There are fifty-two private universities in Bangladesh, and the President is Chancellor of each one, meaning a Vice Chancellor runs the day-to-day operations of these universities. On the President's behalf, Kabir invited me to give the North South University convocation speech. I was honored, of course, but I knew I would need to discuss the matter with Arthurine. I knew she would be thrilled. I also knew she would insist on going with me.

That night, I brought up the opportunity. She reminded me that her grandfather was an observant Muslim from Calcutta. She somehow knew that Calcutta was less than a hundred miles from Dhaka, the national capital of Bangladesh. Indeed, she also knew that they spoke the same language in Dhaka as in Calcutta, *viz.*, Bengali. She also knew that Bangladesh and the Indian state of West Bengal once comprised Bengal. No one in her family had ever been to India. Arthurine would be the first to travel so near her grandfather's native country and state.

The next day, I accepted the invitation to deliver the Convocation address at North South University with one condition. My wife also must be invited. She was. We were in Dhaka for about fifteen days. Every morning and every afternoon, I made a presentation on different topics to government officials, businessmen, community leaders, or students.

Several days before the Commencement, we attended a Bangladesh wedding, a syncretic fusion of Indian and Muslim traditions. Arthurine dressed in an emerald sari with a choli underneath. She was invited to have a formal picture taken of all the women.

I sat at our table and looked upon the stage at the beautiful, colorful Indian dresses, and I could not help but notice Arthurine. She looked as Bangladesh as the Bangladesh women. Her grandfather would have been proud.

The day of the Convocation was a day of tight security provided by Bangladesh military men. After all, the country's president, Iajuddin Ahmed, was in attendance and sitting at the head table. I was deeply honored to sit next to the President, and I respected him immediately from the first of several substantive conversations.

I could have spoken on any number of business topics, but I chose instead to speak about purpose and integrity. I emphasized spiritual development and maturity, perhaps an odd placement of emphasis for a man of Christian up-bringing who is addressing an audience of Muslims. Before wrapping up my Convocation speech, I thought I would leave them with a little story.

Finally, I want to leave you with a story. A little more than twenty years ago, I learned that my father had terminal cancer. I moved across the country so that I could be close to him during the last year of his life. Indeed, I was with him when he passed away.

You think of so many things under such conditions, some strange and inexplicable. I found myself thinking, what do I mean when I say, "my father?" I know what I mean when I say, "my house" or "my automobile." The word "my" connotes ownership. I own my house, I own my automobile, but I did not own my father.

So, I kept thinking, what do I mean when I say, "my father?" I finally concluded that I meant I owned a special and unique relationship to him. After his funeral, it occurred to me that I meant the same when I said, "my students." I did not own my students, but I did own a special and unique relationship to them. My special and unique relationship to my father did not end when he died. He did not become my ex-father or my former father. He was still my father. In the same way, the special and unique relationship to my students does not end with final grades being posted upon the completion of my course.

For that reason, I have no former students, no ex-students, and no old students. All the students I ever had, they are still my students. They are my students for life.

I concluded the speech with one of my beliefs regarding people I care about. I don't believe in saying goodbye. I believe in saying see you later. I told them I cared about them and hoped to see them later. Afterwards, countless graduates and their families wanted a picture taken with me. Everyone had good things to say about my speech. Newspaper and television coverage picked up the emphasis on spiritual development and maturity, and they also seemed moved about "my students for life." They also wrote and said they hoped to see me later.

In 2008, we were invited by the President to return to Bangladesh to be the Commencement speaker for Northern University Bangladesh. We were in Dhaka for seventeen days. I made fifty-one different presentations on fifty-one different topics to fifty-one different groups. These presentations did not include my Commencement speech. On this second visit to Bangladesh, we decided to wear Bangladesh clothing rather than our American clothes. This small gesture made a big impact on the people. Wearing their clothes was an expression of acceptance that meant a lot to them. Indeed, we loved the country and the people so much that we adopted Bangladesh as our second country and those we met adopted us into the Bangladesh family.

A PROPER UNDERSTANDING OF FAITH AND RELIGION

When I was growing up, I often went to my father to ask him what a word meant. He always said, "Do you want a definition? Or do you want to know what it means?" I never wanted a definition. I wanted to know what people meant when they used a particular word. I remember a girl saying to me that she was "resigned to the fact" or perhaps used the word "reconcile." I didn't know what she meant. I went to Dad.

"Well, if you want to know the definition, we'll look it up in the dictionary. If you want to know what it means, I can tell you what it means."

Dad was good about that. He was not big on definitions. He always knew the meaning of words.

My experience has been that people have differing degrees of difficulty with faith because they don't know what it is. I never have found dictionary definitions of the word "faith" helpful at all. Invariably, a dictionary will tell us that faith is "unquestioning belief in God." Or that faith is "religion." A significant part of faith deals with understanding the seasonality of spirituality, understanding the seasons of spiritual growth. In turn, we need to understand what faith and religion are, understanding what faith and religion mean.

First, evidence is an outward sign or indication that furnishes some kind of proof. In turn, proof deals with cogency. Cogency suggests compelling agreement with an argument because of the sheer validity and soundness of its reasoning. Validity, in turn, deals with the impossibility of an argument breaking down. The reason the argument does not break down is because of its absolute conformity to correct reasoning. A valid argument evidences soundness, flawlessness in reasoning, and solidity in the grounds on which it is based. Proof is that degree of cogency arising from evidence that convinces the mind of any truth and thus produces belief. Proof is the effect of evidence. Evidence is the medium of proof.

Faith

What, therefore, is faith? In the fewest words, faith is belief not based on proof. Faith is belief not arising from evidence. In this sense, belief is conviction of the truth or reality of something, but the conviction is not based on grounds that are sufficient to support positive knowledge or proof. Usually, faith is belief that is based on personal experience and personal knowledge rather than on proof arising from evidence that because of its validity and soundness convinces the mind.

Marketing and advertising, for example, rely heavily on testimonials in certain kinds of commercials. Consider advertising campaigns for, say, laundry detergents. The ads present testimonials that are statements about personal experience intended to encourage belief in the efficacy of a product. In other words, testimonials in these commercials are used in lieu of proof arising from evidence.

When a dictionary defines faith as "unquestioning belief in God," it means that simple faith is conviction of the trustworthiness, the reliability, the truth, and the reality of God not because we have proof arising from evidence or positive knowledge, but because we have *personal* experience and *personal* knowledge of God in our lives. Knowledge *about* God is not the same as knowledge of God, which is experiencing God in our lives. Knowing God is trusting in something that is not physical. Simple faith is not cogent, not forcible in a physical sense. Simple faith is belief not based on proof.

Religion

Many times, I have been asked, "What is your religion?" My answer usually is "I'm a Christian." I don't add that I am skeptical about the fundamental details. For some reason, this answer stuns some people and astounds others. Most people say back to me, "Well, I didn't expect you to say that! I expected you to say you're Catholic, Baptist, or something like that."

There is an old joke that goes something like this. You know someone is Assembly of God because he will say, God says. . . . You know someone is Church of Christ because he will say, Jesus says. . . . You know someone is Baptist because he will say, the Bible says. . . . You know someone is Episcopal because he will say, it seems to me. . . .

There is a relationship between faith and religion, but the two are not parallel. Religion deals with a relationship to God. Indeed, religion is a relationship to God as manifested in faith and form of worship. The particular nature of faith colors the form of worship and religion, that is, a relationship to God.

Denomination deals with names and designations. Roman Catholic is a name given to a form of worship based on faith in Jesus Christ. Methodist is a name given to a form of worship based on faith in Jesus Christ. Baptist is a name given to a form of worship based on faith in Jesus Christ. Episcopalian is a name given to a form of worship based on faith in Jesus Christ.

Roman Catholics, Episcopalians, Methodists, Baptists, and other Christian denominations share a religion. What is the religion? Christianity. They give their forms of worship different denominations, different names, even though they have a common faith and a common religion. Different denominations are different names given to indicate different forms of worship, not different faiths and religions.

DIFFERENCES: ENDS AND MEANS

When I am invited to speak on spirituality *per se* or as a component of overall integrity, I speak from the only *personal* perspective I know. I was born into a Christian family in the same way that others are born into a Jewish or Muslim home. I speak from a Christian point of view. It's what I know best. I have total respect for other religions, however. I fully respect the Jewish and Muslim religions. In each case, religion is the same in terms of the end. Religion is a relationship to God. The end is the relationship to God. In each case, religion is different because the relationship to God is established and maintained through different *means*.

I'm afraid that many people talk about a relationship to God as though they own God. Because they own God, no one else can have a relationship to God unless it is established and maintained through the same means as their own. This way of thinking in terms of ownership is a creedal perspective taken to an extreme, which is dangerous. In effect, the belief is that, if it's not done my way, it doesn't count, it doesn't take.

To me, what is important is the end rather than the means. For believers, what is important is to establish and maintain a relationship to God. This relationship to God is the end, and it is an end that is common to Christian, Jewish, and Muslim religions. We differ in terms of means.

Some people cannot handle differences, any kind of differences. They marry people like themselves. They seek the company of those like themselves. If they are white Protestants, they marry white Protestants, and all of their friends are white Protestants. They cannot handle being in the company of black, Hispanic, or Asian people or people of Catholic denomination or of Jewish or Muslim religion.

Other people can tolerate differences. These people recognize differences. When placed in an atmosphere of differences, they can suffer through the experience and endure it without any sense of permanent harm. They are able to put up with differences.

Other people are difference seekers. I am a difference seeker. If all my friends were like me, I know I would be bored. I like being in the company of people who are different from me. Everywhere I have lived, my friends have been different from me. Consulting and related work has taken me around the world, at times for months. I worked in the Soviet Union in 1988 as a negotiator as well as consulting in Indonesia, Turkey, Nigeria, Dubai, China, and more. People of different cultures, traditions, and religions are interesting to me.

THE JEWISH CONNECTION

When I lived in Gainesville, Florida, most of my friends were Jewish. For a time, our daughter, Amanda, went to a Jewish summer camp in North Carolina every year. Camp Mountain Lake, a Jewish camp owned and operated by "Uncle Al" and "Aunt Nan" Savage of Miami. Nevertheless, Amanda fit. They thought her name was Amy Davidson. My best friends on the economics faculty were Phil Friedman, who is Jewish, and Harold Black, who is black. I loved Harold even though he was a Georgia fan. Indeed, he was one of the eight black students who were the first African-Americans to be admitted to the University of Georgia. My best friend was Nancy Horowitz. Her husband, Ira, is Jewish. I loved Ira even though he was a Yankees fan. I enjoyed the differences. I am like a magnet. I am attracted to opposites. Unless I am mistaken, opposites are attracted to me.

When I lived in Gainesville, I always contributed to the United Jewish Appeal. I made an annual contribution, and I responded with a contribution each time someone called me regarding a special cause. One night, I received a telephone call from someone in the local Jewish community. She asked me for a specific amount based on my history of giving. I readily agreed, telling her immediately that she could count on me for that amount. Then, she said she didn't know me, couldn't remember ever meeting me or seeing me at the synagogue. I began to explain that I was not Jewish. She cut me off in a piercing high-pitched whine.

"Not Jewish! What's your name doing on our list? That, I can take care of myself."

She apologized for calling, told me I didn't have to send any money, told me no one would ever bother me again because my name had been taken off the list, and hung up before I could get in another word. I sent my check anyway, and it was in the amount she stipulated. Money speaks louder than words, and my name was not taken off the list. That she couldn't take care of herself after all.

At about the same time, a Jewish friend, Raphael Lusky, was ill. He was an Israeli. Raffie had been an air force pilot in Israel before going to MIT to earn a doctorate in economics. He was one of our assistant professors in the economics department at the University of Florida. One day, he found a knot on his leg. It grew bigger quickly. It was cancer. Raffie needed blood. I had the same blood type that Raffie needed. For the first time in my life, I donated blood. I donated blood to Raphael Lusky. My blood didn't go into a blood bank. My blood went directly into Raphael Lusky.

Raffie fought the disease as courageously as he fought for the national defense of his country when he flew fighter jets. When Raffie died, I went to his funeral service at a local synagogue in Gainesville. It was deeply moving. I looked around and saw Christian and Jewish people in tears over the loss of someone we loved and respected. I saw Christian and Jewish people who could handle differences. They didn't just tolerate differences. They were Christian and Jewish people who were difference seekers.

DIFFERENCE SEEKING REDUX

I am a difference seeker. I don't believe I was born a difference seeker. I've learned to appreciate differences and to seek differences. In my case, difference seeking is learned.

There is an old joke about a country boy who was walking down a road with only one shoe on. Someone yelled out, "Did you lose a shoe?" He yelled back, "Nope. I found one!"

Differences are like finding two shoes to make one pair. In the business lexicon, complements are products that complete a set, *e.g.*, bagels and cream cheese, peanut butter and jelly, red beans and rice, breakfast cereal and milk, hotdogs and hotdog buns, gin and tonic.

Electromagnetism is one of the four fundamental forces in nature. The other three are gravity, the strong force responsible for binding protons and neutrons in the atomic nucleus, and the weak force responsible for particle decay in radioactivity. Teachers still bedevil their students with the question of whether gravity is stronger than electromagnetism. When the discussion winds down, a teacher points out some iron filings on a tabletop along with a magnet. Then, he or she delivers the punch line.

"It takes all the gravity of the entire Earth to hold those iron filings on the table top."

He or she picks up a small magnet from the table and holds it over the iron filings. The iron filings appear to leap from the tabletop to the magnet. Then, he or she shows students the iron fillings on the magnet.

"This tiny magnet I purchased at a dime store produces enough electromagnetism to overcome the gravity that it takes the entire Earth to produce."

Electromagnetism is responsible for interactions between charged particles. The same magnet that attracts particles with different charges also repels particles with the same charge. Magnetism in relationships is the same way. When two people are attracted because of their differences and interact in a relationship such as marriage, the differences can be charming and endearing at first. In time, however, the differences can seem less and less charming and endearing. The same differences that were charming and endearing can become grating and irritating. In time, the differences that attracted can repel. The same magnet that closes distance when it attracts opens up distance when it repels.

A story is told about the famous evangelist, Billy Sunday. After one of his fiery sermons, someone came to him and said, "Mr. Sunday, you rubbed my cat the wrong way." Billy Sunday retorted, "Well, brother, you better turn your cat around the other way."

When someone seeks differences and is attracted to differences, the magnet should be remembered. The same magnet that attracts also can repel. Like the Billy Sunday cat, you might need to turn the magnet around the other way so that it attracts rather than repels. Some people have turned he magnet around many times.

ENTROPY

Faith is a process. Although faith is not natural in the sense of chemistry and physics, it seems to be governed by some of the same laws. A simple statement of the First Law of Thermodynamics is that, in any physical process, energy can be neither created nor destroyed. Sometimes, this Law is called the "conservation of energy" because it says that energy will be conserved in any physical process even though it may be converted from one form to another. The Second Law of Thermodynamics states that physical processes are irreversible because some energy is always dissipated as heat. In other words, you cannot go from energy to work and back to energy again without some energy being dissipated as heat and thus lost to the physical process.

I think that the equivalent of these laws also affect faith. The concept of entropy comes from thermodynamics. It serves as an adjunct of the Second Law. The concept of entropy suggests the inexorable tendency of any closed system or process in the physical universe to slide toward a state of increasing disorder. Entropy deals with disorder and randomness that come from degradation of matter and energy to an ultimate state of inert uniformity. Within any physical process is also a process of degradation, a process of running down, a trend to disorder. Entropy is a measure of unavailable energy.

Faith, I believe, is subject to entropy. Faith is a process in which some energy is dissipated and lost to the process. As the energy from faith is dissipated, it is unavailable. Over time, disorder overtakes faith, and faith runs down and ultimately reaches an inert state unless new energy is invested continuously or discretely in the process. In other words, as energy from faith is dissipated, energy must be replaced to avoid a trend to disorder and inertness.

SPIRITUAL STRUGGLE

Spiritual growth is a lifelong struggle. At one time, I suppose I thought spiritual development and maturity are a destination. Once you arrive, you are there. From my own experience, I discovered that the spiritual characteristic of our individualities is more like a lighthouse. A lighthouse is not a destination. A lighthouse gives direction. At times, the spiritual characteristic of my personality gives me a bright light that indicates a strong direction and clear purpose. At other times, the spiritual side of my individuality gives me a dim light that indicates no clear direction and only obscure purpose.

I think I know what faith is. At times, I find faith simple and easy and real. At other times, I find faith to be complicated and difficult and otherworldly. At times, I need no proof arising from evidence, and I have great faith. At other times, I require great proof, and I have very little faith. The struggle with faith underlies my lifelong struggle with spiritual growth and development. Even when I need no proof arising from evidence, I still prefer proof. Even when faith wanes, I have a strong sense of humanism. Human means, human interests. When faith doesn't provide the basis for core values, the shoring of humanism props up and supports me spiritually.

Seasons

Proof arising from evidence makes everything a lot easier. If anyone wants me to believe something, show me the evidence, the validity and soundness of the reasoning, and the proof. I'm a tough customer when asked to believe something for which there is no evidence, no validity or soundness of reasoning, or proof. I find it most difficult to accept the basic tenets of any religion. I also have found that spirituality has seasons like natural divisions of the year. Indeed, my spiritual life itself is highly seasonal, spring, followed by summer, autumn, and winter.

In any culture, certain seasons are designated for legal purposes, religious purposes, social purposes, recreational purposes, and other purposes. The summer season is a natural division of the year. The Christmas season and the Lenten season are cultural. Christmas and Lent are divisions in the Christian year. Rosh Hashanah and Yom Kippur are highly important days, the most important days in the Jewish year, and Passover is cultural in the same sense. Deer hunting season is defined legally with a beginning and an end as artificial as the politicians who make the laws, including laws that govern hunting and fishing.

Characteristics that comprise our individualities experience growth and development. These characteristics also experience seasons. These seasons touch the physical, intellectual, emotional, and spiritual characteristics that make up our individualities, and thus touch our individualities. In particular, the spiritual makeup of our individualities goes through seasons that resemble the natural seasons of the year, spring, summer, autumn, and winter, although these seasons can last much longer than a year. I know that my own spiritual life has evidenced seasonality. At times, I have felt the stirring of spiritual aliveness associated with spring. At other times, I have felt the emptiness of spiritual desolation associated with winter.

From my firsthand experience, I know that my faith, my humanism, and my spiritual growth have seasons. I also know that the only times in my life when I have felt and sensed wholeness and completeness and fullness were times when my faith, my humanism, and my spiritual development were strong and vibrant. When I have been whole and complete, I have felt human as though the breath of life was in my nostrils. During the times of fractured individuality, I felt like I was perishing, living towards death in a dead world. At the times of integrity, I smelled an aroma, a fragrance of life and a fragrance from life to life.

Chapter Six
TEN RULES FOR PERSONAL INTEGRITY

THE UTILITY OF RULES

In economics, the word "utility" means the capacity of a good or service to satisfy a human want or need. Utility is a reference to usefulness and satisfaction. Certain wants and needs motivate the provision of certain goods and services that are fit for their intended use, which is to satisfy these wants and needs.

Rules are established guides for action and conduct. Rules are fixed principles to determine action, conduct, custom, and habit. Rules have utility. Rules have the capacity and power to satisfy certain wants and needs. Indeed, wants and needs motivate the establishment of rules that are fit for their intended use, which is to satisfy these wants and needs.

This notion can be called "the utility of rules." The utility of rules lies in their power to guide and determine action, conduct, custom, and habit. The utility of a personal rule lies in its power to inform a person what to do so that he or she doesn't have to think about it every time.

Gordon Tullock

I was introduced to the utility of rules by Gordon Tullock, a member of the economics faculty at the University of Virginia when I was a graduate student from 1964 to 1967. In the 1960s, Tullock also was a faculty fellow of the Thomas Jefferson Center for Studies in Political Economy. At the same time, I was a student fellow of the Center. Gordon Tullock was an unlikely economist. He never had taken a course in economics. His background was a Foreign Service Officer in the State Department. His only advanced degree was in law from the University of Chicago. He said he learned all the economics he needed to know by browsing around the Chicago law library. In fact, he said that he learned all the economics he needed to know by reading one book, *Human Action*, by Ludwig von Mises.

Gordon Tullock was very smart. He also was a brilliant and experienced debater. I think he had been on the debate team at the University of Chicago. He liked to needle people. Actually, Tullock liked to find each person's button and push it so that the other person went off like a skyrocket. I saw him do it countless times. Tullock was an irksome irritant. I liked him a lot.

While I was a graduate student, I was admitted only twice to the Colonnade Club, an exclusive club for faculty on the grounds of the University of Virginia. It was located on West Lawn between Patterson Alley and Colonnade Alley. The first time I was admitted was at the invitation of W.H. Hutt, a well known economist from South Africa. The other time was when Tullock invited me to join him for afternoon tea.

When I arrived to join him to talk about my doctoral dissertation research, Tullock was engaged in a heated discussion with a sociologist. The heat was one-sided as always. Tullock had heated up the other side while he remained totally calm and serene. Tullock and the hapless sociologist were discussing unilateral disarmament by the United States. They had reached a momentary impasse.

After a momentary lull, Tullock seemed to be lying doggo, concealed and prepared for ambush. "Okay," he said. "Tell me what you think would happen if the United States unilaterally disarmed."

The misfortunate sociologist was oblivious of the surprise attack that awaited him. "Well," he said, "I think the weight of world opinion would force the Soviet Union to disarm."

Tullock broke into his devilish smile, smug with satisfaction of his position. "By 'the weight of world opinion,' I suppose you mean the *New York Times*."

The clueless sociologist tried to divert the issue back to Tullock, still unaware he was about to fall on a well placed punji stick. "Well," he said, "what do you think would happen if the United States unilaterally disarmed?"

Tullock struck with suddenness. "I think we would be captured by Mexico."

The deflated sociologist slipped quietly through the doorway, chagrined and discomfited, one more victimized quarry of Tullock's skill. I was doubled over with laughter. Tullock was an irksome irritant. I liked him a lot.

During my first semester at the University of Virginia, I took graduate courses in economics and mathematics. One of the courses was "Seminar on the Theory of Simple Agreements" taught by Tullock. This seminar was the first of a two-course sequence. The second course was "Seminar on the Theory of Complex Agreements." These seminars were seminal courses on the discipline now known as Public Choice. During these two courses, I quickly learned to like Tullock and to respect him. In the second course, I wrote a paper that he liked. He encouraged me to develop the paper for publication. The paper was published as a monograph by the Thomas Jefferson Center, and an article-length paper based on the monograph was published in *Papers on Non-Market Decision Making,* a scholarly journal now called *Public Choice.* While working on drafts of the monograph and the article, I was a frequent visitor to Tullock's office.

One day, I sat in Tullock's office. We were discussing my dissertation. Tullock had his legs crossed. Tullock was a natty dresser although he wore more tweed and herringbone than absolutely necessary. He was unfailingly well dressed in loafers, slacks, and sport coat. Over the fifty years I have known him, I never have seen him in a suit or in lace-up shoes. I never have seen him without a tie. On this particular day, he wore his signature loafers, slacks, herringbone jacket, and a classic striped tie.

As he sat with his legs crossed, I noticed he didn't have cuffs on his dress trousers, which was unusual in the 1960s. I couldn't keep my mouth shut.

"Mr. Tullock, why don't you have cuffs on your trousers?"

Tullock looked down at his trousers where the cuffs should have been. He said, "Cuffs have no purpose. Their only function is to collect lint. Years ago, I made a rule. Never have cuffs on my trousers. That way, I never had to think about it again."

I couldn't leave it alone. "What do you mean, 'I never had to think about it again?'"

Tullock said, "I'm talking about the utility of rules. The utility of a fit rule is that you never have to think about something again. When I was a boy, I made a rule that I would never steal anything from a store. Since it was a rule, I never again had to think about stealing from a store. Without a rule, I would spend time on every occasion that I go into a store deciding whether or not I'm going to steal something. Over the years, I have saved a lot of decision-making time, which is time that can be devoted to something else."

Richard Feynman

Years later, I was reading a book, *Surely You're Joking, Mr. Feynman!* This book is a wonderful collection of stories told by the late Richard P. Feynman, a self-described "curious character" who won the Nobel Prize in physics in 1965. Early in his career, Feynman was trying to decide whether to stay on the physics faculty at Cornell University or to accept an offer to join the physics faculty at Caltech. He says that when you are young you worry about things and try to decide, but something else comes up.

"It's much easier to just plain decide," Feynman said.

Once you just plain decide, Feynman said, never mind the something else that comes up. The something else that comes up is not going to change your mind. Feynman said that when he was an undergraduate student at MIT, he grew weary of having to decide what kind of dessert he was going to have each time that he ate on campus at a cafeteria or off campus at a restaurant. He decided that it would always be chocolate ice cream. He says he never worried about it again, never had to think about it again. Just plain decide. Make a rule, and you never have to think about it again.

MICROSCOPIC AND MACROSCOPIC RULES

After learning about the utility of rules from Tullock, I made the first of many rules. On the way home in my automobile, I thought about how far I should stay behind the car in front of my own automobile while stopped at a traffic light. While sitting at a traffic light that day, I made a rule. The rule was that I would stay far enough behind the car in front of me to see its rear tires. I never had to think about it again. I never have thought about it again. I still stay far enough behind the car stopped in front of me to see its rear tires. It's a rule.

A number of years later, when I was a competitive long distance runner, I found I couldn't moderate my consumption of ice cream. If I had ice cream in the freezer, I would eat all of it. I would start with a bowl of two or three scoops from the container. Then, I'd tell myself that one side of the container was higher with ice cream than the other, and I would scoop more of the high side to even it out. Next, I would decide that the other side was now higher and scoop out still more ice cream in the attempt to even it out. Sooner or later, I'd eat a heaping bowl of ice cream. After I finished the heaping bowl of ice cream, the ice cream in the freezer would call to me like an insidious, enticing siren, like Circe, the sorceress who enchanted the companions of Ulysses and transformed them into swine.

I made a rule. I decided never, ever to have ice cream in the freezer. I never had to think about it again. Afterwards, I discovered something remarkable. I found moderation of ice cream extremely difficult. I found giving it up extremely easy. I loved ice cream so much that I couldn't moderate my consumption of it, but I didn't miss ice cream at all when I gave it up. I never thought about it again.

The great advantage and the great usefulness of rules is that you never have to think about something again. You just plain decide.

In my life, I've found that I respond well to rules. I recommend rules to others. Not necessarily my rules, but I recommend establishment of rules that are fit for their intended purpose, which presupposes a purpose in the first place. Rules can be microscopic in the sense that they deal with the lowest level of decisions such as how far you stay behind the automobile in front of you. Rules can be macroscopic in the sense that they deal with the highest level of decisions such as how you keep your body as strong and healthy as possible.

Over the years, I have established many rules for my life. These rules are guides to my actions and conduct, guides that I needed. On the other hand, I have failed to establish rules that I needed to serve as guides for my actions and conduct. I also have established rules that I broke for a time before respecting them again. O. Dean Martin, the late minister of Trinity United Methodist Church in Gainesville, Florida, once said of the rules we call the Ten Commandments, "We do not break the Ten Commandments. We are broken by them." Indeed, Maimonides codified 613 commandments in the Hebrew Bible, 365 negative and 248 positive. Mostly, we ignore 603 of the 613 commandments and are broken by ten, the Decalogue. When I established rules and later did not respect the rules, I didn't break the rules. I was broken by the rules. I lost the utility of the rules. Sooner or later, I went back to the rules.

THE TEN RULES

No purpose could be served in enumerating and giving expression to my own microscopic, day-to-day rules. For example, I established a rule a number of years ago to wear over-the-calf socks with a suit. I never had to think about it again. When I was a competitive runner, I had a rule that I wouldn't drink any calories. Later, when I retired from competitive running, I also retired the rule. Over the years, however, I've also ascertained certain overarching rules that govern a large part of our overall lives. Specifically, I enumerated ten rules that apply to all of us. The ten rules have utility for all of us. In other words, all ten rules have usefulness and the power to satisfy certain wants and needs.

These ten rules deal with the physical, intellectual, emotional, and spiritual aspects and characteristics of our lives. These ten rules are fit and useful. If these ten rules are adopted as a guide for conduct and action, all of us will take care of our whole person. In this way, all of us will grow and develop toward wholeness and fullness. The utility of rules, ten rules. You just plain decide, and you never have to think about it again.

1. SWEAT EVERY DAY

The first rule is: *sweat every day*. Boy or girl, man or woman. Establish a rule that you sweat every day. Our bodies were not created for idleness. Our bodies were not created to exercise the brain only. For the purposes of physical health, physical strength, and physical stamina, we must have a strategy. To achieve these purposes of health, strength, and stamina, one strategy is to establish a rule. Sweat. Sweat every day. This simple rule is a strategy. You never have to think about it again.

When I turned thirty, I began to jog. At first, jogging required dogged discipline but later became fun, something to which I looked forward. Eventually, I entered races. I entered 5Ks (3.1 miles), 10Ks (6.2 miles), and marathons (26 miles, 385 yards). At one time, my running regime entailed 114 miles per week, more than five thousand miles annually. If anyone chooses to run more than one hundred miles weekly, he or she is running for some purpose other than basic physical fitness. For the purpose of basic physical fitness, a daily twenty-minute jog is enough. In other words, a daily jog of two miles is enough. Or walk thirty minutes at or under a pace of fifteen minutes per mile. Or swim. Or ride a stationary bike. Or use a treadmill. Just plain decide. Establish a rule that you sweat every day. In addition, bear in mind that muscle loss after age forty-five is one percent per year. Resistance or strength training also should be included in a physical fitness regimen.

I Don't Have Time, and I'm Too Tired

Many excuses are convenient alibis for not exercising. These excuses are too, too convenient. The excuses I hear most often are "I don't have time" and "I'm too tired."

First, consider the time excuse. Time is democratic. Rich or poor, we all have twenty-four hours in a day. "I don't have time to exercise" means "I don't place priority on time to exercise." Establish a rule to sweat every day, and you never have to think about it again. After placing high priority on time used to exercise, the time is there after all.

Second, consider the "I'm too tired" excuse. Physical exercise is energizing, not enervating. When too tired to exercise, it's a good time to exercise. Physical exercise gives energy. Physical exercise does not take energy away. When I first began to run, I often found myself tired and sleepy when I came home from campus. After I ran, I found the sluggishness dissipated, and I enjoyed a vital evening attributable to the physical exertion. Establish a rule to sweat every day, and you never have to think about it again.

Other Customs, Other Habits

When you sweat every day, you also tend to gestate other changes in your life. One change in your life leads to another change. When I was running more than a hundred miles every week, I lost my taste for red meat. I also lost my taste for chicken skin and for fried food of any kind. Fat in either red meat or chicken skin and fried food just didn't taste good any more. My body was sending me a message, telling me something. Fat takes a long time to metabolize, as much as twenty-four hours. For that long time, fat is tying up red blood cells in the metabolism process, thus employing red blood cells that are not available to carry oxygen.

After eating red meat or fried food, I found my running performance measurably and significantly diminished. I felt downright sluggish. My workouts were poor. I didn't establish a rule to eliminate fat from my diet. I didn't need a rule. I just lost my taste for fat in red meat, chicken skin, or any other food. I found myself craving carbohydrates such as pasta and rice mixed with protein such as black beans. My routine diet changed for the better when I began to sweat every day. My improved diet required no discipline. My tastes simply changed. I rarely eat red meat. I still do not eat fried foods. I still do not eat chicken skin. I mostly eat seafood and vegetables.

Almost always, people who establish and respect a rule of sweating every day also develop other customs and habits that are beneficial to good health. I think these valued by-products of sweating every day are due to a growing focus on the body and taking care of your body. These people eat more of the foods that we now know are good for you and less of the foods that we now know are bad for you. Eating better and drinking less are beneficial by-products of the rule regarding daily exercise. In almost all instances, these by-products are not the result of additional rules. These by-products are not the result of additional discipline. They are outcomes of the basic, underlying rule to sweat every day.

For people who want to develop and maintain a disciplined program of exercise, I recommend *The Aerobics Program for Total Well-Being,* written by Kenneth H. Cooper, M.D. This book deals with all forms of physical activity leading to sweat, and it details how much of each form of sweating is needed for physical fitness. In fact, the book deals with exercise, diet, and emotional balance. More than any other person, Dr. Cooper is the man who started America running. His earlier book, *Aerobics,* first published in 1968, started me running and sweating, sweating every day.

Drink Plenty of Water

Of course, when we sweat every day, we need to drink plenty of water. Thirst is a symptom of dehydration. If we experience thirst, our body is telling us that we are not drinking enough water. A rule of thumb for daily water consumption is a half-ounce per pound of body weight. Therefore, a person weighing 128 pounds should drink a half-gallon of water (sixty-four ounces) daily. Set a half gallon bottle of water in the refrigerator, and see if you drink it over the course of a day. If you weigh more than 128 pounds, you should be drinking more than a half-gallon of water. If you weigh 256 pounds, you should drink a full gallon of water daily.

You should never suffer from thirst. Keep in mind, however, that vegetables and fruits are constituted of a lot of water. Vegetables and fruits are water-rich. When you eat vegetables and fruits or drink vegetable or fruit juices, you don't need as much pure water. The key, as always, is to listen to what your body is telling you. Thirst is a message that your body is sending you. The message is, drink more water systematically so that you don't suffer the symptoms of dehydration.

2. DON'T START WHAT OTHERS ARE TRYING TO QUIT

The second rule is: *don't start what others are trying to quit.* For the purposes of physical health, strength, and stamina, one rule rises above all others, paramount over physically exercising, taking vitamins and minerals, or eating the right foods. One rule contributes more to physical health, strength, and stamina than any other. If you smoke, quit. If you do not smoke, don't start.

Smoking is not a habit of ignorance. Ignorance means uninformed. Everyone in America is informed and, indeed, well informed about smoking cigarettes. Cigarettes kill people. Cigarettes make your body sick and unhealthy. Cigarettes rob your body of physical health, strength, and stamina.

Smoking is not ignorant. Smoking is stupid. People who are well informed about the known deleterious effects of smoking but still choose to smoke cigarettes may be smart people, but smoking is a lapse of intelligence, an act of stupidity. Smart or not, smoking is crassly foolish. Smart or not, smokers are strangely and inexplicably in a dazed and benumbed state of mind about smoking and its killing consequences.

The Ugliness, Recklessness, Harmfulness, and Deadliness of Smoking

I do not understand smoking. People don't smoke because they enjoy it. People don't smoke because it gives them pleasure. People smoke because they are addicted to a drug, *viz.*, nicotine, and they smoke to avoid the withdrawal symptoms. People light up a cigarette to avoid the withdrawal symptoms of nicotine denial.

I do not understand smoking. I have stopped at a traffic light and seen what I am sure is an otherwise intelligent and caring young mother light a cigarette in a closed automobile with small children as passengers. In this stupid and uncaring way, this mother subjects the tender, developing lungs of her own children to the killing effects of cigarette smoke in the closed automobile.

I do not understand smoking. I have seen people sit in an expensive restaurant, prepared to spend a hundred dollars a person on fine dining. Then, they light a cigarette, which decimates the capacity and power of taste buds to distinguish tastes.

I do not understand smoking. I have seen beautiful women, who have spent substantial amounts of money to present themselves to attract men, and then light a cigarette and thus repel men because of the ugliness of a cigarette dangling from an otherwise attractive mouth. I have seen beautiful women, who have spent substantial amounts of money to purchase an expensive fragrance that carries the diffused essence and scent of flowers about their bodies, and then light a cigarette and consequently stink from the overriding odor of cigarettes in their clothes, on their hands, on their bodies, and on their breaths.

I do not understand smoking. I have seen people sit in a doctor's waiting room, coughing and hacking and hawking up phlegm, waiting for a physician to heal them or relieve their symptoms, when they could be treating themselves by removing the cause of the ailments that brought them to the doctor's office in the first place, *viz.*, smoking cigarettes. I have seen my own father die in my arms from lung cancer caused by smoking Camel cigarettes.

Whatever We Do, We Recommend to Others

I do not understand smoking. Nothing is worth what smoking does to us and to our loved ones. Nothing. What smoking does to the smoker is bad enough. What smoking does to others is even worse.

Whatever we do, we recommend to others. When a father has his own children as passengers in his automobile and drives that automobile recklessly, he recommends reckless driving to his children. When a father has his own children as passengers in his automobile and drives that automobile while drinking, he recommends driving while drinking to his children. When a father eats junk food in front of his overweight child, he recommends eating junk food to the overweight child. When a father smokes cigarettes, he recommends smoking to his children. Nothing is worth what smoking does to us and to our children. Nothing.

Discrimination Against Smokers

Over the years, I've known a lot of corporate recruiters and human resource managers. When we talk privately over lunch or dinner, they have credibly sworn to me that they never knowingly or willfully discriminate on the basis of race, gender, religion, or national origin. However, they have told me that they would never knowingly hire a smoker. The usual reasons given are that smokers run up health insurance costs and that they are less productive, taking time from work to smoke or working with the distraction of not being able to smoke. They also have told me that smokers are stupid, and they are not interested in hiring stupid people. Such recruiters and managers are very clever about finding out whether someone is a smoker.

Never Too Late

Many people who smoke are trying to quit. All kinds of products and programs have been developed to aid people who are trying to quit smoking. People who are trying to quit smoking deserve our help and support in this positive direction for their lives.

People who are trying to quit smoking should serve as a powerful example to young people who might start smoking. When these young people see how difficult quitting smoking really is and how much time and money are spent on quitting smoking, they ought to see that preventive measures are highly superior to later corrective measures. The problems of smoking can be prevented by not smoking in the first place. Prevention is highly preferred to correction. However, the damage from smoking can be arrested by quitting.

I shouldn't say it is *never* too late to quit smoking. For my father, it was too late to quit smoking Camels once he had terminal lung cancer. In general, however, it is not too late. Anyone who smokes is damaging his or her lungs and heart. We are told that every cigarette smoked reduces life expectancy. Anyone who has smoked has damage. The damage can be arrested and, within limits, reversed upon quitting.

Sweating and quitting smoking go well together. They are complements, like a right shoe and a left shoe make a pair, like peanut butter and jelly make a sandwich. Sweating and quitting smoking are complements, completing a set or a pair of strategies, a set or pair of rules that jointly achieve the purpose of physical health, strength, and stamina.

Let me say once against that smoking is not a moral issue. Smoking is a physical issue. It is a health issue. People who smoke are not immoral. Smokers are merely stupidly and foolishly inuring themselves to the known killing consequences of their smoking.

Drinking, Gambling, Abusing Drugs

Smoking is not the only addiction with disastrous consequences. Many people are trying to quit drinking. They may be alcoholics who lose everything, their families, their homes, and their jobs. Or they may be people who function in their day-to-day lives and on their jobs, but who in clever ways mask and hide the degree and extent of their drinking problem from their employers, their families, their friends, and others.

I know people who have established rules regarding their drinking. A business acquaintance sets a limit of two drinks a day. If he misses either one or both drinks on a given day, he does not make it up on another day. Another business acquaintance established a rule that he never drinks during the week, Sunday through Thursday. These rules have utility for the men who established them.

Some things that go without saying need to be said. Drug abuse, whether prescription drugs or otherwise, is something no one should start. Once started, drug abuse should end. Period. Furthermore, many people cannot control their gambling. Some of these people establish rules that limit their gambling to controllable levels. I know someone who likes to play blackjack at a casino. When he plays, he takes a hundred-dollar bill. He buys a hundred dollars in chips, and when the chips are gone, he is gone. In this way, his gambling is controlled and limited to losses of one hundred dollars.

If you start something that other people are trying to quit, then quit when you find that you cannot control it. Or establish a rule that will keep the something under your control. Or establish a rule after you find it's a problem. The rule sets genuine limits that bring the problem under control and keep the problem permanently under control. Let me say again, I found I couldn't moderate my consumption of ice cream. I gave up having ice cream at home. I didn't give up ice cream altogether. I still buy an occasional cone of ice cream. The amount of ice cream is measured and controlled by someone else. By making a rule that I never have ice cream in my freezer at home, I established a rule that limits my consumption of ice cream to controllable amounts that are comfortable for me.

Moderation is not the answer in many cases. Abstinence is the only path. The rule is abstinence in the case of marijuana, cocaine, heroin, opium, or other drugs. In the case of such drugs, the rule is simple. Never, ever, do such drugs under any circumstances. Period.

Rabbit Tobacco

I am reminded of the time I was listening to radio news back in the late 1960s or early 1970s. A story out of Nebraska was reported. It seems that farmers in Nebraska discovered the "rabbit tobacco" they smoked as youngsters was actually marijuana. It grew wild all over the state. Hemp had been planted so that the tough fiber could be used for cordage. The Nebraska legislature undoubtedly included a number of men and women who had smoked "rabbit tobacco" as youngsters. The question was whether to legalize what legislators had smoked in their youth.

My mother had told me about smoking "rabbit tobacco" when she was a girl growing up in Mississippi. I seemed to remember that the military planted hemp all over Mississippi. After hearing the Nebraska story, I couldn't wait to ask her more about "rabbit tobacco." When I saw her two or three months later, I asked her to describe "rabbit tobacco."

"Well," she said, "it was bright green. It had slender leaves that were jagged and fanned out like a man's hand."

I asked her about how they prepared it. "Well," she said, "we pulled it out of the ground and laid it upside down on a big rock or something like that. Sometimes, we would hang it upside down from a tree branch. We let it dry out in the sun. When it dried, we crumbled the leaves off the stems, threw away the stems, and that was our rabbit tobacco. We rolled it up in cigarette papers and smoked it."

I asked her about what it did to her and how she felt when she smoked it. "Well," she said, "we would just laugh and laugh. It made us real silly. And hungry. It made us real hungry."

I didn't have the heart to tell her. She would have died if she knew she smoked marijuana. As an act of kindness, I never told her.

What Determines How Fast Our Bodies Age?

In Dr. Kenneth Cooper's book, *The Aerobics Program for Total Well-Being*, he writes about the rate at which bodies age. He asks the basic question, "Who determines how fast [our bodies] age?" He answers his own question. "You do!" He continues by saying,

"And here are three main things, mostly likely in this order that accelerate the aging process:

Cigarette smoking

Inactivity

Obesity

If you wish to slow down the aging process in your own life, I am convinced that you must eliminate all three of these factors."

To slow down the aging process in your own life, Dr. Cooper says, you must eliminate cigarette smoking, eliminate inactivity, and eliminate obesity. The first two rules for personal integrity address all three factors. Sweat every day, and don't start what others are trying to quit. A corollary of the second rule is, once you start what others are trying to quit, join the others who are trying to quit and quit with them. Sweat every day. No smoking. You will find that you lose weight because you will burn up more calories, and you will find that your eating habits change as a byproduct of exercise.

3. GET ENOUGH SLEEP

The third rule is: *get enough sleep*. America has become a nation of people who suffer from sleep deprivation. More than twenty percent of us suffer from significant sleep deprivation. We just don't sleep enough. We know that a good night's sleep as a matter of routine and pattern means better health, better mental state, greater productivity, and fewer accidents. Some of us require more sleep than others, and some of us require less sleep than others, but all of us need enough sleep to meet our own personal requirements. Establish a rule to sleep enough. Operationalize the rule. Making a rule to sleep enough is fine, but establishing a routine that is concrete and measurable is better.

I hate to be awakened by an alarm clock. I might set an alarm clock just to ensure that I won't oversleep, but I almost always wake up before the alarm sounds. In other words, I don't use an alarm to awaken me in the morning. I wake up on my own. Actually, I tend to wake up at daybreak. Year-round, I am up no later than 6:00 every morning, including Saturday and Sunday.

To get enough sleep, I know what time I have to go to bed at night. I stay up later on Friday and Saturday nights, but I take a nap on Saturday and Sunday afternoons. The only times I ever rely on an alarm is when I have to rise at, say, 4:00 for a plane flight or whatever. I just have a rule that I won't depend routinely on an alarm clock to wake me up. If I depend routinely on an alarm clock to wake me up, I know that my body is telling me that I am not getting enough sleep routinely.

Natural Sleep

To be truly restful, sleep should be natural. Natural sleep is self-generated rather than induced by drugs, including alcohol. To know the time when you naturally awaken, you must be yourself for a period of days long enough to determine your natural time to awaken. If you drink a six-pack of beer every night, you aren't yourself when you go to sleep. You don't rest fully from your sleep because the natural stages of sleep are disturbed by the presence of substantial alcohol in the bloodstream and thus in the brain.

Some of us have genuine sleep disorders that make falling asleep and staying asleep extraordinarily difficult. For such people, medicating themselves with alcohol is not the answer. Taking over-the-counter or prescription drugs is not a solution to the problem. Alcohol and sedatives treat symptoms rather than remove the root cause of the problem. Find the root cause of the problem, address strategies to make the root cause of the problem go away, and the problem goes away with it.

I'm not saying that rules regarding sleep also are rules against alcohol. Personally, I enjoy a glass or two of wine with dinner. I enjoy a glass or two of wine in a social setting. When I am sitting in the stands at a ballgame, I enjoy a hot dog and a beer or two. A routine or pattern of drinking too much every night before going to bed will disrupt natural sleep, however.

Getting enough sleep deals with the quantity of sleep. Getting enough natural sleep deals with the quality of sleep. Getting a good night of sleep and rest deals with both the amount of sleep and the quality of sleep.

4. CONTINUE TO LEARN OVER A LIFETIME

The fourth rule is: *continue to learn over a lifetime.* I like old sayings. One old saying is, "You can't teach an old dog new tricks." To most people, I suppose this old saying is an excuse or an apology. To me, it means we need to work against becoming an old dog. As Dad said, as long as you learn new tricks, you'll never be an old dog! In the 1960s, someone in his nineties began to learn Spanish. Perhaps the man was Bertrand Russell. When asked why he was learning Spanish at his age, he said, "If I don't start now, I won't get it in." Such people are never an old dog. Even in his nineties, he was learning new tricks.

Learning involves a will to gain knowledge or understanding of something or a will to gain a skill in something by study, instruction, or investigation. If you consider learning to be a process and if you make a rule that learning will be a lifelong process, then you never have to think about it again. At any given time in your life, you should be learning something by study, instruction, or investigation. In some ways, learning is another word for exercise, in this case exercise for the muscles of the mind and its intellect. As long as you're learning and working out the intellectual characteristic of your individuality, you're staying alive intellectually and staying in shape intellectually. You're taking care of your intellectual health, strength, and stamina. In the process, the things learned are rewarding and fulfilling.

In my own life, I've had a lifelong love affair with learning. In every case, learning has come through study, instruction, and investigation. I formally studied economics and learned it through a terminal degree in the discipline. I received years of instruction in economics from some of America's best economists, including one Nobel Laureate, James M. Buchanan.

On my own and without formal instruction, I have studied literature, history, theology, and physics. By the time I was graduated from high school, I had read enough to have the equivalent of a literature major in college. I've read critically all of William Faulkner. When reading *The Sound and the Fury*, I learned to build up a family tree of the characters in a Faulkner novel. In the case of this particular book, written in stream of consciousness, I also learned to build up an account of the events that occur so that my mind can organize and assimilate the story. Years later, I still have my copy of *The Sound and the Fury*. On an inside page of the book, my rendition of the family tree of the characters and my account of the events occurring in the book are still written there.

Cooking as Learning

I learned to cook from my mother. When I left home, I missed her country cooking. I missed her biscuits in the morning. I missed her creamed corn, her mashed rutabagas, her candied yams, and her other country dishes. When I visited her, I watched her cook. She never used a recipe for anything. I just watched her to learn what she put into what she was cooking. Back home in my own kitchen, I guessed at measures of each ingredient. Through trial and error, I discovered her recipes. I still use them.

My obsession with discovering her recipe for biscuits didn't work at first. I watched her make biscuits and figured out her recipe. However, my biscuits didn't come out the way her biscuits did, high and light. I finally found I had to use her recipe, and I had to use her method. She mixed the ingredients in a bowl. She touched the dough ball as little as possible. She took the dough ball out of the bowl, put it on a floured board, and rolled it around only enough to flour the outside of the dough ball. Then, she squeezed off a little ball of dough, rolled it around in her hands as little as possible to shape it, and put the shaped dough in an iron skillet. This technique is called drop biscuits. She totally filled the iron skillet with biscuits. When she filled the iron skillet with biscuits, the biscuits had only one direction to expand when placed in the oven. Up. Those biscuits rose. Because she filled the iron skillet with biscuits, they rose and had no crust on the sides. Well, the biscuits on the interior had no crust on the sides. The biscuits on the outer edge of the iron skillet had a golden crust on the side touching the iron skillet. Through trial and error on both recipe and method, I learned how to make her biscuits. I still make them.

Operationalizing Rules

Rules with respect to learning have utility. I do not think making a rule to learn is sufficiently operational. To have utility, I think that rules must be operational, which makes them concrete and measurable. When a rule is operational and measurable, you know whether or not you're respecting the rule. For example, I have a microscopic rule about reading a book at all times. As soon as I finish one book, I immediately begin another one because I don't want to find myself between books.

One night in the 1960s, I had a hundred pages or so to read in John Steinbeck's book, *The Grapes of Wrath*. I couldn't put the book down. I finished it at about 2:00 AM. I was emotionally overcome by its ending, in which Rose of Sharon breast feeds a starving man with the milk of human kindness from her breasts. I knew I would have trouble sleeping. I stuck with my rule to begin another book. I never go to sleep at night not having a book I'm reading. Having finished one, I had to begin another. I went downstairs where my books were located at the time, and I looked for a book I felt would put me to sleep. I quickly decided on Steinbeck's non-fictional book, *Travels with Charlie,* his account of traveling around the country with an old one-eyed standard poodle named Charlie. Rather than being bored to sleep as I expected, I was totally absorbed. I stayed up the rest of the night and finished it.

The next morning, I thought about the only other reference to "grapes of wrath" I could recall. In 1861, abolitionist Julia Howe composed the *Battle Hymn of the Republic* after visiting a Union army camp on the Potomac River near Washington, D.C.

> *Mine eyes have seen the coming of the Lord:*
> *He is trampling out the vintage where the grapes of wrath are stored;*
> *He hath loosed the fateful lightning of His terrible swift sword:*
> *His truth is marching on.*

In Biblical references, "grapes" represent people or nations judged or destroyed by God because of their wickedness. In other words, there is a final harvest of the grapes, a final harvest of the wicked. In the bloodiness of the Civil War, Julia Howe foresaw the inevitable divine event when Jesus returns to judge all people and all nations.

A Pain in the Neck

In April 1992, I had surgery for a ruptured disk in my neck. My doctor said it looked like an old injury that had degenerated over the years until the disk finally ruptured. He thought it probably was the final outcome of an injury incurred while playing center in high school football and butting nose guards.

After surgery, I had a month of convalescence at home. In that month, I read. I read all the time. I decided to keep an ongoing list of books that I read for the remainder of my life. I sat down at my computer and created a directory for books, and I have kept the list current from that time. I average about six books a month. Each time I make an entry of all information that I log for each book, I am reminded that computers also are something that I chose to learn as an adult.

George Leonard once wrote a book, *Education and Ecstacy,* in which he suggested that learning might be the purpose of life. Well, I'm not so sure about learning as the purpose of life. I think of learning rather as a means than as an end. Certainly, learning is a means of gaining knowledge about or of understanding the purpose of life and, in this sense, giving purpose to life. However, learning is not the end to which life is purposed. Still, a never-ending journey of learning is critical to living a life of integrity, a life of wholeness comprised of physical, intellectual, emotional, and spiritual characteristics that are growing, developing, and maturing throughout our lives.

I once introduced a friend of many years as an "old" friend, and my "old" friend told me he had reached the age when he didn't like to be called an "old" anything. Now, I'm old enough that I understand my "old" friend completely. I especially don't ever want to be an old dog. I keep from being an old dog by continuously learning new tricks. I keep the intellect in me growing and developing and maturing through learning.

In May 2005, I attended two graduation ceremonies, both my own. First, I was graduated from the School of Theology of the University of the South (Sewanee) for completion of the four-year program of theological education (by extension), otherwise known as Education for Ministry. Only two weeks later, I was graduated from the School for Ministry, a two-year program offered by the Episcopal Diocese of Louisiana. Still learning new tricks.

5. CREATE SOMETHING FROM NOTHING

The fifth rule is: *create something from nothing*. Production is any activity that creates economic value. Bringing something into existence as though from nothing is almost legerdemain, a slight of hand that adds value. Creation can take many forms, arising from physical, intellectual, emotional, or spiritual origins. In other words, creation can be informed by any of these characteristics.

I know an artist, a very good artist whose paintings are exhibited and purchased by galleries, collectors, and interior designers. Her medium is oil, generally. She expresses *herself* in her paintings. Her personality is extroverted, directed outward. She is active and expressive. Her paintings are creations of extroversion, large and filled with color and form.

When she is painting, she is happy and fulfilled in every characteristic of her individuality. If asked, she will tell you the fulfillment is attributable to self-expression, the expression of her personality and individuality, the expression of self through art. She also will tell you that the fulfillment goes beyond that. It also involves making something from nothing. She looks at raw canvas that has been prepared with gesso. As she looks at the unpainted canvas, she sees something. As she paints, she brings something new into being. She originates something as if from nothing. In so doing, she discovers something about herself through expression of self. Through sale and gift, she shares this expression and creation with others.

Cooking as Creation

I am a writer. I have had ten books and more than thirty scholarly articles published. Words are my medium of creation and expression. However, I have experienced the joy of creation and expression in other ways. One way is cooking. After mastering some of my mother's recipes, methods, and techniques, I was given Julia Child's book, *Mastering the Art of French Cooking*, for Christmas one year. I began to cook my way through it. I was thrilled at the process of creation. Creating something as if from nothing. I discovered I was good at French cooking. I began to invite people to my home as guests for dinner parties. I would do all of the cooking.

Once in Florida, I invited six people to join us for dinner, and I planned my first Beef Wellington. One of the six was Ronald Coase, the Nobel Laureate. With others sitting in the living room, relaxing and drinking a glass of wine, I was in the kitchen. I was not relaxing and drinking a glass of wine. I was facing my moment of truth. I had followed all instructions of Julia Child's recipe, and I finally placed the Beef Wellington in the oven. If I failed, I had eyewitnesses to my failure waiting in the living room, waiting to enjoy fine dining, waiting to eat Beef Wellington. The Beef Wellington was perfect. I had eyewitnesses to my perfection. Thank you, Julia Child. I was proud of my creation. I think the others were impressed and probably surprised and amazed. There is an old saying, "Prepare for the worst, and you'll never be disappointed." I think they were prepared for the worst, but they were not disappointed. I think they were extremely pleased with their dinner of Beef Wellington.

After Julia Child, I began to cook my way through Craig Claiborne's *New York Times Cookbook*. I never had a failure with either Julia Child or Craig Claiborne. At some time in the early 1970s, I went beyond the pleasures of using someone's recipe, say, Julia Child's recipe for cream of spinach soup or Craig Claiborne's recipe for black beans. One of the great pleasures of cooking is creating your own original recipes. I began to experiment with Italian cooking. Through trial and error, I created a number of recipes. Spaghetti sauce. Cannelloni. Lasagna. I decided to put spinach in my lasagna along with two sauces, a tomato and basil sauce and a white sauce that Italians call *besciamella*.

One time, I prepared lasagna for about seventy-five men who were members of the Methodist Men's Club of Trinity United Methodist Church in Gainesville, Florida. As usual, I put spinach in the lasagna. As the cook, I was the last to be seated to enjoy the lasagna. I overheard two men talking at a nearby table.

One of them said to the other, "You know, this is the best lasagna I've ever eaten."

The other one said, "Yeah. It's the best I ever ate. But what you suppose the green stuff is in here?" The first one said, "That ol' boy's from Miss'ippi. It's prob'ly turnip greens."

When you create your own personal, original recipes, you feel clever and accomplished. The more recipes you create and the more you cook from your own original recipes, the more your background contributes to additional creativity. The creation of your own recipes and actualization of these recipes into real meals are so easy. You just take known ingredients and assemble these ingredients into an original form. Yet, the process of recipe creation is expressive and fulfilling.

Community Service: Engagement, Not Involvement

Creation takes all forms. An interesting and fulfilling form is community service and community development. In this case, your involvement is thinking and acting in terms of something much bigger than yourself. Working in the community to develop its people more fully or develop its economy more fully is a process of creation. Working in the community is expressing yourself through serving the best interests of the community in which you live, building something as if from nothing.

Involvement alone is not creation, but engagement is. Involvement and engagement are different. If you're sitting in an automobile with the transmission in neutral and people get behind the automobile and push, you go in whatever direction the people push the automobile. You're involved with the automobile. If you're sitting in an automobile and shift the transmission into drive, put your hands on the steering wheel, and step on the accelerator, you will go in whatever direction you drive the automobile. You are engaged with the automobile. When you are engaged with the community in which you live, you are engaged in creation.

I've been fortunate to be engaged with leadership of communities in which I have lived. In Mobile, Alabama, I worked with Ken Dean and Wally Lee to create a "Goals for Mobile" program. For two years, I was Chairman of Goals for Mobile. We assembled one hundred leaders in the Mobile area for a two-day working conference to develop a consensus on the highest priority goals for Mobile. Some of these leaders were unaccustomed to working together or even talking to one another. We used the goals to drive the annual programs of work for city and county governments, Chamber of Commerce, and civic organizations. I was proud of what we accomplished over the years as the result of Goals for Mobile, which became an annual conference for accountability and further refinement and development of goals and strategies for accomplishing goals.

I believe everyone needs to have a passion. One of the best books written about passion is by Ralph Leighton, *Tuva or Bust!* It is the story of Richard Feynman and Ralph Leighton and their attempts to travel to Tuva, actually Tannu Uriankhai, which is an historic Mongolian region of the old Soviet Union. Feynman, who was a Nobel Laureate in physics, died two weeks before travel approval was forthcoming. The book is a story of pure passion.

After reading the book, I told a friend, "Anyone with a passion should read this book." I paused a moment and added, "Anyone without a passion also should read this book."

Passion as Creation

When I resigned in 1994 as Dean of the College of Business Administration at the University of New Orleans, the Associate Dean also resigned. His name is Phil Jeffress. After resigning, Phil told me he always had wanted to act on stage, but he never had tried out for a part.

One day, Phil told me he was auditioning for a play to be staged in the New Orleans area. He told me he was trying out for the part of Atticus Finch in *To Kill A Mockingbird*. It was his passion. He got the part and made his acting debut in the starring role. I was there on opening night. Phil was good. In fact, he was better than good. It was a passion. Phil created something as if from nothing.

Passion is an intense, driving feeling or conviction, usually focused on something creative. I think we need to create. No one is without creative ability and capacity. For one person, it's painting or sculpting. For another, it's writing. For others, it's developing original recipes, providing leadership in the community, gardening, restoring classic automobiles, public speaking, managing a political campaign. Creation lies in the process of making something as if from nothing, bringing something new into being.

I have found creation to be a human need, a need that can be satisfied through the means of rules. A rule that deals with creation as a process, a continuous and never-ending process of taking known ingredients and assembling them in original forms as if making something new from nothing. It is a rule that has utility, in the sense that the rule has the power to satisfy a human need.

6. LIKE YOURSELF

The sixth rule is: *like yourself.* Studies show that those who think well of themselves are less vulnerable to life's setbacks and struggles. To state it somewhat differently, people who like themselves are less likely to be wounded painfully by inevitable struggles and reversals. Americans pay more attention to self-esteem than the rest of the world put together and then some. However, studies of wellbeing seem to underscore the power of healthy self-esteem, which basically is nothing more than liking and respecting yourself. We Americans have found that the best indicator of general satisfaction with life is satisfaction with self.

To express our respect for others, we often say, "He is a good and decent man" or, "She is a good and decent woman." Satisfaction with self is when you can say to yourself in a healthy way, "I am a good and decent person." Again, studies show that healthy self-esteem that ensues from liking and respecting yourself grows from achieving realistic goals.

Setting goals in the first place gives some meaning to actions and conduct related to the goals. The goals should be realistic. I love symphonic music. Especially Mozart. I am a fanatic lover of Italian opera, especially Verdi and Puccini. If I had decided at any age to be a symphonic orchestra conductor, I would have chosen an unrealistic goal. I was not born with the genius for music. The only instrument I play is the radio. I love chess. I once was a member of the United States Chess Federation. If I ever had chosen the goal of becoming a Grand Master, I would have chosen an unrealistic goal. No amount of study and hard work on my part ever would have resulted in my becoming a Grand Master or the conductor of a symphonic orchestra.

Realistic Goals

Healthy self-esteem is directly related to achieving realistic goals. When achievement falls short of unrealistic goals, frustration ensues. Setting the bar far higher than any realistic expectation of clearing it is also setting us up for efforts and attempts in vain, thwarting us by running counter to making headway, bringing us to nothing to show for our efforts and attempts. In other words, unrealistic goals set us up for frustration and failure. Yet, most of us build in a gap that stretches us a bit.

The old exhortation, "Aim for the stars," is expressive of the idea that even halfway to an unreachable target is better than all the way to a lesser but reachable one. I'm not convinced. Aiming for the stars and not making it to the stars often lead to frustration and a sense of failure. We can find greater satisfaction and contentment by making our expectations more realistic and our goals congruent with our expectations. Contentment comes from limiting our dreams and our goals to the wherewithal we have. When we do not have the human means to achieve a dream or goal, we feel defeated. In this case, the feeling of defeat is actually frustration by prevention of success.

Avoiding Invidious Comparisons

In addition, we must avoid invidious comparisons to others who we see on a rung or two higher on the ladder. The ladder can be good looks. It can be income and the standard of living that income can support. The ladder can be job success. It can be athletic ability. These comparisons can diminish how much we like and respect ourselves so greatly that self-esteem is fatally wounded.

I am an economist. Over the years, I've known countless young economists who had an opportunity to work at a federal agency, say, as Deputy Assistant Secretary for Tax Policy in the U.S. Department of the Treasury, Washington D.C. In general, these young economists were extremely bright and accomplished scholars and teachers who had a highly promising career in academics. When they went to Washington, they were soon cursed with ambition. Whatever their position, they wanted the next higher position. When they had the next higher position, they wanted the next higher position. They were never contented, never satisfied, and never happy. After all, there is only one highest position in Washington. In any cabinet, there is only one highest position. Many of these young economists were broken by the Washington experience, finding that they were good economists but lousy politicians. Many of them left academics after their governmental experience.

When I was an assistant professor on the economics faculty at Iowa State University, I once invited other junior faculty members to my home one evening for cocktails. Four of us sat and talked. We were highly competitive people. We were trying to earn tenure. We were striving for promotion to associate professor. We worked hard on our research and tried to get our research published in scholarly journals.

When we were more relaxed, one of them said to another, "Jim, I feel inferior to you because you know so much mathematics. You're an expert on spectral analysis."

Jim said to still another one of us that he felt inferior to him. When the frank discussion was over, we discovered that each one of us felt inferior to another one of us. We had a dab of sense, and we knew that all of us couldn't be inferior. Each one of us simply had feelings of inferiority that came from making comparisons to another one of us founded on some highly limited basis such as mathematics, statistics, history, writing ability, or creative ability. The experience was healthy for all of us.

Like Ourselves, Like Others

I think we like others more when we like ourselves. I think others like us more when we like ourselves. When we like and respect ourselves, we also grow in our capacity to like and respect others. We are focused on building ourselves up rather than breaking others down. This focus carries over to our relationships to others in our lives.

In a marriage, for example, we need to have our focus on building up rather than breaking down. In other words, a wife needs to have her focus on conduct that will build up her husband and her relationship to him. A husband needs to have his focus on conduct that will build up his wife and his relationship to her. Neither should engage in conduct that breaks down the other or breaks down the relationship to the other. When a wife does not like or respect herself, she is not likely to behave or act so that her behavior or action indicates she likes and respects her husband.

From my experience, nothing good comes from "always" and "never." The husband says, "You always bring that up," or "You always make a mess." The wife says, "You never take out the garbage," or "You never take me anywhere." Always and never are breaking down words.

When we don't like and respect ourselves, we also tend to focus on our own inadequacies. This focus carries over to a focus on the inadequacies of others in our lives. For example, a husband can make an issue of his wife's inadequacy in some area of their relationship. This issue can take the context of an invidious comparison to other wives. Other wives do this, or other wives do that. Since his wife does not do this or that, she is inadequate. Focusing on or making an issue of a wife's inadequacy in this way has two huge, unintended, negative effects. First, the wife has to cope in some way with hurt feelings and feelings of inadequacy. No wife can be the equal of other wives in every area imaginable. Second, when a husband makes an issue of the inadequacy of his wife in comparison to other wives, he invites his wife to compare him to other husbands. No husband can be the equal of other husbands in every area imaginable. The outcome is that both wife and husband are focused on the inadequacies of the other one. No wife and husband can sustain this focus on inadequacies and maintain a healthy marriage for long.

The underlying root cause of problems of this sort is usually a person who does not like and respect herself or himself. Such people often try to build themselves up by breaking down others in their lives. These misguided attempts are ruinous for all parties concerned. Indeed, I don't believe we like and respect ourselves when we know we are breaking down someone else. If the root cause of the problem is not liking and respecting yourself, the solution lies in strategies to build up yourself so that you increasingly like yourself and respect yourself. This focus on building up rather than breaking down will carry over to relationships with others in your life.

For many years, I didn't know myself well. I didn't want to know myself well. I think I was afraid to know myself well. I suppose I was afraid to know myself well because I feared I wouldn't like myself and wouldn't respect myself. I finally was willing to be vulnerable enough to know myself better. When I knew myself better if not well, I found that I liked myself and respected myself. I respect what I have achieved. I respect my motives and purposes. A healthy self-esteem is life's best defense against the otherwise daunting wounds of life's inevitable struggles and setbacks.

7. ACT HAPPY

The seventh rule is: *act happy.* O. Dean Martin, late minister of Trinity United Methodist Church, once said in an off-handed way, "It is easier to act yourself into a new way of thinking than it is to think yourself into a new way of acting." Acting does not mean a manifestation of insincerely to give merely an impression of happiness contrary to your own inner thinking. Acting means regulating your behavior to bring thinking into conformity. Acting means taking action.

When you feel unhappy, you cannot think about being happy and wait for some introspective inspiration suddenly to manifest happiness. You have to start acting happy, meaning to regulate behavior to engage, pursue, and prosecute actions that bring about a new way of thinking. You cannot mope and dwell in the world of the unhappy. Instead, you behave in a manner to comport with the inner mental attitude you want to engage, pursue, and prosecute.

Attitudes Follow Behavior

Dean Martin was right. Studies show that attitudes follow behavior rather than the other way around. In other words, attitude does not shape behavior. Attitude follows behavior. Attitude is shaped by behavior. Attitude is a feeling or mood, whereas behavior is the way in which we act in response to feelings or moods. Our actions can shape our feelings and moods. This point is the one made by Dean Martin. Act yourself into a new way of thinking, a new way of feeling, and a new attitude. Behave yourself into a new attitude, a new feeling or emotion, a new mood.

Acting happy when we are not is not being phony. Being phony is attempting to fake something with the intent of deceiving others. In the sense given it here, acting happy is a genuine attempt to shape our innermost feelings through appropriate and worthy actions. A behavior of happiness can shape an attitude of happiness, a feeling and mood of happiness. We need to act happy even when we are happy. When we have the attitude of happiness, we need to follow through with the act of happiness. We need to act on the attitude.

Earl Monroe

When I was dean of the business school of the University of South Alabama and lived in Mobile, Alabama, I was a member of Rotary International. When I was installed as a member of the Mobile Rotary Club, I was installed along with a young man named Earl Monroe. He was not Earl "the Pearl" Monroe of NBA fame, but rather he was Earl "the Dentist" Monroe. Afterwards, Earl and I always looked for each other at Rotary meetings. When we saw each other, we sat together.

One day, I missed Earl. I missed him again the next week and the next week. Finally, I sat in sorrow when I heard the president of our Rotary Club announce that while vacationing in Mexico, Earl had contracted a rare virus that attacks the spinal cord. Earl was in the Rotary Rehabilitation Hospital in Mobile. Earl, it was announced, would be a paraplegic for the rest of his life. At the moment I heard the news, I remembered the day that Earl and I stood together when we were installed as members. I remembered all the days when we looked for each other and sat together at Rotary meetings. I imaged Earl in Rotary Rehab confined to a wheelchair.

One day, my telephone rang. It was Earl. He said he wanted to see me and talk with me. When Earl came to my office in his wheelchair, he had a big smile on his face. It stayed on his face. He made small talk as usual. He eventually came around to the purpose of his visit to my office. Referring to his condition, Earl said, "This is a great opportunity. I've always been interested in stocks and bonds. As long as I was doing root canals, I couldn't do anything about it. Now, I can. This is my big chance to start over. I want to do something I'm really interested in. I want to go back to school and study finance. What do I have to do to get into the MBA program?"

After Earl left that day, I sat quietly and reflected privately about what I had just seen and heard. I recalled a woman I had seen on television news only weeks earlier. She lived in a canyon in California. A fire swept through the canyon, and all of the homes in the canyon were destroyed. Her home was one of them. All others who were interviewed were emotionally overcome. Men and women whose homes were destroyed cried and collapsed in devastation. Yet, this one woman had a smile on her face. I'll never forget what she said. Smiling, she said to the reporter, "I've always wanted to start over again. This is my big chance."

I immediately admitted Earl to the MBA program. When Earl finished the MBA program, the graduate faculty unanimously agreed that Earl was the best student we ever had in the MBA program. When Earl finished his degree, he went into business providing financial services to physicians and dentists. He was good at what he did because he enjoyed what he did. Earl acted happy. Earl took action to bring about a new way of thinking.

Laugh

One way to act happy is to work on your sense of humor. Think about funny things to say. Listen to funny things that others say. At one time, I made up new "old sayings." Some were twists of existing old sayings. Others were malapropian combinations of two old sayings. Some were just new old sayings. Such as, "People who live in stone houses should not throw glasses." And, "I'd give my right arm to be ambidextrous." And, "A fool and his money are a girl's best friend." And, "A man who holds his nose to the grindstone is a bloody fool." And, "Single-ply toilet paper is just as good as double-ply if you use twice as much." Or, "Two can live as cheaply as one for half as long." Cheesy, but anybody can do it.

Think about puns. A fraternity man and his girlfriend parked in a Georgia state-owned park alongside a steep-walled canyon. She tried to make her fraternity boyfriend pin her. He refused. They struggled. He finally fell down, and she succeeded in securing his fraternity pin for her dress. She was pinned in one fall by Georgia's Gorge. Catching onto the pun is helped if you remember the old wrestler, Gorgeous George. A man went to a party in a penthouse and discovered an exact clone resembling the man in every detail. The clone began to use vulgar language. The man objected to the clone's foul language. They began to struggle on a balcony, and the clone fell to his death. The man was arrested for making an obscene clone fall. The minister of a church in Franklin, North Carolina, placed a Christmas wreath in its sanctuary. Afterwards, the minister heard a voice saying that music would come from the wreath only once. The minister decided to record the music and market it as "The Sole Music of a Wreath of Franklin." The famous skier, Peekaboo Street, endowed an intensive care unit. It's called Peekaboo ICU. Cheesy, but anybody can do it.

I believe the more we think about funny things, the easier it is to act happy. You find that thinking up funny things to say and listening to funny things others say are good ways to act yourself into a new attitude. Let us all hope that God has a sense of humor. I once found myself asking, "What did Winnie the Pooh and John the Baptist have in common? They had the same middle name." Even worse, asking, "When Jesus was a baby, do you think he could crawl on water?" Still worse, asking, "When we receive the body of Christ at mass, is he naked or does he have clothes on?" Holy cow!

8. FOSTER CLOSE RELATIONSHIPS

The eighth rule is: *foster close relationships.* Close ties to other people translate to better physical and emotional health. Closeness of relationships is a uniting of identities, a coincidence of interests. When we have closeness to family members or friends, we have a mutual sharing of painful feelings. The sharing of pain is *divisible* so that the pain of wounds is *divided* by the number of close people in our lives and thus is diminished accordingly. In this divisible way, we don't need to bear all of the pain of our struggles and setbacks. The pain is dispersed over the close people in our lives. When we have closeness of family relationships and closeness of friendships, we also mutually share joyful feelings. We share our joyful feelings that ensue from triumphs and successes in a *multiplicative* way. In this way, joyousness is *multiplied* through sharing the happiness and contentment with the number of close people in our lives. Having a lot of close relationships allows us to *divide the pain* in our lives and to *multiply the joy.*

Personally, I have to work hard to foster close relationships. I am introverted and introspective. My nature is to watch a football game alone in the privacy of my own home. My idea of going out to dinner is to go out with my wife. I have a strong sense of directing my interests upon myself. I have to work against my nature to foster close friendships, and I have to work against my nature to sustain and develop these close friendships. I have to work against my nature to invite friends over to watch the Super Bowl with me or accept an invitation to watch college bowl games on New Year's Day with others. I have to work against my nature to invite another couple to join my wife and me for dinner at a fine restaurant or to accept an invitation to the home of another couple for dinner. I do it, but I have to work hard and continuously to overcome my nature. The product of continuous hard work at overcoming my introverted personality is a number of close friends who I care deeply about and who care deeply about me.

Chris

When I was the business school dean at the University of New Orleans, I met a young African-American student named Chris, and I met his mother. Chris was struggling in school. Since he enrolled in the university as a business student, he never had made a 2.0 grade point average for any semester. As I talked with Chris and his mother, I knew that this young man was bright. Yet, his grades did not reflect his intellectual ability. I told Chris and his mother that I would take a direct interest in him. I introduced him to my staff of secretaries and advisers. I asked him to meet with me at least once a week. All we did was to provide an infrastructure of support, an infrastructure of close relationships that he was lacking. For the first semester of this direct interest, he achieved a 2.5 grade point average. For the second semester, he earned a 3.0.

The secretaries wanted me to hire him as a student worker. I did. The secretaries later told me that he was the best student worker we ever had. Still later, I spoke about Chris to a friend of mine who was the general manager of the Royal Orleans Hotel. He offered Chris a desk job in what I regard as one of the best hotels in New Orleans. Chris was prepared for a career in the hospitality industry. After graduation with a major in Hotel, Restaurant, and Tourism, Chris went into housekeeping management and quickly was promoted to regional housekeeping manager for a major hotel chain. All of this success started with an infrastructure of close relationships to support him. I think we grossly underestimate the vitality and importance that close relationships and strong support have in our lives.

They Busters

In management consulting, I often work with top management. They engage me to assist them in improving their costs and productivity. In 1991 and 1992, I worked for top management of a large company, and the process I brought to the company resulted in savings of annual operating costs in the amount of forty million dollars. They were happy. I kept thinking I should have worked for a percentage rather than my hourly consulting fee.

The process I brought to this particular company is the set of methods and techniques associated with continuous quality improvement. These methods and techniques morphed into Six Sigma in the 1980s. I've been working with companies and bringing these methods and techniques to companies for more than thirty years. Two cornerstones of the quality movement are a focus on the proper understanding of quality and on employee involvement. As a management consultant specializing in quality as a means of improving cost and productivity, I work with all levels of management from the Chief Executive Officer down to first-line supervisors. A lot of this work is training.

I train people to recognize that quality is a focus on meeting or exceeding the needs, requirements, or expectations of your customer. What people do not always recognize is that the customer may be someone within the company or within the plant. If you are a maintenance mechanic, your customer is the operator who runs the machine or equipment you maintain. Quality maintenance is maintenance that delights the operator of machinery and equipment, meeting his or her needs and requirements. In a process of continuous quality improvement, maintenance mechanics and operators must recognize that they are part of a team and that meeting and exceeding the expectations of the ultimate end-use customer of the final product critically depends on every worker within the company meeting and exceeding the expectations of other workers who are his or her customers within the company.

On one occasion, I was training first-line supervisors. Some of these supervisors were in operations and others in maintenance. After the basic training, I formed four groups of five people each to go through what I call the "More or Less Exercise." Each group was asked to write on an easel pad what it agrees that supervisors will do more and what it agrees that supervisors will do less as the result of the continuous quality improvement process. Most of these groups will fill up two or three pages of behaviors or actions that they believe supervisors will do more or will do less.

One day, a group of supervisors went to the front of the room to make its presentation to the others, and the leader of the group flipped over a cover sheet on his easel pad to reveal a three-line catena that said it all. Written in large, red, block letters was:

MORE WE

LESS I

NO THEY

The leader of the group turned the page again. On the next page was a single word written in large block letters: THEY. Around the word, these men had drawn a circle. Diagonally across the circle and the word, these men had drawn a line. The message was clear: THEY BUSTERS. These men suggested that a THEY BUSTER sign should go up on every bulletin board in the company.

You Busters

This simple three-line catena from business practice also applies broadly to all kinds of relationships. For example, it can be modified a little to apply to marriage. If a husband and wife adopted this catena, I think it would read:

MORE WE

LESS I

NO YOU

A husband and wife are well advised to begin more sentences with the word "We." A husband and wife are well advised to begin fewer sentences with the word "I." A husband and wife are well advised to begin few if any sentences whatsoever with the word "You" when the word is followed by the word "never" or the word "always."

A husband and wife are well advised to avoid "you" altogether. The few times that the word "you" is good are not worth the overwhelming number of times when it is used to blame, accuse, or find fault. The husband gives up saying, "You look lovely, my dear," which is a good thing to say. He also disdains saying, "You never get ready on time," and he gives up saying, "You always start these arguments." He forgoes saying, "I know how you are," and he gives up saying, "I should have known what you would do." It's not worth it.

A Better Husband, A Better Father

After working with a particular chemical company for eighteen months, I received a telephone call one day from a senior vice president. He was a man for whom I had utter respect as a manager and a leader. The president of the company felt the same way about him. The president of the company once told me that this vice president was so good that he'd be willing to work for him.

The vice president had called me on many occasions for advice or just to tell me about something. This time, I listened as he told me that as the result of the consulting and training I had brought to the company, his manner of management and leadership had changed. "My way of managing and leading has changed," he said. "I couldn't go back to the old way. I want to thank you for training and redirecting us and for what you've done for me personally. That's not the reason I'm calling. The reason I'm calling is to tell you I carried home what you taught us. It has made me a better husband to my wife and a better father to my children. The reason I'm calling is to thank you for that."

Fear of Rejection

The training I provide deals at times with establishing a culture in which people are encouraged to speak up. The best ideas come from those who are closest to the work. People must feel comfortable while telling others about these ideas. If the supervisor has a "shut up" style of managing people under his supervision, then the "speak up" culture will not flourish. In this context, training deals with fear at times. With twenty supervisors in attendance, I go around the room sometimes and find out what their fears are. I hear the usual things: snakes, heights, public speaking, death, crippling injury, and so forth. I've made two observations about these sessions. One observation is that we all have fears of some kind. Another observation is that, probing beneath the surface, the greatest fear we have is rejection.

Rejection is a fearsome expectancy and a terrible experience. The fear of rejection is far greater than we ever imagined. Rejection is a form of discarding someone as unsatisfactory or useless. Among the worst words to hear from someone is, "You're worthless," especially from someone who matters. These words are never forgotten. What lies behind rejection is the fear of isolation and solitude, separation and detachment from others.

Acceptance

When we foster close relationships, we foster a culture in which the fear of rejection is managed. My experience has been that the fear of rejection varies directly with distance. The likelihood of rejection is lesser when the relationship is closer. In marriage and in business, I have found that the closer the relationship, the lesser the likelihood of finger pointing and the lesser the likelihood of rejection. There is no role in which fostering close relationships fails to improve our lives.

If rejection is what we fear the most, acceptance is what we seek. Reception, approval, agreement, recognition are forms of acceptance. I remember a retired NFL linebacker telling me with tears in his eyes, "My daughter told me last night, 'Dad, I appreciate everything you do for us.'" This huge, tough man was overcome with emotion by simple recognition and acceptance. Acceptance, what we seek, what moves us.

What about running around with the wrong crowd? Your mother was right.

Close relationships with the wrong crowd are not healthy. I once tried to say the same thing to my daughter without the corny content. I'm not sure I improved on it a whole lot. I said to Amanda, "It is better to despair of loneliness than to be in the company of the wrong people." You be the judge. I'd give it a gentleman's C, maybe a C minus. All I can say is that, after all these years, Amanda and I have decided how we feel about it. We laugh about it.

9. CONTROL YOUR OWN DESTINY

The ninth rule is: *control your destiny.* We now know about the effects of stress on our lives. Stress is the pressure and strain and tension attributable to external forces not under our control. Stress is common to all of us. The stress of moving, the stress of a death in the family, the stress of a divorce, the stress of losing a job, the stress of starting a new job, and the stress of deadlines are typical stresses that are common to all of us. Other stresses are idiosyncratic. The stress of flying bedevils some of us, while the stress of heavy traffic or the stress of financial problems frustrates, torments, and otherwise maddens others. When we cannot control external forces, we can only cope with the stress that ensues from the lack of control.

Life is filled with uncertainty, and life is filled with the stress of an uncertain future. Many people believe in fate and destiny. To these people, where we end up and how we get there are inevitable and immutable, foreordained, and inescapable. Fate may make good fiction by William Faulkner and Thomas Hardy, but fate engenders a culture of maximum stress, the stress of waiting to see what external forces have in store for us. A life based on a belief in fate is a life of coping with stress rather than preventing stress. One strategy for preventing stress is controlling what happens to us.

Strategic Planning

As a management consultant, I have facilitated strategic planning for a number of large and small businesses and large and small not-for-profit organizations such as public school systems, city governments, charitable organizations, and churches. Strategic planning borrows language from the military lexicon. In military usage, strategy means positioning your own forces advantageously prior to actual contact with the enemy. Strategic planning for a grocery store chain, a law firm, a city, or a school system is the same, *viz.*, develop a vision for your organization, determine your mission, shape strategies for achieving your vision and accomplishing your mission, and deploy your resources advantageously to accomplish objectives driven by your vision and mission. In this way, you decide what you want your future to look like, and then you determine specific actions that must be taken to actualize and achieve the future you want.

By definition, all of us have a future. Strategic planning is a process of deciding what you want that future to look like and acting on what must be done to realize that future that you've planned for yourself. Strategic planning is not goal setting. Strategic planning is goal setting plus a plan to achieve the goal.

I recall a friend who owns several car dealerships. I once had a meeting with him right after lunch. I asked him how things were going.

"Great!" he said. "I really feel good about things right now. I took senior management through strategic planning this morning."

My experience is that strategic planning is a process that takes most businesses six to nine months to complete. I was curious about what he meant by "strategic planning." When I asked him, his answer did not reflect strategic planning. "We came up with some great goals." He had engaged in goal setting, not strategic planning.

Another friend once told me that he always had a goal of retiring when he was fifty. He was nowhere close to being able to retire because he never had a financial plan to accomplish his goal. He had engaged in goal setting, not strategic planning.

I once knew a woman who said she would give anything to be able to play the piano. This statement was simply an extravagant hyperbole. She never had given as much as a minute of her time or a penny of her money to take even a single piano lesson. She would have told a better story if she had said that she was unable to play the piano because she was never willing to do anything whatsoever to learn. She never planned.

Failure to Prepare is Preparing to Fail

Most of us do not plan. We do not think strategically. When we do not plan and when we do not think strategically, life does seem to be a matter of fate and destiny. When we plan and think strategically, we control a number of factors that determine our fate and destiny. When we plan and think strategically, our fate and destiny are to a great extent the fate and destiny that we make for ourselves. When we control our own destiny, we take the stress out of our destiny. Instead of coping with the stress, we prevent the stress. We are living in control of our lives rather than living our lives under the control of external forces. Studies show that the few of us who feel in control of our lives also have extraordinary positive feelings of happiness. The few of us who have power over circumstances also have improved health and morale.

We can plan. We can think strategically. A husband and wife can talk about where they want to go, which is goal setting, and how they can get there, which is planning. They can talk about what must be done to accomplish their goals. If the actions that must be taken to look a certain way in five to eight years are not done, then they won't be where they want to be in five to eight years. They write down what they want to look like physically, intellectually, emotionally, spiritually, financially, and in every other way that is important to them and the future that they want for themselves. They write down strategies that if acted upon will result in accomplishment of each objective related to accomplishment of the overall mission. They write down the actions that must be taken to look a certain way that they have chosen. They have just taken control of their lives.

Strategic planning is not goal setting. It is goal setting plus. The plus is an honest assessment of strengths and weaknesses with respect to vision and mission, an understanding of opportunities to minimize the weaknesses and to exploit the strengths, a determination of strategies to accomplish the mission, a commitment of resources necessary to support the strategies, a consensus on who is going to sponsor each of the strategies, a timeline to indicate when each task of each strategy will be undertaken, and regular and periodic accounting of progress made on each task of each strategy. If everything that must be done is done in a timely way, then the husband and wife have their best chance to be where they want to be in five to eight years and to look like they want to look.

10. HAVE A BELIEF SYSTEM

The tenth rule is: *have a belief system.* I mean a working belief in the truth, value, and trustworthiness of core values fundamentally based on the principled tenets of humanism, secular or religious, or the doctrinal belief in God.

Before becoming a business dean in 1981, I was an ordinary member of the business faculty at the University of Florida for ten years. For most of that ten-year period, I taught large sections of undergraduate courses. Up to 1,250 students when I taught on television. Countless students came to see me in my office. Sometimes, their agenda was the course itself. Sometimes, it was problems in their personal lives such as problems with girlfriends or boyfriends, problems with mothers or fathers, stepmothers or stepfathers, problems with money or drugs or alcohol, problems with direction in life or direction for a career.

Often, I would conclude after a lengthy conversation, perhaps several lengthy conversations, perhaps several lengthy conversations punctuated with tears and sobbing, that the young man or woman sitting before me had no sense of purpose, no animating spirit. Rebellion was a common thread woven into the fabric. Sometimes, I discovered these young men or women had distanced themselves from his or her upbringing. Students rarely brought up the humanism or religion common to their families. Students might know they were rebelling against their parents, but they didn't realize that they also were rebelling against the faith, religion, or other common beliefs of their families.

In talking to such students, I saw time and time again the effects of distancing yourself from traditional and customary beliefs. I always tried my best to help these young people with the immediate and concrete problem that they brought to me. I used a process that led the two of us to agree on what the problem was. We had to agree on the problem itself, and then we had to agree on the root cause of the problem. In this way, we dealt with the causes of problems rather than with the symptoms of problems. Next, we developed strategies to make the root causes of the problem go away. Sooner or later, we might talk about core beliefs and perhaps religion if relevant. I never, ever attempted to influence young people about faith or religion. I had too much integrity to manipulate young people who often are vulnerable to undue influence. I had too many strong feelings against manipulating people of any age, and I did not want to be a party to it under any circumstances.

Sooner or later, the discussion might turn to core values based on some belief system. I might find a need to bring such concerns to the front burner of discussion. A young man might have a problem with his father. He rebels against his father and anything his father values. The rebellion against his father leads to a rebellion against his father's beliefs, perhaps his father's religion.

"I know you and your family are Jewish," I would say. "When is the last time you were in a synagogue?"

Generally, the answer was a long time ago, perhaps before he left home for college. These young men would talk at length about their upbringing, going to Hebrew school, recalling their bar mitzvah, generally talking about their particular culture and their basic beliefs.

Eventually, after listening carefully, I would say, "I think you need to go back to your synagogue."

Almost always, he did. At times, I asked these Jewish young men if they could tell me what a synagogue was. They could. Most of them knew the Greek origin of the word. Two Greek roots taken together translated as "a bringing together." What better place for reconciliation than a place set aside for bringing people together, and bringing people together with other people who share a common belief system and corresponding values. Reconciliation is a great theme of faith, religion, and, for that matter, humanism.

A young woman might be Christian, perhaps Roman Catholic. Our conversation would center on agreeing on the problem and its root causes, what was working and what was not working. When pertinent, we would find ourselves talking about beliefs, faith, and religion.

"You're Catholic. When did you last go to mass?" Invariably, the answer was in terms of a long time.

"I think you need to go back to mass," I would say, "and I think you need to keep going to mass."

Almost always, she did. Almost always, these students talked at length about their faith, religion, or humanistic belief system and the role it played in their childhood and adolescence. They talked about core values of their upbringing. They talked about how these core values had gone missing from their lives. Each had lost his or her way, lost whatever focus they had on the spiritual dimension of their lives, lost the sense of purpose.

The Need for a Belief System

My experience has been that we need a belief system. If not a belief in the rituals and ceremonies of organized religion based on a relationship to God, we need a belief in the universal truths of human means exercised on behalf of human interests. People who are Christian, Jewish, or Islamic have formalized relationships to God based on their respective religions. These people need that faith and religion particularly when engaged in struggles and enmeshed in setbacks. People of faith and religion have secure beliefs that enable them to cope with adversity and rebound from adversity. People of faith and religion readily recover their sense of wellbeing.

Faith and religion are not the only belief systems, however. Whether secular or religious, humanism centers on the commonality of human values, human worth, and human capabilities. As a belief system, humanism is concerned with the best interests, needs, and wellbeing of people, individuals and any collectivity of people. Such humanists need their beliefs in the same way that people of faith and religion need theirs.

People find social and cultural support in the infrastructure of their belief system. People find a strong sense of long-term hope and a strong sense of purpose in life when they have a belief system. Humanists and those associated with some form of organized religion often have the needs of other people alongside their own needs at the hub of their lives. This tendency alone, this attention to others and their needs, has been identified in happy people.

When I struggled with spiritual growth, spiritual development, and spiritual maturity, I never lost my beliefs altogether. My beliefs and humanism merely have had their ups and downs. The ups and downs act on other aspects of my individuality, act on the physical, intellectual, and emotional sides of my life. In this way, the ups and downs act on my sense of wholeness and integrity. Beliefs are drivers. Beliefs drive the other interrelated parts that add up to make and complete the whole.

CHARACTERISTICS OF BEST MANAGEMENT

Sound managerial decisions are based on a solid foundation of adherence to certain basic principles. At a minimum, capable managers must be competent to identify and pursue accomplishment of goals; recognize the nature and importance of profits; know their customers, products, and markets; and know their employees and understand incentives and motivations. This overview suggests that best management is not merely being a boss. Anyone can be bossy and order others about, but being effective in managing work and leading people requires knowledge in addition to power. After all, when a leader says, "Follow me," the leader presumably has knowledge about where he or she is going and how to get there.

Setting Goals and Crafting Strategies

Presumably, the basic, fundamental, ultimate goal of any business is to maximize the value of the firm, although this presumption is far from settled. One measure of the value of a firm is market capitalization, sometimes called market cap. Market capitalization for a corporation is number of its outstanding shares of common stock multiplied by the price of a share of its common stock. In this sense, market capitalization is simply the market value of a company measured by the total value of its common stock. From week to week in mid-2011, Exxon Mobil and Apple battled for the top spot in market cap, but Apple's share price soared. Consequently, Apple distanced itself well beyond Exxon Mobil, indeed to become the company with the highest market cap in history, more than six hundred billion dollars.

Recognizing the Nature and Importance of Profits

Since the ultimate goal of a business presumably is to maximize the firm's value, the principal means presumably is to maximize profits. Recognizing the nature and importance of profits is critical. The general public and the business community itself typically think of profit in terms of an accounting concept. In the simplest sense, profits are generally understood as the difference between sales revenues and costs. Often, this definition of profit is called accounting profit. However, the invested capital of owners is the equivalent of non-purchased inputs used in production, and these owners expect a return on their invested capital. Economic cost includes all "out-of-pocket" costs and the opportunity cost (the return on equity forgone when it is invested by owners in their own business) of invested capital. In other words, economic cost includes forgone return on invested equity capital that could have been earned if invested in another company of equal risk.

Economic profit is the difference between revenue from sales and economic cost, which includes both out-of-pocket costs and the imputed opportunity costs of non-purchased inputs represented by invested capital in the large, modern enterprise. This simple concept has been elevated into a model for managerial decision making called Economic Value Added (EVA). In the EVA framework, net operating profit after taxes (NOPAT) is made using debt and equity capital, and a charge for this debt and equity capital is subtracted from NOPAT. If the cost of capital is less than NOPAT, value is added to the firm. If the cost of capital is more than NOPAT, value is reduced.

Knowing the Customer, Product, and Market

Best managers know their products and their product markets. They analyze and understand competitive conditions in their product markets, including a deep sense of the internal rivalry among incumbent firms as well as forces that would intensify competition and thus threaten profitability. In addition, capable managers know their customers. Nowadays, businesses are driven by the attempt to meet if not exceed the needs, requirements, and expectations of customers. Best managers also know the factors that affect sales of their products and know something about the sensitivity of sales to each of these factors. For example, they know how sensitive sales of a particular product are to the price of the product itself, to the prices of competing products, to per capita income in the market area, and to advertising outlays. Understanding a company's customers, products, and markets is integral to competitive analysis, and competitive analysis is critical in formulation of business strategies.

Knowing the Worker, Understanding Incentives and Motivation

Best managers know their customers and know their needs and requirements. Best managers also know their workers and know their needs and requirements. Capable managers have a firm grasp on the role of incentives and know how to shape incentives to induce proper effort from workers. Indeed, incentives are shaped and implemented to energize and animate people in an organization to reflect the organization's "personality," which is its organizational culture.

Like human personality, organizational culture tends to be unique to a particular organization, and this organizational culture is concerned with custom, tradition, and shared beliefs about organizational life. In this light, culture in an organization is seen as the pattern of assumptions found to be useful in coping with the internal and external environment and taught to new members as the "correct" way to perceive, think, and feel about their work. The culture in an organization is a powerful determinant of individual and team behavior. It affects virtually all aspects of organizational life, ranging from the ways people interact with each other to how they perform their work.

Incentives deal with motivation, which literally means provision of an incentive and thus a reason to move to action. In other words, incentive is something that induces action or motivates effort. This meaning is so well known that we sometimes speak of incentives as inducements. In addition to a narrow financial approach to incentives and motivation, several points need to be made briefly.

A number of people have observed that most organizations are overmanaged and underled. Grace Hopper was one of these people. Rear Admiral Grace Murray Hopper (1906-1992) was a remarkable woman. She was the first woman to be awarded a Ph.D. in mathematics at Yale University (1934). In 1952, she first conceived of compilers, which were computer programs that translate computer languages used by programmers into a form accessible to computers. She developed FLOW-MATIC, the forerunner of COBOL (Common Business-Oriented Language), the first commercial high-level programming language. She was the third programmer on the famed Mark I, an electro/mechanical computer built by IBM and delivered to Harvard in summer 1944 for use by the U.S. Navy.

In November 1985 at the age of 79, the nomenclature of Grace Hopper's rank of Commodore was changed to Rear Admiral. She thus became one of the few women admirals in the history of the U.S. Navy. She retired on August 14, 1986, in a ceremony aboard the U.S.S. Constitution in Boston. After retirement, "Amazing Grace" worked as Senior Consultant for DEC (Digital Equipment Corporation) until eighteen months before her death on 1 January 1992. She was buried with full Naval honors at Arlington National Cemetery on 7 January 1992.

Rear Admiral Hopper once said, "You manage things, and you lead people." The general idea is to manage work and lead people. Management is highly directive in dealing with workers. When managing workers, it is meant to exert control over workers. Leadership relies on inspiring and motivating workers. Leadership depends on vision, which must be detailed, communicated, shared, and supported. Leaders articulate a vision, develop strategies to accomplish the vision, and then inspire, motivate, and align others to accomplish the vision. All of these leadership roles deal with people, whereas management deals with work. Hence, managers in their role as leaders adhere to the locution that you manage work, but you lead people.

Another giant of the twentieth century also dealt with incentives and motivation, emphasizing the central role of leadership rather than management. Dr. W. Edwards Deming (1900-1993) was a remarkable man, truly one of the most influential people of the twentieth century. He earned his doctorate in mathematical physics from Yale (1928). Along with Dr. Walter Shewhart (1891-1967), Deming is regarded as a founder of the quality movement worldwide and certainly was its spokesman throughout his life. Dr. Deming emphasized transformation. He developed fourteen principles for transformation of an organization from what it is to what it can be and ought to be. He argued that transformation required leadership. Throughout his lifetime, Dr. Deming said that the aim of leadership is not to find and record the failures of people but to remove the causes of failure so that people can do a better job.

Emphasis should be placed on team as well as individual incentives. An example from mining illustrates the hazards of emphasizing individual performance alone. When a phosphate mining manager was asked if he had told other mining managers in the same company about a breakthrough idea he had implemented, he said, "Hell, no! Let them figure it out the hard way just like we did." In fairness to the manager, it must be said that he was acting in response to company incentives, which motivated people to behave in this way. Historically, the way to get ahead in the company was to elevate one's own job performance above that of rivals for advancement. The longer this particular mining manager could keep his breakthrough idea from other mining managers, the longer his mining results would look better by comparison to the performance of other managers. Of course, keeping the breakthrough idea from being implemented in other mines operated by the company harmed the overall performance of the company itself and harmed the interests of owners. The company moved to change its culture so that incentives motivated managers to act in concert as a team for the advancement of company goals and objectives.

Organizational Integrity Follows Personal Integrity

Best managers realize that incentives are meant to motivate the people of an organization, to energize and animate people to behave in a certain way. They also know that the culture of organizational integrity is the collective attitudes and behaviors of people in the organization. Indeed, "corporate culture" is a newcomer to the business lexicon, entering the language in the late 1980s. To grow, develop, and maintain a corporate culture of organizational behavior, the nutrient substance is personal integrity. When the organization is populated from bottom to top with people of character and personal integrity, the organization is a body of persons sharing a culture of personal integrity. Organizational attitudes and behavior follow personal attitudes and behavior.

Organizational integrity follows personal integrity. Organizational behavior follows personal behavior. Organizational misbehavior also follows personal misbehavior. Personal integrity implies parts that make up wholeness. Personal integrity is properly understood as growth, development, and maturity of the parts so that wholeness, completeness, and soundness are realized. Organizational integrity is the collective of personal integrity. Absences of personal integrity, deficiencies of personal integrity, and lapses in personal integrity lead to lack of organizational integrity, deficiencies of organizational integrity, and lapses in organizational integrity. These nutrients feed organizational misbehavior.

Once again, it can be said that organizational integrity follows personal integrity. Pursuing personal integrity thus is good for the person and good for the organization. Personal integrity is pursued and achieved through growth, development, and maturity of the physical, intellectual, emotional, and spiritual parts that make up the whole person.

COME ON, GET HAPPY

Thomas Jefferson was the founder of the University of Virginia and author of the Declaration of Independence, both cited on his tombstone. When he wrote the Declaration of Independence, he stated that, "all men are created equal, that they are endowed by their Creator with certain unalienable Rights." He wanted to state that these rights are life, liberty, and property, the latter following the lead of John Locke. Instead, he was persuaded to write, "that they are endowed by their Creator with certain unalienable Rights, that among these are Life, Liberty and the pursuit of Happiness."

Jefferson was making a political statement, but in making a political statement, Jefferson suggests that the pursuit of happiness is a worthy, protected, inalienable undertaking. Indeed, the pursuit of happiness is a right endowed by our Creator. Moreover, Jefferson states that governments are instituted to secure these rights, including the right to pursue happiness. We Americans have a divinely created right to pursue happiness.

None of us wants to end his or her life like Quasimodo, the hunchback in Victor Hugo's classic book, *Notre-Dame de Paris (The Hunchback of Notre Dame)*. In the movie version, the last scene is that of Charles Laughton as Quasimodo sitting atop Notre Dame between the gothic gargoyles that project elaborately from the cathedral roof. Hopelessly in love with the gypsy girl, Esmarelda, he asks plaintively in abject sorrow and woe, "Why was I not made of stone like them?"

Mr. Burke, my Spanish teacher when I was a freshman at the University of Southern Mississippi, told us that "get" was the first word he taught to immigrants who wanted to learn English as a second language. "You can get anything," Mr. Burke said with a laugh. You can get up and get down, get on and get off, get married and get divorced, get a job and get unemployment benefits, get sick and get well. You can even get happy, pursue and know true happiness. Come on get happy. . . . It's quiet and peaceful on the other side.

There are no guarantees in this world. Except maybe a guarantee that your best chance to get happy, to pursue and know true happiness, is to sweat every day, don't start what others are trying to quit, get enough sleep, learn continuously over a lifetime, create something from nothing, like and respect yourself, act happy even when you don't feel happy, develop and sustain close relationships, control your own destiny, and have a belief system.

These foregoing ten rules have utility. The rules have usefulness. You can use them to secure personal integrity in your life. You can use them to pursue happiness, get happy, and stay happy.

THE AUTHOR

Dr. J. Ronnie Davis is a native of Shreveport, Louisiana, but grew up in Pascagoula, Mississippi. He was graduated from the University of Southern Mississippi with a bachelor's degree and a master's degree in economics. His doctorate in economics was earned from the University of Virginia, where he was a student of James McGill Buchanan, who won the Nobel Prize in Economics in 1986. His doctoral dissertation, *Pre-Keynesian Economic Policy Proposals in the United States During the Great Depression,* won the prestigious Tipton R. Snavely Award, judged by Ronald H. Coase who won the Nobel Prize in Economics in 1991.

From 1967 to 1971, Dr. Davis held a faculty position in economics at Iowa State University and from 1971 to 1981 at the University of Florida. Now a professor of economics at the University of New Orleans, he previously served three universities as their business school dean, including the University of New Orleans from 1989 to 1994. Previously, he was Dean of the College of Business and Management Studies at the University of South Alabama from 1983 to 1989 and Dean of the College of Business and Economics at Western Washington University from 1981 to 1983.

Dr. Davis has been recognized as an exceptional teacher, winning numerous awards for teaching and mentoring students. He teaches Managerial Economics in the MBA program. Dr. Davis has been Teacher of the Year in the College of Business Administration at the University of New Orleans. EMBA students in New Orleans and Puerto Rico have recognized him numerous years as Teacher of the Year and as Mentor of the Year.

Dr. Davis has been published widely in economics and political science. He is the author of more than thirty articles in scholarly journals, including *American Economic Review, American Political Science Review,* and *Economic Journal.* For more than twenty years, Dr. Davis was Editor of the scholarly journal, *Public Finance Quarterly,* renamed *Public Finance Review* in 1997, which is an international journal for the study of the public sector of the economy published by Sage Publications in California. He is the author of ten books, ancillaries, and monographs dealing with the history of economic thought, public finance, and managerial economics. His most recent book is *Economics for Executives: Principles, Practices, and Strategies.*

Since 1971, Dr. Davis has worked around the country and world as a management consultant. His extensive consulting has involved engagements in strategic planning, management auditing, and improving cost and productivity. He learned quality methods under the tutelage of Dr. W. Edwards Deming. Dr. Davis is regarded as an authority on Six Sigma. Most of his consulting experience has been in the chemical and automobile industries. His clients have included *Fortune* 500 companies as well as small businesses, cities, public school systems, federal government agencies, and law firms.

Because of his academic and consulting experience in the United States and around the world, Dr. Davis has earned a wide and deep platform of followers who know his reputation, who respect his character, and who seek his advice. Over the past ten years, he has been a frequent speaker on the topic of integrity, both personal integrity and organizational integrity. He also has been engaged to train executives as well as hourly workers to act on and commit to personal integrity. In response to their behest to write it down, he has written *Organizational Behavior: The Case for Personal Integrity.*